AF616528

COBDEN
and his
KATE

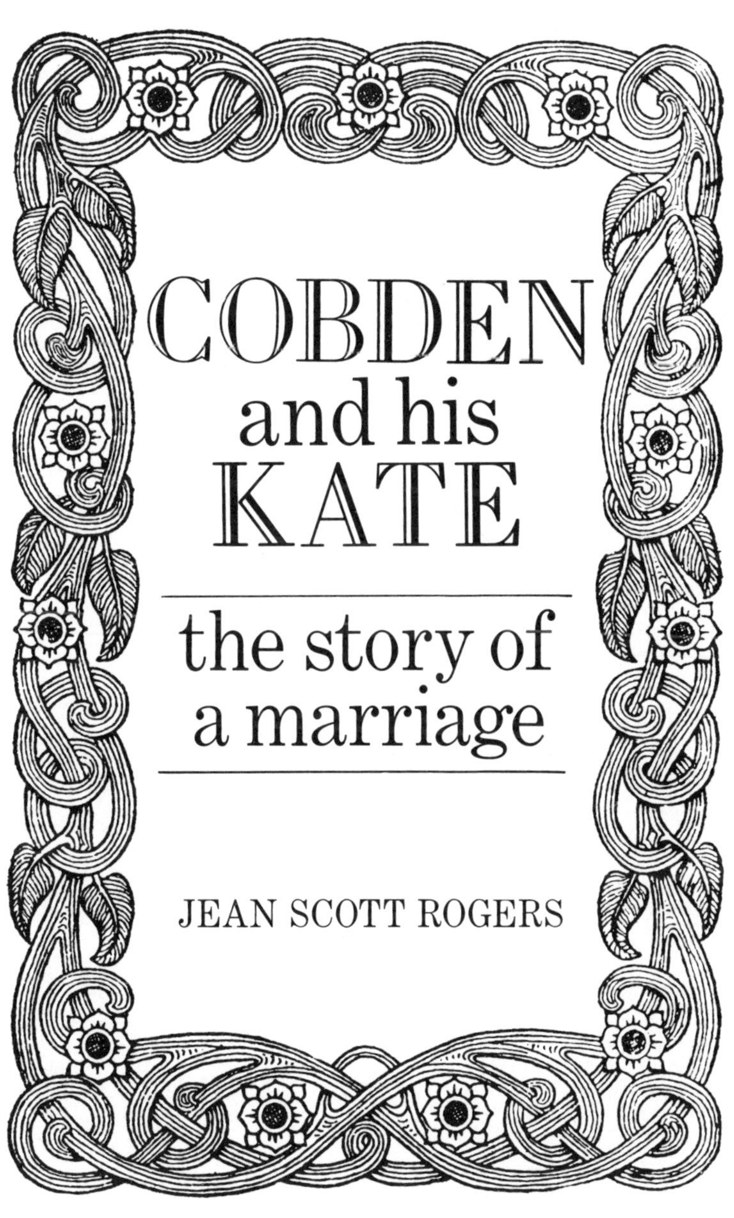

COBDEN and his KATE

the story of a marriage

JEAN SCOTT ROGERS

HISTORICAL PUBLICATIONS

First published 1990
by Historical Publications Ltd
32 Ellington Street, London N7 8PL
(Telephone 071–607 1628)

ISBN 0 948667 11 7

Typeset by Historical Publications Ltd
and Fakenham Photosetting, Fakenham

Printed in Great Britain by
Biddles Ltd, Guildford and King's Lynn

Contents

Acknowledgements

Grateful thanks are due to the following: the British Library; the West Sussex Record Office and the County Archivist for access to the Cobden Manuscripts, by courtesy of the Governors of Dunford House; Julia Bellord, Elizabeth Cobden Boyd, Joan Clayton, Janet Grant Ogilvie, Lyla Osbiston and Walter E. Smith.

The Illustrations

Plates VI and X are reproduced by kind permission of the ILN Picture Library. All other illustrations, excepting plate II, are reproduced by kind permission of the West Sussex Record Office.

To the memory of my good friends
Felix and Martine Hilton
who made this book possible

Introduction

This is the hitherto untold story of the marriage of Richard Cobden and Catherine Anne ('Kate') Williams, the beautiful Welsh girl he chose to be his wife and who was to prove a buoyant helpmate to this physically delicate but indomitable man. Their twenty-five years together is recalled here in their own words or those of their friends, collected from letters and diaries.

Cobden has his own unique niche in British political history, for it was he that was the prime mover in the League to abolish the Corn Laws and to establish the principle of free trade between nations.

The importing and exporting of grain had been subject to legislation in Britain from the reign of Edward III in the 12th century, but these laws did not assume political importance until the Corn Law of 1815, which prohibited the importation of grain until the domestic price reached almost two pence per lb. This meant that a labouring countryman, whose average wage was ten shillings a week, had to pay one shilling for a loaf of bread. In an age when large families were the norm this was a cause of considerable hardship.

The Corn Laws were finally repealed in 1846, thanks to the highly efficient and strenuous agitation conducted throughout the country by a group of Manchester industrialists led by Richard Cobden, the radical Quaker politician John Bright, and their fellow members of the Anti-Corn Law League.

Repeal, in the words of Cobden's first biographer, John Morley (*The Life of Richard Cobden*, 1879), was 'the one finished triumph with which Cobden's name is associated', and he added, 'it is a tolerably safe prophecy that no English statesman will ever revive a tax upon bread'.

On 16 April 1839, in the first issue of the modest organ published by what was then the Anti-Corn Law Association, Cobden wrote a history of the Corn Laws; and from then on their abolition was the cause to which his considerable talents were devoted – but which was to have disastrous results for him personally.

In researching these two very different people I have never ceased to marvel at the courage of Cobden – the 'International Man' – the devotion of Kate and the stamina of both. In so doing I have grown to feel something like affection for their very human weaknesses – an affection I hope may come to be shared by the readers of this work.

Jean Scott Rogers
Suffolk, 1990.

CHAPTER ONE

'Mrs Fitz'

John Nash's porticoed church of All Souls, Langham Place, in the London parish of St Marylebone, was less than twenty years old when, on the morning of Thursday, 14 May 1840, a small group of people met there to witness a marriage.

The groom was 36 year old Richard Cobden, second son of William Cobden, unsuccessful farmer and timber merchant, and his wife Millicent Amber. Born on 3 June 1804 at his father's farm at Heyshott, near Midhurst in Sussex, Richard was the bright one in a family of eleven children. He had grown to manhood physically undermined by five years at Bowes Hall in Yorkshire, a school run by a Mr and Mrs Clarkson and said to have been the model (though model is hardly the word) for Dotheboys Hall in Dickens's *Nicholas Nickleby*, where the fees for himself and brother Charles were paid by a relative. Their mother died aged 48 of typhoid fever in 1825, after nursing the sick child of a neighbour. The gentle, ineffectual William died in 1832, from which time Richard became, virtually, head of the family. Two of his ten siblings had already succumbed to tuberculosis and Richard himself had a serious illness in 1835. By 1840, he was already a much travelled man with a prosperous business in the calico-printing trade, an Alderman of Manchester and headed for a parliamentary career. Surprisingly, he was still a bachelor. Whatever his motives when he finally proposed to the young Welsh woman to whom he was romantically attached, he made a good choice, although many of his friends had doubts as to its wisdom at the time.

The bride was Catherine Anne Williams, one of seven children of Hugh Williams, timber merchant (but described on the marriage certificate as 'Squire') of Machynlleth, Montgomeryshire and his wife Elinor Evans. Born on Christmas Day in 1815, the year of the Battle of Waterloo, Catherine Anne was at school with one or more of the Cobden girls and then became a governess – about the only means whereby a gentlewoman could earn a living in those days. She was 25 when she accepted Cobden's offer of marriage – some would say a tardy one – and became his dearest 'Kate'

Witnesses to the marriage were Kate's elder brother, Hugh, a lawyer, Elizabeth Smith of 73 Newman Street, Oxford Street, and two of Cobden's brothers – Frederick, the eldest, and Charles.

In the paper-backed notebook in which Cobden recorded his honeymoon journey on the Continent, the entry for his wedding day could hardly have been more laconic: 'May 1840 14 Thursday – ½ past 11 at All Souls Langham Place. Afterwards to Winchester.' They were to be away for ten weeks, touring France, Switzerland, Germany and Holland.

Having at last proposed to Kate, Cobden wrote a letter to Hugh Williams on 27 March 1840, an uncomfortable mixture of pomposity and commercial jargon: 'My dear Sir, – To you as the elder brother, in London, of Miss Williams, I think it is my duty, both in deference to her wishes and your own claims to address myself under circumstances that will probably be wholly unexpected by you – I yesterday in a personal interview elicited the hand of your sister and although I cannot feel justified in saying that I was formally accepted, the result was such as to call for this explanation of my view to you – I shall only add that I leave to you the right and duty of satisfying yourself, on behalf of Miss Williams, of the eligibility of one who pretends to the high honour of becoming the guardian of her happiness.'

This letter, written from the Victoria Hotel in Euston Square, ends in best calico-printer's style: 'Awaiting the favor [*sic*] of your reply I remain my dear Sir Yours faithfully Richard Cobden.'

Kate was no stranger to the Cobdens, and it seems from the warmth of their letters that the whole family welcomed the news of the engagement. On 27 March Cobden's eldest surviving sister, Priscilla, Mrs William Sale, wrote to her future sister-in-law:

'My dear Brother Richard has given me permission to address you as my dear Sister elect, and I hasten to offer you my very sincere congratulations on the happiness you have in anticipation. You have indeed my dear Kate made choice of one who will study to render you the happiest of women. But before I say more in praise of our good dear Richard, allow me to assure you of the pleasure we shall feel in welcoming you back to Manchester as our near, and dear Sister...I long to hear from you again, as in future our letters will be free of all reserve, at least I should wish them to be so, you will gratify me my dearest Girl by treating me as your Sister. Our dear Richard will I suppose soon leave you, but I expect will very often have *particular business* in Town.'

Priscilla's phrase 'free of all reserve' suggests that Kate's former correspondence with Cobden's sisters had been guarded, as there was no official engagement, and they had no idea of his intentions towards their friend.

Mary Cobden wrote to Kate from the Cobden home in Quay Street on 30 March: '*Most gladly* do I avail myself of dear Richard's consent to my offering you a welcome into the Cobden family, pray dear girl accept the *Most hearty* one I could give you...' Soon after writing this, Mary was sent to join Kate in London.

Only one sheet survives of the letter Cobden wrote to Kate from Manchester on 2 April, addressed to Newman Street: '...Sarah and Priscilla will write to you I hope one or the other daily. Expect a long letter from the former tomorrow. They will have much news to tell you – I hope you will write to them whenever you have leisure. But they will not expect you to tax yourself with writing to us all. There is a little pocketbook with a cover of beads, which I bought in Berlin last year [actually 1838] for my intended, long before I knew the object. It is now packed up in wadding ready to be sent to my darling Kate. Sarah begs her kindest love as well as Priscilla. I have taken a kiss from Baby [his nephew, Willie Sale] for you. Give my regards to your brothers.'

Hugh and John Williams, both solicitors, were practising from an office in Verulam Buildings, Grays Inn Road, but whether they also lodged at Newman Street is not clear.

Cobden goes on: 'It shall not be many days before I see them and you again. Present my kindest love to Mary who I hope will remain till the last moment with you. Believe me my sweetest Kate your affectionately attached Richard.' At the foot of the sheet he scribbles: '*Write, write, write!*' This was to be a plea often repeated throughout their married life. Cobden was a prolific letter writer, and words flowed effortlessly from his pen, but Kate, alas, possessed no such facility, as can be seen from the numerous scraps and drafts which survive and which for some unknown reason she failed to tear up. During the 25 years that they were husband and wife he wrote to her almost every day when his parliamentary or other duties kept them apart. Kate treasured these letters, but little or nothing of hers survive.

In the interval between her engagement and her marriage, Kate went with Mary to visit Kate's parents in Wales.

'My dearest Kate,' he wrote on 30 April, 'I have remonstrated with Cobby [his elder sister Sarah] for not having told me before that you were always known [at school] as the *late* Miss Williams. Cobby tells me that I shall find all that out and a great deal more in due time, but I reply that it will then be '*too-late*' – I consider that I have a fair ground for divorce against Cobby – What shall I do with breakfast kept waiting every morning till 9 or 10 o'clk – Oh Mrs Fitz – Mrs Fitz – Mrs Fitz!'

On 2 May Cobden acknowledges what must have been something of a letter-bomb from her: 'My dearest Kate Your very severe letter of this morning has put me upon my good behaviour. I sit down to write in all penitence and contrition, with your awful little letter lying before me, which in truth looks like a combustible piece of firework, that has exploded in my hands – I hardly know what to say, to regain your favour, and reestablish myself once more in the good page of the good book of my Kate...I have tried to picture to myself your lovely face, all clouded with frowns, as you sat down to upbraid me with neglect. But the terrible vision is too much for my poor nerves – I turn away from it as a terrible phantom that has no real foundation in truth...She may write in letters of gall, with a *steel* pen upon crimson papers, sealed with black wax, and inscribed with a motto of vengeance – but even though every letter breathe wrath and vengeance I shall not be able to change the visions that in her own natural and lovely form haunt my mind day and night...'

Such outpourings might have come from a lovesick youth and not from a man in his thirties. There is more of the same: 'Last night, my dearest Kate, I dreamed of you, and was awoken by the intensity of the illusion. I thought you were in the room! Strange thing for me, who sleep with so much earnestness that I scarcely ever awake in the night, even from one year to another, I did awake to a very terrible disappointment. It was just the break of day and I went to the window to look out upon the quiet scene of the garden and the church beyond. You can't imagine how lonely I then felt! Shall I tell you the reasons for my dream last night? Dear Mary had been telling me just before she went to bed that you my love had dreamed of me. Tell me, my dear Kate, if you have dreamed of me since. Let me console myself with the fancy that you do not always forget me, even in your sleep...How can I tell you all the pleasant little chat that has passed between Mary and me? – We have talked about you incessantly. I have heard all the news about the dresses and I have seen the patterns of the silks, need I say how highly I approve of your taste! – I have ordered a dress of the enclosed to be finished for you – tell me my Kate if you like it – The same pattern in blue or green would have been better – but neither colour becomes you so well as pink – Tell me by return if you approve it if not I will not send it. Your my dearest for ever devoted(?) Richard.'

It was not until 5 May that the shy and diffident eldest Cobden, Frederick, wrote his letter of welcome to his future sister-in-law: 'My dear Miss Williams, I am conscious of being rather awkward at any form of expression of my feelings, and will therefore not trouble you with a long epistle; believe me I shall most heartily welcome you as one of our family in the confident assurance that unalloyed happiness to my brother and yourself will be the result of the union. Pray accept the accompanying trifle, and with it my sincere wish, that your own best, and fondest hopes of happiness, may be more than realised; and believe me. Yours most truly F.W. Cobden.'

Sarah Cobden's reaction to her brother's marriage is not known, but some years previously, when Cobden had been on a holiday in Wales, she had said in one of her letters to him: '...I am sure you must have had a most delightful trip into Wales and with such pleasant company too. I wonder it had not been almost too much for you. You say in your letter that you don't think you shall require any advice from me as the lady with whom you are amorous is, or has been, a governess herself but of course the advice *she* will give you, will be of this nature namely either to come next time with a *ring*, or else conduct her immediately to the *Hymenial* [*sic*] *altar* which sort of advice I would strongly advise you not to follow although my opinion is unasked and will be perhaps *unheeded* which is not my fault perhaps you will consider it is jealousy on my part for fear I should lose my chance of having the education of the children which you know has always been promised me.'

Whether there had been pressure on Cobden from any other quarter against his marriage it seems that he and Kate had the support and approval of his family when they set off together on 14 May 1840. They spent the first night of their married life at Winchester, travelling by train next day to Southampton, where they put up at the Star Hotel and paid a visit to Netley Abbey before crossing on the ferry to the Isle of Wight.

Cobden kept his diary throughout the tour, at first in a small, neat hand, but later the entries show signs of haste or, possibly, boredom. Ten weeks of strenuous sightseeing, even in the company of his dearest Kate, must have been a tiring business, both physically and mentally for a man of his delicate constitution. In the diary he used the first person plural throughout; its pages contain few direct references to Kate, but his letters to Frederick give an insight into the active part she played on the tour. Cobden had reason to be writing to his older brother for he was now closely linked to him in business. The previous year, Cobden had dissolved the very successful partnership which had existed between him and Messrs Sherriff Gillett & Co, and from 1 January 1840 Frederick became his partner. What disastrous results this change was to bring were not evident when Cobden was on his honeymoon, but he obviously felt it necessary to keep closely in touch with Frederick about the affairs of the business. That done, he found time to give his brother a vivid account of the highlights of the tour. Writing to him from Geneva on 20 June he tells him that at Chambray, capital of Savoy, 'we found a party going to Geneva, who took our carriage and all its contents, excepting a carpet bag, with which Kate and I have started for the mountains, intending to make a tour of a week, and then go to Geneva to resume our former civilised mode of travelling. Our first excursion will be remove from Bourg St. Maurice, over the little St Bernard into the Vale of Aosta, and after spending a day or two in that valley we intend to cross by the Great St Bernard, to Martigny. Kate says she is determined to have an adventure before she returns; and what in the name of womanly curiosity think you has she decided upon in preference to all other exploits? Nothing less than the passing a night in a monastery, with a monk for her *fille de chambre*, will satisfy her! so we are resolved to ascend to the Hospice of Great St Bernard, the highest habitable spot, and the only monastery in the world where women are allowed to sleep under the same roof with its sworn bachelor inmates!

'The heat has been excessive ever since we left Paris; and at Lyons...we suffered extremely...We are now upon high ground, and feel the advantage of an altered temperature...my wife is a superlative travelling companion. For fatigue she can beat her husband – and she *thinks* of everything. She desires her kindest regards to you, and all the family circle, – not forgetting the dear little baby...Kate will write to the dear girls (to whom our especial love) after we have eaten some trout, with the monks of St Bernard, and romped with their dogs...We shall come out upon the Simplon route near to Leuk [Loeches] the bath where Konig is boiling in descending from the Great St Bernard, we may perhaps take him by surprise and catch him in his bathing-dress. Believe me yours very truly R. Cobden.'

'After leaving the Hospice (little St Bernard) went across a plain upon which they say Hannibal encamped – I care not whether or no – In the evening a thunder storm such as had not been known at St Didier for many years came on. Flashes of lightning in quick succession lighted up the alps, so that Mont Blanc for an instant became visible to the minutest particle of its vast extent – then followed an interval of total darkness – Again the rocks, mountains and glaciers were by a magical effect brought into the glare of a bright but ghostlye [*sic*] light – to be followed by the most solemn darkness – We went to bed in the midst of this sublime scene. Towards 2 o'clk in the morning we heard the tinkling of the cowbells which continued throughout the forenoon – We were told that this arose from the flocks of cattle that were going to the mountains to spend the summer.'

The diary entry telling of their ascent to the Great St Bernard shows that a great deal of physical effort, not to say danger, attended Kate's 'adventure'. They were mounted on mules, and there is no mention of their having a guide: 'It was snowing...The road after proceeding a half hour was carried up the face of a steep, and almost precipitous mountain by a series of zig-zag windings which carried us at last far into the clouds and we could see nothing but a fathomless-looking abyss below...It was excessively cold and the snow drove full in our faces with a strong wind. After going upwards for an hour and a half the path led over snow sometimes above the Mules knees – I could now hardly endure the cold especially in my feet.'

During his years at Bowes Hall Cobden had contracted frostbite, and nearly lost several toes, and all through his life had to have his boots specially made, so this exposure must have been particularly hard on his feet.'Kate,' he writes, 'advised me to keep them close the Mules sides which I found an excellent mode of getting warmth. In the midst of our distress and whilst we could hardly see a dozen yards ahead for snow we heard a loud barking of dogs in a deep tone startled us and looking up saw two of the far-famed dogs of St Bernard coming bounding through the snow towards us. They paused for a moment when nearly close, and then continued their course – It is impossible to express the crowd of emotions that crossed our minds, as we first heard the sounds and caught sight of these interesting animals – Cold and comfortless as we were it gave us the cheering assurance that the Hospice was near...

'After we had changed our linen and Kate had got rid of the ice which hung like diamonds all over her hair, we sat down to a comfortable repast with the brother – a very gentlemanly man who did the honours of the table quite like a man of the world – poured out our wine, and then in a laughing way drank our health in the English fashion talked to Kate and told her among other things that she should be a prisoner there until the weather was clearer. Kate had brought a basket of cherries as a *cadeau* for the *religieux* which was conveyed to them. I was told in answer to my enquiries that ladies could not dine with the brothers in a body but that one of them by turn, took the office of receiving the visitors, if ladies were of the number, but if gentlemen only were of the party take their dinner in the refectory with the community.'

The Cobdens were at Weisbaden on 22 July, where they 'looked in a little at the gambling table at the Cursaal, then looked round at the shops and bought a specimen of the carved stags horn for which they are so famous in the neighbourhood.'

Up at six on 23 July, Cobden and Kate went to the well 'where we drank hot water tasting like chicken broth. We next bathed in the same kind of water...' Next day their Rhine steamer trip to Rotterdam started at six. They had a five hour stop at Dusseldorf, where they 'went on shore to look at the town, which with its beautiful promenades its botanical gardens &c was highly pleasing.' On 25 July they sailed into Dutch territory, arriving at Rotterdam where Cobden noted that the 'houses and everything we saw bright and clean beyond imagination.' After 26 July they were off again by public diligence for Haarlem by way of The Hague and Leyden. At Haarlem they 'went to hear the organ' before taking the train for Amsterdam, where they had dinner and took their customary exploratory walk. Back to Haarlem by rail on 27 July, and on by coach for Rotterdam. An exacting schedule for a young woman already carrying her first child.

On 28 July they boarded the steamer *Batavier* and sailed from Rotterdam for London.'We made a very calm and pleasant passage in 26 hours.' The life that lay ahead of them was to prove less 'calm and pleasant', but at that moment everything seemed set fair: they were in love, Kate was pregnant and Cobden already committed to the campaign which was to bring about the repeal of the Corn Laws.

CHAPTER TWO

Married to the League

On their return from their first Continental tour together, the Cobdens made their home at 21 Quay Street, Manchester, a large old house, later to become Owens College, which Cobden had bought for himself and his relations in 1836, when his calico-printing business prospered.

In spite of her pregnancy, Kate was soon drawn into the activities of the Anti-Corn Law League. By 29 October, she was helping at a tea-party for some 850 people, held in the 'handsomely decorated' Corn Exchange in Manchester. According to Cobden's friend Archibald Prentice, a journalist and one of the creators of the League, this had been 'a brilliant occasion'. The little governess from Machynlleth now wielded a silver teapot and listened to her husband and the other speakers holding forth on the aspirations of the League.

The Quay Street house had for some time been the rendezvous of the local Literary Society, and Sir W.E. Watkin in his book *Alderman of Manchester* writes of meeting Kate at a 'ladies night'. He describes her as 'a Welsh lady, then beaming with the beauty of youth'. The writer, Mrs Elizabeth Gaskell, who met her about a year later, described her in a letter to a friend as a '...very pretty woman, pearls and white lace, and jet black hair and eyes, and an exquisitely clear olive complexion without a particle of colour.' Kate's hair seems to have been her most striking feature, and many years later an old admirer, who had known her as a little girl in Wales, was to write to her recalling the sweet shop where '...a pretty little school-girl in frock and pinafore named Kate Wms, came sometimes to buy her sweets and sours...perhaps you also may remember the petite beauty, with her sable silken curls...' After Cobden's death an old school friend, a pupil at 'Miss Ellenthrop's', wrote her condolences and asked if any of her children had 'beautiful black hair'. The time when this remarkable hair was to turn white almost overnight was still many years in the future.

Kate's first child, a boy, was born at Quay Street on 12 March 1841. Cobden sent a note to brother Frederick to let him know that she was in labour: 'The Doctor is here – He talks of being released before four o'clock. Can you come to dine at 2? Yours affectly R.C.'

Things did not go quite as swiftly as anticipated, for later that day Cobden sent a second note: '5 min pst 6 – a fine boy – Both doing well R.C.' Kate's firstborn was christened Richard Brooks on 2 June.'The important ceremony comes off today at ¼ past 1 at St Peter's,' he wrote to Frederick.'John Brooks and you to be sponsors.' Brooks was their neighbour in Mosley Street, a member of a firm of bankers, but I found no evidence that he played any further part in Dick's life after his christening.'Will you be good enough to go or send to Broughton for the girls?' Cobden goes on: 'Priscilla will I hope stand. I have written to Fiers.' Charles Fiers, a Swiss, had married Cobden's sister Sarah, and the couple were then living in Manchester. Later they went abroad and made their home at Torre Pelice near Piedmont in the Italian Alps.

After her first confinement Kate spent some time staying in the home of a friend of Cobden, Edmund Ashworth, a founder member of the League. In September 1841, they moved to Leamington, where they were neighbours of John Bright and his family. When visiting relations in the town on 13 September Cobden called on Bright to condole with him on the loss of his wife, Elizabeth, who had died three days earlier. This meeting was to prove a crucial one for the two men, because it was then that Cobden said to Bright: 'When the first paroxysm of your grief is past, I would advise you to come with me, and we will never rest till the Corn Law is repealed.' Kate's younger brother, John, had a house in Leamington, which he was on the point of selling, and this Cobden now rented for six months, with John as their lodger.

Kate was unwell after the move – a fact which Cobden attributed to the weather – but which was probably due to the early malaise of her second pregnancy.

1841 was in every way momentous for the Cobdens, seeing not only the birth of a son and heir, but also Cobden's election as Member of Parliament for Stockport, which he had contested unsuccessfully in 1839. On 25 August he made his maiden speech. In September a committee of ladies was formed to organise a Free Trade Bazaar, to be held in the Theatre Royal, Manchester, early in 1842, with the object of raising funds for the League and bringing sympathisers into closer personal contact. Kate found herself chosen as President. The preparations for the bazaar meant involving herself in entertaining – something she was quite unaccustomed to – and she seems to have relied on her brother-in-law, Frederick, for help, for Cobden writes to him: 'Kate would be obliged if you would come down here at 12 o'clk and select ½ doz champagne and 3 bottles of port for the ladies of the bazaar.

Jackson has the key but Kate is very desirous that you who know how *matters ought to be* in the cellar should take a survey of the wine.'

An account from Mrs Amber, Court and Fancy Dress Maker of 5 Hanover Street, Hanover Square, a relative of Cobden on his mother's side, shows that in November that year (1841) Kate had been on a shopping expedition in London. Her purchases included 'A Rich Black Genova Velvet Sutherland Cloak lined with silk £6 .16.6d; A ditto Dress lined with silk and long sleeves £5.15.0. Pair Tulle demi Sleeves 11/-, A morning Cap trimmed with velvet, £1.8.0. A dark Sable Muff £6 .16.6, a ditto Victorine Tippet £7.10.0, Silver convolvulus Wreath £4.4. Pair Silver Ear Rings £2.2.0, Deal case &c 6/6. The total was £45.9.6 and suggests that the newly-elected Member for Stockport and leading light of the Anti-Corn Law League wished to be sure his wife could hold her own among her fellow stallholders.

The bazaar was held from 31 January to 10 February 1842 and raised close on ten thousand pounds for the cause. Kate and, presumably, the other 'ladies of the bazaar', duly received an ornamental certificate, decorated with symbolical corn sheaves 'In grateful acknowledgement of her unwearied exertions'. She was to keep it for the rest of her life.

Cobden had suffered serious qualms about press reaction to the bazaar, as he admitted to George Wilson, the man who had taken J.B. Smith's place as Chairman of the League Council and who was responsible for the regional re-organisation, completed the following year: 'I remember twelve months ago feeling apprehensive that the monopolist papers would have deterred the ladies from appearing as sellers at the stalls by their blackguardism-...Now what marked change is seen in those papers; not a joke or attempt at ribald wit. All is fair and even laudatory. In this fact alone I see a great moral triumph of the League...'

By this time (1842) the finances of the League were improving, but Cobden's own business affairs were already causing him some anxiety, and he was finding the continued upkeep of the Quay Street house a burden. On 10 March he wrote to Frederick from London asking him to take the necessary steps to exonerate him from 'the charge of taxes at the Quay Str. house after this qtr. It will be necessary,' he prompts his brother, 'to consult with a collector or experienced man of some kind...as to the mode in which you must proceed to escape the tax man – I believe it will be necessary to put all the furniture into one room. Let no time be lost as the qtr day is close at hand.'

To avoid paying rates on the property Cobden had seemingly asked Kate to let him know what items of furniture she would like brought from the old house to their new quarters in Leamington. Her choice had not been altogether practical, for he exclaims on 1 May: 'I will endeavour to attend to your request respecting the things you want from Quay Street but I really can't suppose that you want to have the large plate chest! I could not bring it with me unless I hired a special train!'

The following month found Kate with Cobden in his London lodgings at 15 Upper Seymour Street, and it was there that her second child was born on 26 June. Cobden reported the event in a formal letter to her elder brother Hugh: 'My dear Sir, your sister was safely brought to bed this morning at 3, and a fine little girl has been added to my household. Both Mother and baby are I am happy to say doing well. Kate, at whose request I am writing desires me to present her love to you and believe me in haste My dear Sir Yours faithfully Richard Cobden.' On the same day he wrote, less formally to Frederick: '...the nurse says it is a very fine baby – as usual. Please communicate so much to our circle.' They called the baby Kate.

In Leamington began the close friendship with Priscilla Bright, who was keeping house for her brother, and caring for his daughter Helen. The friendship was to endure throughout Kate's lifetime, and it was to Priscilla that Kate entrusted the young Richard when the time for her second confinement approached. Like her father, Priscilla was a Quaker, and she kept the anxious mother-to-be informed of the little boy's progress in a series of affectionate letters written in the manner of the Friends.

Frederick was still living at Quay Street, working at the Mosley Street office, and supplying Cobden, from their joint business, with the funds for the Leamington establishment. The method adopted by the brothers for transferring cash by post was for Fred to send a half note in one letter followed by the other half by a later post, in case – presumably – of loss or theft in transit. On 19 September, soon after they had settled in John Williams' house, Cobden asks Fred to let him have '£20 for household purposes...We have the car at the door and are off to Warwick to see the thatchers fair and an ox roasted in the Market Place, and all sorts of things besides.' On 22 October he tells Fred: 'Kate and I shall come to Manchester on Tuesday. We shall leave the boy here. Will you let a fire be put in our room in Quay Street for a day or two – Kate will only stay about three days, and then return here. I shall stay longer in Manchester.' On 24 October Cobden acknowledges the safe arrival of the notes and tells Fred: 'Kate and I shall come in the afternoon of Tuesday. We are going to Birmingham tomorrow evening to sleep at Sturge's.' Joseph Sturge (1793–1859), philanthropist, was one of the first members of the Anti-Corn Law League. A further request was made for cash on 9 November – this time for £30 '...and be pleased to send me by the luggage train (when you have leisure to seek it out) a dozen each of port and sherry...The weather is remarkably fine and we are constantly in motion. I have nearly got rid of my cold, and Kate is better but not quite well...the boy looks like a cherub-butcher.'

On 18 January 1843 Cobden, at the height of his 'agitating' tour of the North, wrote buoyantly to Kate from Stirling: 'My dearest Kate. We left Edinburgh on Monday morning and crossed over to the Fife shore by steam boat. Upon landing we were met by a crowd of people with a band of music and we walked up to the beach in regal state between a couple of rows of people who cheered the Free Trade party heartily...'

Cobden had already received the Freedom of Glasgow on 11 January, now followed Stirling, Dundee and Edinburgh. From Perth he writes to her that 'although we had only given them a few hours' notice we were invited by the Lord Provost, and Corporation to the Council chamber where the freedom of the City was presented to me.' In Edinburgh he caught one of the colds which were to plague him throughout his life, and tells Kate he is taking a hot bath in an attempt to get rid of it.'...I am glad to have such good account of the children – But the time is at hand when we must exercise great self-control in treating them. Our affection must be shown rather by wise management than exhibitions of transports of love. The little things will very soon begin to have their character formed and we must take care that it is not spoilt by an exhibition of increasing kindness.' After receiving the Freedom of Edinburgh he says he will turn his face 'joyfully southwards'.

But there was to be no joy awaiting the triumphant agitator on his return to Manchester. Their 'very fine baby girl' had died on 27 January, leaving Kate in a debilitated state. Cobden wrote at once to Hugh Williams with the news: 'My dear Sir, I write to you from a house of mourning – our dear little girl has been snatched from us – She was seized with convulsions on Wednesday, and to add to my distress I was absent from home when her pure spirit departed – Poor Kate has been confined to her room since and unable to write – She is now more tranquil and resigned. I have lost no time on my return in giving you this sad tidings – Believe me my dear Sir Yours faithfully Richard Cobden.' The sudden death of her baby was the first blow Kate suffered in her marriage. A later loss was to leave her far from 'tranquil and resigned', but in 1843 she had youth to help her through the ordeal.

Cobden enlisted the help of his brothers in arranging the child's funeral in Prestwich Churchyard, telling Frederick to send Charles to ask the Prestwich clergyman to officiate. On 30 January he wrote to James Mellor, father of Martha Mellor who married Cobden's journalist friend William Paulton, and of Alice Hargreaves, with whom he had obviously had an appointment: 'Owing to a distressing family affliction, (the sudden death of a very fine child) I am withdrawn for a brief period from public matters, and shall not be able to take part in the proceedings of this week either in Manchester or Liverpool.'

Cobden's friend, Joseph Parkes, at that time a Parliamentary Solicitor, wrote to condole with him on the death of little Kate. Writing from the Albion Hotel, Brighton on 2 February, where he was convalescing after an illness, he begs Cobden to: '...take care that you do not break down in Health. *You* are I am sure, and with a quick natural circulation, working a one hundred horse power Engine at 130, and take care that you do not explode a boiler or break your piston rod...Let me sympathise with you and Mrs Cobden on the sad loss of your child...Your worst grief is the first anguish of the *Mother's* grief...You, in the *necessity* of your public exertions, will soon recover your tone of mind; for *men must* return to the business of life.'

That month, Kate was to share with her husband trouble of a very different kind.

In readiness for the session, Cobden had taken new lodgings at 8 Connaught Terrace, Bayswater. It seems that the old apartments in Seymour Street had been more to his liking. From these lodgings he tells her on 16 February, the day before he spoke to such disastrous effect in the House: 'My old annual attack of inflammation in my right eye has visited me at a most unlucky moment, I have been detained at home for two days, and fear it will be quite impossible for me to go down to the House this evening – However, I have sent word to Villiers [Corn Law Reformer and Free Trader] that if the debate is likely to close tonight, he must send a messenger and a cab for me, and I will assuredly go down and fire a shot at all risks before the division.' His attendance on 17 February, on the fifth day of the debate, was to lead to the worst moments in his parliamentary career.

Just before the opening of the 1843 session of Parliament, Mr Drummond, Prime Minister Sir Robert Peel's private secretary, was shot in Parliament Street by a mechanic from Glasgow named Daniel M'Naghten, and died from the wound. M'Naghten was tried and acquitted on grounds of insanity. A rumour quickly spread that his target had been the Prime Minister, which had a disastrous effect on Peel, highly sensitive as he was to physical pain. The affair also produced a crisis in Cobden's public life which must have shaken Kate when she read the newspaper reports. On 17 February Cobden, speaking in the debate on a part of the Queen's speech at the opening of Parliament which referred to the present distressing state of the country, said he held Peel 'individually responsible for the present position of the country.' This produced a furore in the House, and Peel temporarily lost his usual composure. He is reported to have said, 'with signs of agitation', 'Sir, the honourable gentleman has stated here very emphatically, what he has more than once stated at the conferences of the Anti-Corn Law League, that he holds me individually responsible for the distress and suffering of the country...' By then the place was in an uproar, and Cobden found it impossible to explain himself, although he attempted to: 'I have said that I hold the right honourable gentleman responsible by virtue of his office, as the whole context of what I said was sufficient to explain.' In the end, Peel, although very stiffly, accepted his explanation.

Cobden gave his own account of that hectic evening to Frederick: 'The affair of last Friday seems to be working more and more to our advantage. It has been the talk of everybody here, from the young lady on the throne, down to the back-parlour visitors of every pot-house in the metropolis. And the result seems to be a pretty general notion that Peel has made a great fool of himself, if not something worse...'

Cobden's opponents used the Peel affair as ammunition against the League: they even said that he had ruined his political life. The word 'Downfall' was used by Lord Brougham. However, as Cobden wrote to Kate three days after the scene in the House: '...The whole gossip of the clubs has been for the last few days about nothing but Peel and his attack upon me and upon Roebuck [the Quaker philanthropist] and if I may believe my ears the general opinion is very strong against both. As for Brougham he is a privileged old humbug, and nobody expects any consistency from him. He is I believe a very insincere man, and nobody ought to put any faith in his word – There has been a correspondence between him and Bright, the letters of the latter are admirable, and put Brougham completely in the wrong, and lecture him with great truth and severity upon his shameful proceedings. If they should be published they will attract a good deal of notice.

'We hold our first weekly League meeting at the Crown and Anchor tavern tomorrow, and when I shall make a reply to Peel's atrocious insinuation against me. I expect we shall soon have possession of the metropolis – for there is a great disposition felt to be present at our meetings...Give my regards to your host and hostess and all the circle, and with many kisses for the little man...'

'My dearest Kate You are really becoming a very spirited politician – Your description of the hon. little member for Bath that he is not worthy to be a football for honest politicians is really not so bad – and it is very much in accordance with all that I hear from people up here – But after all I feel far less indignation against Roebuck than Brougham who is his evil genius and tempted, and who I suspect prompted him to the course he took – Brougham is a very bad fellow and is trying to damage the League in every possible way, and is doing all in his power to serve the Tories...

'Our meeting last night at the Crown and Anchor was the most extraordinary affair I ever saw. Nothing like it has taken place in London for 24 years. Not only was the large room crammed, but the entrance hall stairs and passages also and thousands were unable to get in at all – As the people who were inside would not leave we put a detachment of lecturers into the entrance hall who mounted a table, and lectured the audience who crowded passages, and stairs. There were two speeches going on at the same time, and the cheers of one meeting were occasionally heard by the other. My reception was very warm indeed. The audience were determined to whitewash me from the dirt attempted to be thrown upon me by the Tories – I expect in about two months we shall be ready to hold a meeting in Palace Yard – Tell this to Mr E.A. [Edmund Ashworth] for he once predicted it must come to that – The fellow *in the House* will be much more civil in proportion as the enthusiasm grows outside --

'I fully expect however that the *pack* will give tongue upon me when I next get up to speak – if so I shall be ready with a rebuke for them...My time is almost taken up with this perusal of the letters I am getting in approbation of my speech – it has roused a fire of enthusiasm in my favor [*sic*] all over the country, and made me more prominent and notorious than I could have wished. Give my kind regards to your kind host and hostess and tell them how much I blush when I think of the family party that have billeted themselves, under their roof – How long do you think of inflicting yourselves upon them? – I am beginning to be homesick – but don't flatter *yourself* – I am I mean anxious to see the little man – I had half inclined to run down on Saturday, but really I think I should be laughed at if I were only able to stay for a night, and so I determined to put it off a week, but don't be surprised if you see me the following Saturday kiss the little man and remember me to your party, and believe me yours ever affectionately Richd Cobden.'

Meetings of the Anti-Corn Law League were taking much of Cobden's time in the March of 1843. On 8 March he writes to Kate that he is disappointed at not having heard from her, and tells her that the League are preparing to hold their weekly meetings 'in the Drury Lane Theatre, which will make a good display in the Metropolis. We find that M'Cready [*sic*] the Lessee is a Liberal.'

Macready had already played an unwitting part in the shaping of Cobden's future by turning down his comedy *The Phrenologist*. Had this been accepted it might have set Cobden off on a very different career. As it was, he received no encouragement from the famous actor-manager, who returned his manuscript, saying he already had three other plays on his desk on the same subject. Cobden tore up his and that is the last we hear of any literary endeavour on his part.

Previously the League had held their meetings at the Crown and Anchor and the Freemasons' Tavern, but these venues they had outgrown, hence the hiring of Macready's large theatre, and it was there that seven meetings were held between March 1843 and the beginning of May that year. Writing to Frederick on 11 March, he told his brother: 'Wait till we have held two or three weekly meetings in Drury Lane Theatre, and you will see that we are not the men to be put to the ordeal of a middle-class jury. Our metropolitan gatherings are bona-fide demonstrations of earnest energetic men of the shop-keeping class, a large proportion under thirty years of age.' Cobden, who was staying with their friends, the Potters, at Buile Hill, was then 39.

On 12 March he tells Kate that he is going with John Williams to Southampton, to attend an Anti-Corn Law meeting on 13 March: 'John and I arrived here yesterday at ½ past 1 and this morning we took a fly, crossed the ferry, and went to take a view of Netley Abbey – There I found things much the same as when we paid the ruins a visit. There was the kitchen, the chapel, the cloister, the burial ground, but we had none of the fine foliage and bright flowers shining in the sunshine which we beheld when you and I were there…We went down to the old Castle, near the river, and saw the same woman and her children with whom we had a talk.

By the way I can scarcely bring myself to believe that it is almost three years since we were there together.'

The meetings were proving steadily more successful: 'We had a most glorious meeting last evening in Drury Lane as you will see by the paper which I now send you. I never saw such a sight as it presented when I came upon the stage, and old hack as I am I really felt awed at the assembly. From the floor to the roof it was one vast mass of human heads – It seemed as if the house was wainscoated with human faces. I was of course very well received – '

In spite of these political triumphs Cobden was unhappy about his personal life. On 22 March he writes to Kate: 'Your letter to day gives me a fair view of yr plans, but I hardly know what to say or do – It is quite impossible we can continue to live apart in this way – I wd rather give up Power than submit to an entire separation from *the boy* – to say nothing of a third party – yet I really don't see how we are to manage in London. If you do come up here you must necessarily enter upon a certain circle of acquaintance, and our present lodgings are not fit for you to receive yr friends there – and I can't afford a house at the same time that I am keeping the Quay St. establishment up. If you go to the Seaside it has occurred to me that you might perhaps like to be at Margate or Ramsgate or Brighton where I could come on the Saturday – *There* you would not be obliged to enter upon a circle of acquaintance...I am not satisfied with our mode of life, and I cannot settle into any plan which separates us for half the year – I think you are quite right in keeping Charlotte Smith about you, for it wd be impossible for you to be without a friend with you...We are going to have a splendid meeting tonight at Drury Lane, and I shall enjoy it very much as a spectator, not being about to take any part in it – Mrs Cooke Taylor and her party are going to have a private box – With kisses for the little rascal and regards to you all Believe me Ever affectly Richd Cobden.'

On 24 March he tells her: 'I have recd a present for you, which I now enclose – It is the first rewards *you* have had for my labours.' He himself has received 'a printed velveteen for a dressing-gown with a wheatear upon it'. A few days later he is reproaching her for not writing: 'I suppose you are an advocate of "reciprocity treaties", and that you are quite determined not to exchange letters with me unless you get an *equivalent* in return. You are resolved to have as many imports as exports. This I presume accounts for your not having sent me one letter since Sunday. I shall not be able to keep up this "reciprocity treaty" so regularly as I could wish as a *Free-*

trader, owing to my horribly pressing engagements...It is a cold east wind and I am very ill-tempered – so take care of your good behaviour.'

On Sunday 2 April he writes from Norwich reporting a 'Bumper' meeting: '...about 4,000 people in a large and magnificent Gothic Hall.' Back in London, he writes to her on 7 April, tired but triumphant: 'Our visit to Norfolk was altogether satisfactory but cruelly tiring to me, – for at Yarmouth we were put into a kind of black hole for heat and suffocation. I did not tell you that little Smith the Sculptor was taking a bust of me – being quite resolved to exhibit your husband's beautiful features in Marble! As I could not go to his Studio to sit he comes to the lodgings where he has fixed up his clay bust for modelling – It stands in the back room and behind the screen wrapped up in a wet cloth when he is away. Your brother did not know it was there when he came home and going behind the screen he suddenly saw something raised up on a level with himself in the indistinct form of a human head covered with a white cloth which made him start! Little Smith has a great many orders for copies of the bust...'

The reference to John Williams coming 'home' suggests that his younger brother-in-law was sharing Cobden's lodgings at this time.

The question of Dick's schooling is concerning Cobden. In a letter of 26 April he says: 'I am by no means an advocate for his beginning too early to learn his letters – after all a learned child is nothing better than a learned pig. It is only when the intellect is tolerably matured that learning is of much use.' On 3 May he tells Kate that he is going to speak at Drury Lane again, 'our last appearance on that stage – Mrs Selby the landlady has just applied to me for an order to admit her and a friend...'

The last of the series of meetings was held on 3 May: 'Last night we had the most splendid gathering in Drury Lane ever held. There must have been at least 5,000 people present. Every part of stage, box, and gallery was crammed, and the enthusiasm was unbounded. There were more ladies than usual present. We are shut out for the future from the theatre by the Tory committee. Wilson [George Wilson, Chairman of the Anti-Corn Law League] talks of trying to get Vauxhall – '

On 17 May he is in contrite mood when he writes to Kate: '...say every kind thing to your cousin, and express my contrition for all my neglect, which I fear is a part of my nature not the necessity of my circumstances – I *neglect everybody*, even my wife and child. I was in such a whirl yesterday that I allowed the post to go before I could write to you, and afterwards I suffered pangs of conscience enough to satisfy even your vindictive nature! My speech was like cayenne rubbed in with vinegar.'

18 May 1843. Cobden to Kate: '...as respects the visit to Tunbridge Wells your brother and I will endeavour to run down to look about us – But there would be no harm in your writing to Mrs Thomas Smith to ask her how she likes the place and whether she can recommend it.'

In this letter Cobden tells Kate she should make use of Frederick 'in the trouble of removing as you would of me.'

There is a gap in the exchange of letters between husband and wife at this point. Kate was in Tunbridge Wells with young Dick when Cobden wrote on 4 July to tell her he would be coming down to see her: '...will be at Tunbridge station at 1 o'clk. If the weather should be fine and you are disposed to come and bring me back in a fly be good enough to meet me at the station. But you must not come without the boy.' If wet, he tells her, he will take the omnibus.

On 12 July Cobden is writing in lighter mood from London: '...I am in danger of being selected king over the Welsh Rebeccas [protesters chiefly against toll gate charges]. I am engaged to pay a visit to Hereford on the 20th when I shall be heard of I suppose in South wales, and perhaps shall have a deputation from the principality inviting me to become prince of Wales. Will you be princess? Ask the little man if he would wish to be prince of Wales elect? If so we must have him re-christened David or *Taffy*. I really sometimes have great misgivings whether he will not be spoilt and petted too much. Let me hear how you are employing your time.'

On 28 July he tells her: 'I got back last night too late for post and am now on the start for Chelmsford. I hope you inquired at the library the result of the Durham election and learnt that Bright has won a great victory – It is a glorious blow for repeal. We are going to hold a meeting at the Crown and Anchor tomorrow night to address the Durham people, and so I fear I shall not be able to see you till Sunday morning. The Hereford meeting was all right.'

By 1 August Cobden was feeling the strain of the tour.'I have just got a letter from Mr Edwards, the Barrister who is on the Western Circuit, who tells me he saw me at Winchester at the public meeting and was much struck with my bad looks, and therefore he writes to give me some good advice against overworking myself, and then as a good counsellor he talks about my wife and child, and says he is sure *you* will back him in his advice. I do begin to think I am overdoing it, and so have resolved to restrict myself to one day a week...Give my kiss to the little Gabbler for whom I have many inquiries from the Leaguers as well as for yourself.'

On 15 August he writes her what might be called an 'improving' letter: 'There is one quality which I wish you to cultivate, which is that of *self-esteem* which teaches us to despise the fear of being slighted. I want you to have such a good opinion of yourself as not to be offended at the apparent neglect of anybody – There is an old saying which is worthy of notice because other people are apt to believe in its truth: "None fear contempt but the contemptible" – For my part I never am out of temper with anybody for neglecting or slighting me, I always take refuge in a certain self-esteem which tells me I am not despicable, whatever other people may think to the contrary – You would see by your visit to the newsroom this morning that we had a little skirmish in the House last night...'

Cobden was speaking at meetings in Kent in June that year, so possibly spent some time with Kate in her lodgings in Tunbridge Wells for it was from there that he wrote to Frederick on 7 June, reporting the growing success of the campaign. She and Dick were still at Tunbridge Wells when he wrote to her from London on 12 October: '...reached town safe last night at 11 o'clock. Sir Joshua Walmsley came part of the way with me and made me almost promise that you and I would pay him a visit at Renton Abbey before you go to town.'

On 17 November he writes to her from Salisbury that he is glad to find that she is 'in the comfortable asylum of Buile Hill' with the Potters.

That autumn saw growing anxiety in the country over the activities of the Chartists, a movement dedicated to Parliamentary reform which based its campaigning on its manifesto – the People's Charter. On 21 November, he wrote: 'The foolish magistrates have put their heads together, and written to the Home Secretary for 50 London police to keep the peace, and not content with this they have also sent for a troop of horse! Now considering that we have not held one open-air meeting, and that all our lectures and addresses have been given to audiences composed largely of ladies, this is the most amazing piece of foolery I have met with.'

From October 1843 to January 1844 Cobden and Bright were on another 'agitating' tour. On 10 January Cobden wrote from Carlisle to Kate, who was again staying with the Edmund Ashworths at Bolton, and tells her that 'By looking at the map you will be able to follow us...One day we travelled more than a hundred miles by coach.'

On 4 December (1843) he wrote to her from Leeds to 2 Grove Terrace, Broughton, where his sisters were now living: 'My dearest Kate, I will take a mutton chop tomorrow at half past 1 to 2 at home. *Irish stew* is the best way of dressing mutton chops if your cook understands it.' He has had a meeting with Dick: 'I saw the dear little fellow as I passed Rochdale yesterday at the station. You never saw so droll a figure as he represented. Miss Bright had put a fur-tippet on him which nearly reached the ground and made him look like one of the Chinese peasants with a coat of thatch. He was looking remarkably well. The first exclamation he raised was "You rascal!" But he was sadly anxious to go with me in the train. Miss Bright begged to keep him for another week which I agreed to. It is very cold here. Expect me at 2 tomorrow and I hope to find you still rapidly recovering.'

He wrote to her again from the Anti-Corn Law League office in Manchester on 21 December, 1843: '...Have you made any arrangements for Christmas Day – I regret that we cannot meet the members of my family as usual on that day, and should like if you can so contrive to make all other considerations give way for a peaceful and affectionate union of all of us on Monday.' (He does not say where.) 'I hope to meet you at Bury at the Eagle and Child Inn at 12 o'clock on Saturday.'

On 14th January from Aberdeen, he tells Kate: 'Here we are happily at the end of our pilgrimage, and on Tuesday we hope to turn our faces homeward. It has been a hard week's work. After finishing our labours at Perth, I expected to have a quiet day yesterday. We started in the morning by the coach for this place, but in passing through Forfar we found all the inhabitants at their doors or in the streets. They had heard of our intended passage through their town, and a large crowd was assembled at the inn where the coach stopped, which gave us three cheers; and nothing would do but we must stop to give them an address. We consented, and immediately the temperance band struck up, and paraded through the town, and the parish church bells were set a ringing, in fact the whole town was set in a commotion. We spoke to about two thousand persons in the parish church, which, notwithstanding that it was a Saturday evening, was granted to us. It was the first time we ever addressed an Anti-Corn Law audience in a parish Church...I hope we shall last it out for another week...I have thus far escaped a cold, and find my health good; in fact, notwithstanding my hard work, I have been better this winter than ever, having escaped my usual fit of inflammation of the eyes. I think there is a special providence watching over the

Leaguers. Give my regards to your circle and a kiss to the little repealer, and with love to your own little self – believe me, ever yours affectionately, Richard Cobden.'

This is the only occasion I have seen the word 'little' used by Cobden in his letters to Kate.

By 17 January, when he wrote to her from Dundee, he admits he is 'nearly overdone with work, two meetings at Aberdeen on Monday, up at four on Tuesday, travelled thirty-five miles, held a meeting at Montrose, and then thirty-five miles more at Dundee, for a meeting the same evening. Tomorrow we go to Cupar Fife, next day, Leith, the day following, Jedburgh.'

He writes from Hull on 20 January: 'I shall leave this place tomorrow by the train at half-past ten, and expect to reach Manchester by about five o'clock. I am, I assure you, heartily glad of the prospect of only two days relaxation after the terrible fagging I have had for the last three weeks. Today we have two meetings in Hull. I am in the Court House with a thousand people before me, and Bright is stirring up the lieges with famous effect. He is reminding the Hull people of the conduct of their ancient representative, Andrew Marvell, and talking of their being unworthy of the graves of their ancestors over which they walk. We shall have another meeting this evening.'

When he wrote to Frederick on 22 January it was from Newcastle-on-Tyne.'I got here last night from Jedburgh, where we had the most extraordinary meeting of all. The streets were blocked up with country people as we entered the place, some of whom had come over the hills for twenty miles. It is the Duke of Buccleuch's country, but he would be puzzled to find followers on his own lands to fight his battles as of old. Tonight we meet here, tomorrow at Sunderland, the day after at Sheffield, where you will please address me tomorrow, on Thursday we shall be at York, and on Friday at Hull, and in Manchester on Saturday evening.'

The main money-raising event in the history of the Anti-Corn Law League was the Free Trade Bazaar at Covent Garden Theatre in the spring of 1845, which proved to be a nine days wonder, but this time Kate played no part in the proceedings. Instead, she was again staying with the Potters at Buile Hill when Cobden wrote to her about the bazaar on 16 April: '...You want to know what I do with myself on Saturdays, that I forget my lonely wife and children! Last Saturday I went to see the Model of the Bazaar Hall which is being prepared in Covent Garden Theatre. It will be a Gothic Hall 150 feet long and 40 feet high – lighted from above on the outside of the roof – so as to give it the effect, through the transparent and painted linen roof of being covered with glass and the sun shining upon it. The effect will I should say be very glorious and novel, and no doubt it will attract all the world to see it...'

The temporary transformation of the famous theatre was the work of the Grieve brothers, stage designers. That the effect achieved was indeed 'very glorious and novel' can be seen from *The Illustrated London News*, which covered the event in its issues of 10 and 17 May, paying tribute to the work of the Grieve family. There had been a pre-view the previous week:

'On Thursday punctually at 12 o'clock,' *The Illustrated London News* informed its readers on 10 May, 'the doors of Covent-Garden-Theatre were opened to hundreds of well-dressed visitors to the Great Bazaar, in support of the Anti-Corn-Law League...The vast Gothic Hall has been painted, at a great expense, by Messrs Grieve; it is a most effective specimen of scenic architecture. At the upper end of the hall was a large and splendidly decorated cake, weighing upwards of 280 pounds, which had been sent from Bury in Lancashire. The top of it was ornamented with a kind of arabesque work, in portions of which were inscribed the names of the most distinguished free-trade members of the House of Commons.' Cobden described it to Kate as 'a plum cake nearly a yard in diameter'.'This cake,' said the *News*, '...is at the close of the Bazaar to be cut up and distributed to the visitors by the ladies who presided at the stalls.' The Cobdens' friend Mrs Cooke Taylor of Arlington Street, Camden Town, was one of these.'Notwithstanding the check imposed on Thursday, to some extent, by the high prices of admission the Gothic Hall was nearly full in less than an hour after the doors of the Theatre had been opened: and the sale of articles commenced very early, as indicated by the sound of money, which could be heard in all directions. Some elegant stand fire-screens bore the portraits of Mr Cobden, Mr Villiers and Mr Bright, and a splendid piece of Sheffield cutlery, in the shape of a pair of scissors, represented full length figures of Mr Cobden and Mr Bright with the words "Champions of Free Trade". The Bazaar will be opened on Monday next, at the admission of one shilling.'

Further attractions were evidently introduced after the pre-view to increase the scope of the bazaar, and the *News* in its next issue reported: '...To the Shakespeare room the largest additions have been made. It may be regarded as a new Manchester Stall for the exhibition and sale of printed goods, but it also contains some splendid specimens of drapery. Around the room are printed ladies' dresses, of muslin, and similar materials, contributed by Messrs Hoyle & Co., Swanwick and Johnson, Cobden, and several other manufacturers.'

Cobden later reported to Kate: 'Mrs Taylor has been suffering a reaction of languor consequent upon her great exertions in connection with the bazaar', so perhaps Kate, with her dislike of what she called 'bustle' was relieved to have missed it.

But there was another reason why Kate could not have got her self involved in this exhausting event. On 22 November 1844, Kate had given birth to a another daughter, who was also called Kate, and this Kate proved more durable than her predecessor.

CHAPTER THREE

Goodbye to the Corn Laws

Although his business affairs were already in a critical state, in 1844 Cobden chose to seek a house for his family in the Manchester area. After five years without a home of their own the news must have come as a relief to Kate. As on many occasions Cobden enlisted Frederick's help in this search. Writing from London on 14 June he tells his brother: '...As my labors [*sic*] must be less *intense* than heretofore, I shall be able to give more time to my private affairs which Heaven knows have been neglected enough. The first thing to do is to get a house over my head – and no time must be lost looking out – Two sorts of abode are out of the question – I cant be in the town, or in the suburbs in a *row* – I must have a detached place, and whether at two or five miles from the Exchange is of little consequence – Is there anything in the Eccles Road or at Eccles – or at Prestwich or in the old Bury Road past Cheetham. I would rather be on high and dry ground – Is there anything towards Altrincham? Or failing all this anything eligible in Victoria Park? I wish you would at once institute inquiries, and make it your business to look out for the most likely houses at liberty.'

It was this last suggestion which proved fruitful, but some time elapsed before they found a place to their liking. Only on 6 July 1845 was Cobden able to tell Kate: 'My dearest Kate I have just had a letter from Lipton(?) closing with my offer for the house in Victoria Park – the matter is therefore settled – But I suppose we shall not get possession before Easter and then the alterations will require three weeks.' Meanwhile, Kate's lonely life continued. Later that month he is again delayed in joining her: 'I had intended to have gone down tomorrow, but John Brooks is in town, and wishes me to make one of a deputation to Lord Aberdeen, and so I am detained probably till Thursday or Friday...'

The earlier part of 1845 was a period of intense activity for Cobden but he contrived to write almost daily to Kate. On 5 February: 'I was detained in Manchester till the evening yesterday, owing to the fault of the railway clock, which disappointed several other persons. I slept at Birmingham last night, and came up this morning. The bells are ringing for the return of the Queen from the House. I am told by some lookers on, that there was no cheering, and that her little Majesty looked rather glum. Pray kiss the little ones. I begin to feel rather lonely and shall be homesick long before Easter.'

8 February.'...You say you are counting the days till Easter, but I shall not wait so long – depend on it you will see my *apparition* before then if I did not come bodily, for I run always with you in spirit – I have sent you some papers, and hope you will let me have the *Guardian* regular on the day it is published, if you can spare it – '

But he changed his mind about the *Guardian* and tells her on 11 February that she need not send it, as he generally sees it in London the same evening it is published: 'But I hope you will send it away to some of your friends where its free trade doctrines will be of service.' He goes on: 'I met Lord Howick [later Earl Grey] at dinner, as was told you by Miss Bright. He did not convert me to Whiggery, nor did he make any attempt upon my virtue. He is in very good temper with the League, and quite disposed to help us, and to throw the fixed duty overboard. Bright made a very powerful but rasping speech the other night. The milk-and-water people will find fault with him, but he is a noble fellow, and ought to be backed up by every genuine Free-trader.'

20 February: '...I have not expressed my unavailing regrets at our separation to *you*, because I thought it unnecessary to assure you how greatly I feel the separation – Not merely do I long for your company, but the children are as near to my heart at all times – I do not altogether despair of seeing you before Easter. But the questions that are now coming on in the House are all of that practical kind which call for my presence – '

11 March: 'We are certainly taking more prominent ground this session than ever, and the tone of the farmers' friends is very subdued indeed. They never open their mouths if they can help it, and then they speak in a very humble strain. I am quite in a fidget about my speech on Thursday. You will think it very strange in an old hack demagogue like me, if I confess that I am as nervous as a maid the day before her wedding, and I am afraid I shall disappoint others as well as myself. I have sent for Mr Lattimore, who came up and spent an evening with me, on purpose to give me a lesson about the farmers' view of the question.'

'I was terribly out of sorts with the task,' he wrote to Kate after the ordeal was successfully behind him, 'and when I got up to speak, I was all in a maze.' He sent her a copy of the *Times* with the report of his speech and said it was his best.'But I don't think that it was as good as it ought to have been.'

Not only was Cobden worried about the quality of his speeches at this time, but it is clear from his correspondence with Frederick that the state of their business was an added anxiety. He tells him on 7 April: 'I shall certainly be down a week before the Whitsuntide holidays, so as to have at least a fortnight. The fidgets have so got possession of me that I cannot master them. For the first time I feel fairly down and dead-beaten. It is of no use writing all one feels. Entreat J.S. to work down the stock of odds and ends of cloth, and keep down everything as low as possible. And remind Charles again of the critical importance of finding something for the machinery to do in the interval between the seasons. It is of no use writing bad news to me. I can't help it while here.' But by 18 April he had recovered his spirits and tells him: 'I do not see any difficulty in giving adequate attention to the business, and still retaining, ostensibly at all events, the same public position as heretofore. But whether this can be done or not, I shall of course make everything else subservient to the one point in which honour is involved.'

There were times during this session of 1845 when Cobden allowed his exasperation with his wife's preoccupation with domestic matters to show in his letters to her. 23 May: 'I have read the enclosed from Mrs Aitchison: pray throw aside all feeling in this matter and settle it as an affair of business – I will rely on you not allowing me to be stung by gnats in this way whilst I have *lions* in my path to contend with.' It seems Kate's letters to him had been 'doleful', for on 5 June he complains: '...your letters are freighted with bad news – I am sorry to hear that you are not well – and I fear that the constant worry and annoyance to which your mind has been exposed is the cause...Nothing but strict abstinence in eating and drinking keeps me in tolerable health...Bright and I called to-day upon Tom Moore to shake hands with him. D'Israeli invited me to meet him at breakfast the other day. But as it was at 12 o'clk, the hour when our railway Committee sits, I could not go. I should have met Bulwer there also. The little man [Moore] is just the sort of person you would expect to see – a lively brisk little fellow, very polished and gentlemanly, but with the warmth of a poet and Irishman in his manner. But I must say that his head gives little sign to the phrenologist of the force of his genius.'

'You will think I have been very neglectful,' he wrote on 19 June, 'but on Monday and Tuesday I was not quite clear as to your address – I had burned your letter which gave me the No of the house to which you removing – Indeed I put all letters in the fire which only give me pain to look at them. On Wednesday I was to speak at Covent Garden, and being confined all the day in the Committee room, and having to prepare my speech after four o'clock, I knew I should be excused writing.

'I find it very difficult to get up my spirits to appear before a large audience like that at Covent Garden. Indeed I feel myself to be only acting a part, in appearing to speak with energy, hope, and confidence. I can't go through another period such as the present session, to be harassed and annoyed as I have been in every possible way; it would kill me! I have not the least idea when I shall be released from my attendance at the Committee. To-day we have been bored with a three hours' speech from a counsel, who would have nothing else to do if he released us from our confinement. I expect we shall have another week of it at least.'

'I wish you would write me long and agreeable letters,' he begged her on 20 June, 'giving me news of the place, how you employ your time, who your neighbours are, what the boy does with himself, and everything that occurs. You have plenty of time to write, and although I can't send you long letters in return, it would give me great pleasure to get long ones from you. Now I will give you a specimen of my day's work. Our Committee meets at twelve and sits till four. Then the House commences, and lasts on average till twelve. Twice last week I sat till two o'clock in the House, having been under the roof for fourteen hours. Next morning I can't be down till nine o'clock, and scarcely have I got breakfast, and glanced at the Votes and Proceedings for the day, when I must start again for the House. You will, I think, excuse me after this, if I am not a very good correspondent.'

Cobden at this time was corresponding with Mrs Drummond, mother of Peel's murdered secretary, with whom he had often exchanged letters, and her reply to one of his, dated July, shows her understanding of the Cobden's private problems: 'I need not say, dear sir that all and every part of your letter interested me, but especially that part in which there is an allusion to your Domestic circumstances...I can perfectly understand the privation which separation from your family causes, but I cannot agree in thinking that a deprivation inflicted by the pressing nature of your Public duties render your Life either less beneficial to your family or less consonant to high moral principle...and now I have to offer my *kindest remembrances to Mrs Cobden* and when she longs for more of your Company you must reply to her as I did to my Daughter in Law under a similar complaint "Public men are Public property and they who unite themselves to them while they enjoy the honor of their reputation must content themselves with but a small part of their Society" but I doubt not Mrs Cobden is already fully imbued with this sentiment and would much rather have her distinguished tho' absent Husband than some Nobody who is ever at her side.'

If Cobden concealed his business worries from Kate at this time his letters to Frederick whilst tied to London as a member of the Railways Committee verged on the desperate:

'...I will at all risks come down on Friday afternoon by the express train which will land me in Manchester at ten o'clock,' he tells him on the 24th June, 'and I should like to have a bed at your lodgings, and there I must see John Brooks privately on the Saturday morning. I have turned the subject over in every way, and I see no other solution of it than in absolutely withdrawing myself from public life, first having secured such a promise of support from some of my friends as shall secure me from the effects of the shock. I have made up my mind to this, and shall not have a moment's peace of mind until I have fairly got out of my present false position. In fact, I would not go through another four months like the past for any earthly consideration whatever.'

The summer recess of 1845 must have been a far from refreshing one for Cobden, burdened as he was by financial worries. He was, by this time, facing actual ruin. On 15 September he wrote to Bright, telling him of his intention to return to private life. Bright was in Inverness at the time, on a tour of Scotland, and replied on 20 September, telling Cobden: '...I would return home without a day's delay, if I had a valid excuse for my sisters who are here with me. We have been out nearly three weeks, and may possibly be as much longer before we reach home; our plans being pretty well chalked out beforehand.' He begged Cobden not to be hasty: '...The league's existence depends mostly upon you, and that if the shock cannot be avoided, it should be given only after the weightiest consideration, and in such way as to produce the least evil...The victory is now in reality gained, and our object will before very long be accomplished: but it is often as difficult to leave a victory as to gain it; and the sagacity of leaders cannot be dispensed with while anything remains to be done...'

Cobden's letter (which he had begged him to destroy) had ruined Bright's holiday. He could not rest until he had taken steps to help his friend out of his difficulties. What excuses he made to his sisters is not known, but shortly after writing to Cobden he was posting back to Manchester in the rain to rally wealthy friends on his behalf. A group of these promptly came to the rescue with funds and staved off the crisis, and Cobden was enabled to continue the fight for repeal with an easier mind, and give all his energy to the final stage of the struggle.

There is a gap in the correspondence between Cobden and Kate at this time, until he writes to her from Stroud on 4 December: 'My dearest Kate I had reckoned upon getting home on Saturday but Lord Ducie has put the screws upon us. We have no alternative but to sleep at his house on Saturday night, in order to attend a meeting on the afternoon at his neighbouring town of Wooten-under-Edge. We could not resist his appeal. This throws me out in my plans, and I shall not see you till Wednesday. We shall go up to London on Sunday afternoon to sleep there, and meet Villiers, and others for a talk, and on Monday we shall go to Notts, next day to Derby, and on Wednesday home. The *Times* newspaper of today, which has just come to hand here, reports that the Government has determined to call Parliament together the first week in January, and propose total repeal. If this be true, the day of my emancipation is nearer than I expected. But we must be on our guard, and not expect too much from the Government. They will attempt to cheat us yet. Our meetings are everywhere gloriously attended. There is a perfect unanimity among all classes; not a syllable about Chartism or any other *ism*, and not a word of dissent. Bright and I are almost off our legs, five days this week in crowded meetings.'

The only letter that survives from Kate to Cobden – and that probably a draft, as it contains alterations and erasures – is dated 7 December, when she wrote from their new home in Park Crescent, Victoria Park, Manchester.'My dearest Richard, I must fear that you will not be equal to nightly meetings till the assembling of Parliament, though it promises to be earlier than usual from the accounts I hear – However, if one thing can support and cheer you more than an other it is the feeling [crossed out] knowledge that the death struggle is at hand. I understand that they are already arranging plans to celebrate the triumph of their cause at Newall's Buildings – Henry Rawson and George Wilson have to give a grand ball to the Ladies – The Council Room to be continued as a place of rendezvous for congenial spirits to talk over the past and to brew future mischiefs for all those who wish the world to stand still!

'How extraordinary the article of Thursday in the *Times* – of course it has some authenticity or it never would have dared to trifle with the feelings of the country in such [illegible]. Villiers has written to the League to say that the little Queen is highly indignant at not having been made acquainted with the decision of the Cabinet previous to seeing it written in the columns of a public journal and this is here considered as another proof that the *Times* is to be depended upon. However, notwithstanding all this, you are quite right not to relax one nerve till the battle is achieved for there is no knowing how the enemy may yet manoeuvre.

'The boy has been with me the whole of the morning, which will account for some of the blunders of penmanship [a squiggle here] in this epistle. He is never a moment quiet though he has endeavoured his utmost to oblige me whilst writing, for allowing him to be my companion. However a thousand times I rather him fidgety and troublesome than to have the sedate little fellow you describe as being frightened at a little romping. – Marion Higgin staid [*sic*] with me till yesterday. On Thursday we went to Mr Thomas(?) Bright's where Richard had been the two previous days. Their little boy appears in delicate health, having constant sore throat – Mrs Bright struck me as looking rather poorly so I determined upon bringing the boy home with me for from what I saw of their child I concluded that she was unaccustomed to uproariousness – with which God grant we may have ever to combat rather than a sickly constitution. – The Baby is very bonny but shows no great notion of either walking or talking yet.

'I hope to hear from you tomorrow though from opinion gathered at the league I scarcely expect to see you home on Wednesday next. Our united best love Believe me your's affectionately attached Kate Cobden. I hope you have escaped colds. I have had a very bad one but it appears about leaving me now.'

Her letter is continued on a smaller sheet: 'Mr Rawson has just called to inquire if any tidings had come from you today. He desired me to tell you to stir up the Mayor of Nottingham a little as he stands in need of it. Rawson confesses that he would rather see Lord John [Russell] give the Corn Laws to perdition than Peel, for many reasons – In the first place the [illegible] are the most honest of the two and he would have liked to see the League a party in at the death too.'

At the start of 1846 the Corn Bill was going through its final stages, and in his letter to Kate of 23 January Cobden was able to tell her: '...I have no doubt Peel will do our work thoroughly, or fall in the attempt. He will be able to carry his measure easily through the Commons, with the aid of the Opposition, but I have my suspicions that the Lords will throw it out and force a dissolution. Whatever happens, I can see a prospect of my emancipation at no distant date. I am going tomorrow to Windsor, to spend the Sunday with Mr Grote [George Grote, historian of Greece].' He gave Kate an amusing account of this visit on 26 January: 'I spent yesterday at Grotes, about four miles from Slough, and Parkes and Lumley the Lessee of the Italian Opera. We had a long walk of nearly 12 miles round the country, and for want of *training* I find myself like an old posting horse today, stiff and footsore.' A twelve-mile walk in any circumstances, in or out of training, was quite an achievement for Cobden whose feet had been so neglected.'Mrs Grote is a remarkable woman, desperately *blue* in the stocking and quite a philosopher in fact. She is a tall and rather *strange* looking personage, steps out like a man, and stands with her back to the fire to harangue the family party like a regular politician in breeches – You know I am not very partial to these masculine ladies – If I were I should not love you, for you are certainly the very opposite of her – Sidney Smith...used to say when he was going to pay a visit to Grote – 'I am going to call upon the *two* Mr Grotes' – But you must not think me ill-natured – She is a very superior woman intellectually speaking and judging by her kind treatment of two little orphan children, a nephew and niece who are living with her (she has no children) I should say she is also a very kind-hearted person, and then she was very very civil to *me*. Grote himself is a very learned man, but rather lethargic as a *modern* politician, and requires the steam of his wife to bring him into action – He is writing a history of Ancient Greece, upon which he has been engaged for more than ten years, and has only just completed the first two volumes. By the way, Jo Parkes and I occupied adjoining bedrooms – we went to our rooms before 12 o'clock, but he came to my fire and sat gossiping till ½ pst 3 – We came up by train this morning at 10 o'clock. So now you know my history for the last 48 hours.'

Cobden realised what the campaign had cost him in terms of health as well as in wealth. He had to face the fact that he was, in his own words, 'running out of steam'. He wrote to Frederick on 9 February: 'The Queen's doctor, Sir James Clark (a good leaguer at heart), has written to offer to pay me a friendly visit, and talk over the state of my constitution, with a view to advise me how to unstring the bow. He wrote me a croaking warning letter more than a year ago. Since I came up here I have been confined to the house partly to my bed by a cold caught in the left side of my head, and which settled down into pains in the ear and the neighbouring region; the prostration which has accompanied this local attack tells me that I have little reserve strength. In fact I feel "all to pieces". The doctor tells me my constitution is impaired and that I ought to disappear for two years from *English* life altogether. But doctors told me the same story seven years ago.'

He continues: 'As it is possible there may be a paragraph in some newspaper alluding to my health, I thought it best to let you know in case of inquiry. But don't write me a long dismal letter in return, for I can't read them, and it does no good. If Charles could come up for a week with a determination to work and think, he might help me with my letters, but he will make my head worse if he requires me to look after him, and so you must say plainly.'

Wealthy friend, bachelor George Moffatt, in addition to his house in Belgravia, had a rural retreat in Norwood, Surrey. Here the Cobdens stayed once or twice for short rests that winter; as he writes to Henry Ashworth on 19 February: 'I am much better, especially I have quiet in this little cottage, which Moffatt has given up entirely to me, and where nobody can come to talk. All pain has left my ear, but my left ear is deaf, and there is still a discharge of matter from it which annoys me. The severe way in which this local affection has pulled me down has taught me that I have very little reserve strength for such emergencies. Like the railroad people, I have been doing with my constitution in five years what ought to have taken 20...' One of the friends to write anxiously about Cobden's health was Mrs Drummond. Kate answered her enquiry from Norwood on 25 February:

'Our invalid continues to improve in health, but it will be, no doubt some time before he will be thoroughly established in a perfect restoration. And I fear till the Corn Law, is entirely done away with, he will not give himself time for his system to get nourished and strengthened as much as we could desire – However there is now every prospect of his speedy emancipation from political agitation, for events are fast crowding towards a completion of the one thing desired, namely the downfall of the Corn Laws! Our stay here now depends entirely upon the time the division will take place in the House of Commons – A message from the Speaker the other day to Mr Cobden, stated that in all probability the debate would continue till Friday next, in which case we shall not return to our lodgings at "76 Berkeley Street, Portman Square", till that day. Mr C. intends if possible to speak on the subject now before the House, and out of consideration to his health the Speaker has kindly intimated that he will make a *point* of *seeing* him whenever he chooses to speak.' Then, as now, before rising to his feet, a Member must catch the eye of Mr Speaker, and be given the nod.'The opinion is gaining ground in Town, that the measure will pass both Houses, but some people appear to think that very much depends in the Upper House upon the course Lord Stanley will take – The Estimates of the Majority in the Commons vary from 71 to 100. My dear husband begs to unite with me in kindest regards to yourself and your family around you.'

On 7 March, Cobden writes to George Combe, the founder of the Phrenological Society, for whose teachings Cobden had a great regard: 'I am pretty well recovered from my local attack: a little deafness is all that remains. But the way in which I was prostrated by an insignificant cold in my head has convinced me (even if my doctor had not told it) how much my constitution has been impaired by the excitement and wear and tear of the last few years. The mainspring has been over-weighted, and I must resolve upon some change to wind up the machinery, before I shall be able to enter upon any renewed labours. My medical friend boldly tells me that I ought to disappear from political life for a year or two, and seek a different kind of excitement in other scenes abroad.' Cobden confesses that he is 'less and less in love with what is generally called political life, and am not sure that I could play a successful part as a general politician. Party trammels, unless in favour of some well-drafted and useful principle, would be irksome to me, and I should be restive and intractable to those who might expect me to run in their harness. I assure you that during the last five years so much have I been involved in the vortex of public agitation, that I have almost forgotten my own identity and completely lost sight of the comforts and interest of my wife and children.'

On their second stay in Norwood in mid-March came the news that the Queen was about to hold a drawing-room. Kate wanted to attend, but she was frustrated in this very natural wish, as Cobden confided to Frederick on 14 March: '...*my not* having been at a levee is a point that interferes.'

Dick was with the Brights at this critical time. Priscilla Bright writes to Kate to report on 20 March from their home at Greenbank, Rochdale: '...he is very good in spite of his roughness and gets a little more under control I hope – He does not attempt now to go so much to the water near the house – he has found another temptation tho' And one that gratifies every desire, both of *dirt* and *play* – it is the *coal yard* – there he sits hammering coals from morning till night – if I would let him – and comes in as black as the coals he hammers – '

Two days later Cobden is writing to Kate: 'My dearest Kate I have your *short* letter with the postmark Rochdale, but no news, no gossip, oh fie! – and after two days silence! I shall certainly resume my correspondence with old Mrs Drummond, or some other lady who will give me a long newsy letter sometimes...Since I wrote to you George Combe and his lady have come to London. They are lodging at No. 11 Old Quebec St. within three minutes walk of my lodgings, and I have called several times to chat with them – She is a very delightful person and a Siddons – I have had a talk with him about my own future course. He recommends foreign scenes – I have told him our difficulty about the children – He seemed very decided that the first thing we ought to do, is to find some trusty friend in whose family we could place them in England, where their training would be attended to, and where there were other children to play with. I told him that your mind would not be at ease without the children, and that after having given so little of my time or attention to your comfort I should not like you to be deprived of the pleasure of their society – He said that he would like his brother, the Doctor, to see you – he has great influence over the minds of others in the matter of managing children – I told him you were a great admirer of his brother's book, and intended to make it your guide in the training of children but I fear you had been more under the control of *feelings* than his calm reason in your management of the boy – He laughed and said that was usually the way...'

The 'trusty friend' the Cobdens found to take charge of Dick whilst they were away on their continental tour was Miss Eveleigh, a Quaker lady, less well off than she had been, who ran a nursery school in Stockport. Katie was taken under the wing of relations in Manchester.

'In the meantime,' Cobden told Kate in an incomplete letter written to her at that time, 'you can be acting upon the strong probability that we shall spend the winter far away from England – I would advise you to be improving yourself, as much as you can, in French by reading and writing it, and translating...As respects our house, if we leave England for a year I should like to let it furnished, provided we could find anybody that would take care of our things – Do you think such a customer could be got? There will be enough time to think of it when I am sure of being set free.'

In an undated letter to her brother Hugh, Kate tells him she intends to write a journal when they are abroad, 'and shall when any thing particularly interesting takes place make extracts and send them to you if agreeable...My dear husband continues pretty well but I only look upon him as patched up for the present, and will require a long rest of body and peace of mind before we can expect him to be thoroughly recovered.'

Cobden now found himself involved in a round of social activities in which – not for the first time – Kate had no share. He wrote to her almost daily describing his doings. The man who had complained to her of the lions in his path now found that he himself had become a lion of a different sort. The doors of many of the great London houses were now open to him, and everywhere he went he was treated as an honoured guest. This change in his life, brought about by the successful campaign for the repeal of the Corn Laws, could have turned the head of a lesser man. During this London season his letters to Kate are thick with distinguished names, and there is a touching naivety in his obvious delight at being *persona grata* with so many aristocratic or prominent hosts.

But for Kate herself the pattern of life remained unaltered. She had her 'circle' as Cobden called it, frequently referred to in his letters to her, her two children and the management of the Victoria Park house. Whatever her own wishes may have been – and we must assume that Kate, with her good looks and still under thirty years of age, enjoyed social life as much as any other woman – she was virtually a prisoner throughout most of her married life. Cobden had certainly earned his 'run at grass' after the strenuous years of the agitation, but was he perhaps guilty of some insensitivity in describing his social doings? That he was aware of this is shown when he told her that he would really have preferred taking tea with her.

On 11 May: 'My dearest Kate I have been running about sightseeing the last day or two. On Saturday I went to the Horticultural Society's great flower show at Chiswick. It was a glorious and a most charming scene. How different from the drenching weather you and I experienced there. I went in an open carriage with Mr and Mrs Davenport and an Italian Count who could not speak English. She [Mrs Davenport, later Lady Hatherton] is a delightful person, exceedingly amiable and intelligent. She was formerly a beauty of the Grecian Mould – and her bust, taken in her prime, stands in several places in the house...Whilst walking with her in the gardens, I was accosted by Mr Chas Howard (brother of Lord Morpeth) who after shaking hands asked me to introduce him to Mrs Cobden! Mrs Hume and her daughters were inquiring for you. This morning I got up at ½ past 7, and went to the National Gallery [then the home of the Royal Academy] to see the exhibition of pictures. It is a very good display – one of the best ever seen. – There are some beautiful Landseers, and there is Etty with his blazing beauties who sadly want an apron! I went at the early hour in order to escape the heat and the crowd and there I met young Doyle who chaperoned me over the rooms. I also met Mr Lough, the sculptor, who asked me to give him a visit, at his studio where I shall go next Wednesday. We agreed that one of the most interesting female portraits resembled you! Mr Lough told me an anecdote concerning you – Mrs Lough remarked after she met you, that if she were a man, *you* were the woman she would fall in love with...He wished to model your bust, and said you would make a more beautiful head than any there! I have more to tell you – but the post is going. I have mounted white stocks regularly – but I must say I want somebody to look after my toilet a little.'

On 13 May: 'I have two invitations for dinner on Saturday, one to Lord Fitzwilliam's and one to Lord and Lady John Russell, and if I remain over that day, I shall prefer the latter, as I have twice refused invitations from them. I assure you I would rather find myself taking tea with you, than dining with lords and ladies. Do not trouble yourself to write to me every day. I don't wish to make it a task.'

13 May produced two further letters to Kate. In one he tells her he had business at 'the India House', and 'After our interview with the directors, I went over the Museum where were several curiosities from the East – such as old manuscripts, Idols, and paintings. There is the famous toy [now in the Victoria and Albert Museum] which belonged to Tippo Saib, representing a tiger in the act of trampling an English soldier, which it is seizing by the throat. The body of the tiger contains an organ which on being played represents the cries of the victim and the growls of the beast. I thought the boy would have been anxious to have bought the plaything if he had been there – Amongst the paintings is a large picture representing the Schah [*sic*] of Persia hunting with a crowd of youths, all his own sons. The person who shewed me it, pointing to the slight figure of the Schah remarked that he had 100 sons, and 400 daughters, and added that he was a mild effeminate man!'

Also on 13 May: 'I left off my last 'speech' rather abruptly. I was writing it in the library of the House of Commons when the postman came and cut me short. I have now run away again from a very tedious speaker on the factory question, and am going to occupy my time more agreeably upstairs by writing to you. Yesterday morning I took breakfast with Mr Romilly, son of Sir Samuel, and met my good old friend and admirer Mrs Marcet again. She asks all her friends to invite her to meet me, and always requests to sit beside me. It is very odd that none but old ladies fall in love with me, and none but old gentlemen lose their hearts to you...Well today I have breakfasted with Mr and Mrs Lough, and went over his studio, where he has certainly some works of considerable genius...But tell me all the gossip – You see I always let you hear all the flattering things people say about you – but you have nothing for *my self-esteem* in return.'

He was back with his lords and ladies on 21 May and wrote to report to her on 22 May: 'Yesterday I dined with Lord and Lady Fortescue, and met Lords Normanby, Campbell and Morpeth. I sat at dinner between the Duchess of Inverness, the widow of the Duke of Sussex, a plain little woman, but clever, and a very decided Free Trader. I also met Mrs Drummond, the widow of the Irish Under Secretary, and daughter-in-law of our good friend of Edinburgh.

On 13 June he wrote to Kate discussing plans for the children while they are abroad. He wants her to arrange to have both Dick and Katie in the same place because 'You would hear of them at the same time, and not have occasion for a double correspondence,' he sensibly points out, but in the event Dick and Katie were placed under two different roofs.

On 23 June: 'My dearest Kate I have been plagued for several days with sitting to Herbert for the picture of the Council of the League and it completely upsets my afternoons...I have invited the Mayor of Bordeaux to stay with us for a day or two when he is in Manchester. He is a fat old John Bull kind of man, and speaks English well. He is travelling with his manservant who does not speak English. He is a good free-trader and a friend of Bastiat's [Claude Frederick, French economist and free trader]. I expect he will be with us, if no accident happens to the corn bill, on Tuesday next, to be present at the meeting of the council of the League which will be held on probably *Wednesday*.

On 26 June he gives her the news Kate must have longed to hear: 'Hurrah! Hurrah! the Corn Law Bill is law, and now my work is done. I shall come down tomorrow morning by the six o'clock train in order to be present at a Council meeting at three, and shall hope to be home for a late tea.'

'I am going into North Wales tomorrow morning at 7,' Cobden told Bright on 3 July. Next day he wrote to A.W. Paulton, proprietor of the *Manchester Times*, from Llangollen. 'I am going into the wilderness to pray – for a return of the taste I once possessed for nature and simple quiet life. Here I am in one day from Manchester to the loveliest valley out of Paradise. Ten years ago, before I was an Agitator, I spent a day or two in this house. Comparing my sensations now with those I then experienced, I feel how much I have lost in winning public fame. The rough tempest has spoilt me for the quiet haven. I fear I shall never be able to cast anchor again. It seems as if some mesmeric hand was upon my brain or I was possessed by an unquiet fiend, which urges me forward in spite of myself...On Thursday as I went to the meeting I thought that I should next day be a quiet and happy man. Next day brings me a suggestion from a private friend of the Emperor of Russia, assuring me that if instead of going to Italy and Egypt, I would take a trip to St Petersburg, I could exercise an important influence upon the mind of Nicholas. Here I am at Llangollen, blind to the loveliness of nature, and only eager to be on the road to Russia, taking Madrid, Vienna, Berlin and Paris by the way.'

Cobden was still in Llangollen when he wrote to Parkes on 6 July and told him he was on his way to Montgomeryshire 'where my children wait for me at my wife's father's.' Although the visit to Wales (Kate's first as Mrs Richard Cobden) was intended as a holiday, Cobden obviously had no wish to let his correspondence lapse, and he tells Parkes he will be at Machynlleth for the next week or ten days, hinting that he would like to hear from him. Cobden received a hero's welcome in the Principality, as he tells another correspondent on 9 July:

'The good folks in Wales are quite excited by the visit of the agitator – They set the bells ringing in the towns as we passed through and changed horses – for we had neither railroads nor coaches – at this place, the people had been expecting us for two days and they had resolved to take the horses out and draw us into the town. – The night previous to our arrival they descried a carriage with a lady and gentleman approaching the town, and the crowd seized the horses and began to take them out, which so alarmed the occupants that they turned back, and spread the report that there was a *banditti* on the road to Machynlleth! – When we arrived I had a terrible fight to prevent the poor people from making beasts of burden of themselves but all in vain – The horses were removed and the ropes fastened, when I slipt out, and left them to drag the carriage to the door, whilst I followed on foot – Since then we have had bands of music parading the town, the bells ringing, and the usual accompaniments of squibs, crackers, and I fear, *drink*. I don't think anybody, unless it were General Tom Thumb himself, could be more enthusiastically received by these mountaineers than myself.' Brotherton, the recipient of this letter, was himself a free trader and reformer who was then Member for Salford, and had once, like Cobden, been engaged in cotton manufacture in Manchester, but had given up his practice to become a pastor of the Bible Christian Church.

Before he left Wales Cobden wrote to George Combe, the phrenologist and moral philosopher, about the national subscription of £80,000 which had been raised in his favour.'...Now, my dear friend, for a word or two upon a very delicate personal matter. You have seen the account of an ebullition of a pecuniary kind which is taking place in the country, a demonstration in favour of me exclusively to the neglect of others who have laboured long and zealously with me in the cause of Free Trade. I feel deeply the injustice of passing over Bright and Villiers, to say nothing of others; and nothing but the conviction that I am guiltless of ever having arrogated to myself the merit of others consoles me in the painful position in which the public have placed me, of being the vehicle for diverting the regard from me who are as worthy of all honour as myself.

'But I wish to speak to you upon a still more delicate view of this unpalatable affair. I do not like to be recompensed for a public service at all, and I am sensible that my moral influence will be impaired by the fact of my receiving a tribute in money from the public. I should have preferred to have either refused it, or to have done a glorious service by endowing a college. But as an honest man, and as a father and a husband, I cannot refuse to accept the money. You will probably be surprised when I tell you that I have shared the fate of nearly all leaders in revolutions or great reforms, by the complete sacrifice of my private prospects in life. In a word I was a poor man at the end of the agitation. I shall not go into details, because it would involve painful reminiscences; but suffice it to say that whilst the Duke of Richmond was taunting me with the profits of my business, I was suffering the complete loss of my private fortune, and I am not now afraid to confess to you that my health of body and mind have suffered more in consequence of private anxieties during the last two years, than from my public labours.

'With strong domestic feelings and with an orderly mind, which was peculiarly sensitive to the immorality of risking the happiness of those whom nature had given the first claim on me, for the sake of a public object, I experienced a conflict between the demands of my responsible public station, and the prior duties which I owed to my family, which altogether nearly paralysed me. I should have retired from public life last August, had not some wealthy coadjutors in Lancashire forced me to continue at my post, and had they not compelled me to leave to them the cares of my private business. It is owing to the knowledge which my neighbours in Lancashire have of the sacrifices which I have incurred, that the subscription has been entered into, and I wish you to be in possession of the facts, because you are the man of all others whom I should wish to possess the materials for forming a correct knowledge of the motives which compel me to take a course that jars at first sight on our notion of purity and disinterestedness.'

The Cobdens left Machynlleth in the last week in July, slept at Chester and went on by way of Liverpool to leave Dick at Miss Eveleigh's in Southport, before returning home to Victoria Park. Katie was left in Wales with Kate's sister. As Cobden told Bright: 'It was a sad parting but is now over.'

CHAPTER FOUR

Triumphal Tour

At the beginning of their fourteen month continental tour, and for most of its duration, Kate found herself included in many of its highlights. In his first letter to Frederick, written from Paris on 10 August, 1846, Cobden tells him: '...We came from Dieppe to Eu and saw the King of the French – I got there in time to leave my card with his aide de camp just before dinner, and purposed to pay my respects the next morning at 12 – but in half an hour an invitation came for 8 o'clock – I took Kate, and nothing could have been more hearty than the behaviour of the King, Queen, and Madame Adelaide the King's sister. Louis Philippe speaks English perfectly – He knew all about the League and our doings – I don't think it has transpired that I was there; – indeed Eu is too retired for the penny-a-liners, and there was not an Englishman in the place.' This letter contained what was to be a recurring reference to seasickness: 'I suffered terribly on the passage although it was calm, and nobody else was ill – I did not get right for two days.'

In Paris the Cobdens stayed at the Hotel Wagram in the Rue de Rivoli. By 16 August Kate was ill with what sounds like influenza. Cobden's diary records that a Dr Cabarus, a homeopathist, was sent for. On 17 August, leaving Kate in bed at the hotel, Cobden set out to see the King open the chamber of Deputies, which he found 'a theatrical scene – Louis Philippe well cheered'. Next day a banquet was given for Cobden.'About 100 persons in the room – read my French speech which was very well received – splendid dinner. Kate coughed a little today for the first time during her attack – ' On 19 August there was 'A large party in the handsome suite of rooms at Mr Emile de Giradin's...introduced to Victor Hugo...Home late to bed. Kate better today and cough I hope has disappeared.' On 25 August he records that he had had his last French lesson and 'paid *Domville* 100 fr for lessons and grammar.' That day (25 August) he writes to Frederick: 'Kate's health is giving me some uneasiness – She was laid up with a very stiff neck and cold – but although the local affection has gone it has left her very weak. In fact her health is altogether deranged, and she has for two or three days had a slight cough, and occasional flushing of the face with cold and warm fits, and perspirations at night-

...However, I hope we shall find the air of the South of France restore her – We shall go from Bordeaux to Pau the air of which place is much spoken of – But we shall have to remain a couple of days with the Mayor of that place, and I fear there will be a public banquet for me by the town...I am writing to Sir James Clark [physician to Queen Victoria] for advice about Kate – I hope it may turn out an attack of influenza, which I am told is prevalent here...All my plans are of course in abeyance owing to Kate's health.' From Bordeaux on 4 September he is able to give his brother a better report.'...Kate suffered a good deal in coming here, but she is now decidedly better, and I have no doubt a week or two at Pau will set us both up – it is high time we left this place for the Mayor will otherwise kill us outright with feasting...I drew upon Lloyds, in Paris for £200. It was shockingly expensive *there* – but I hope it will be in future cheaper.'

On 7 September he tells Frederick: 'I am glad to say that Kate has quite recovered [from] her attack and I hope she is going to be vigorous.'

It seems that already in 1846 Frederick's health was not good, for, in a letter of 4th September, Cobden tells him: 'I am very sorry however to hear you are not in good health You must take care of yourself – Get all the exercise you can --.' He tells him his own plans are uncertain: 'I can't tell where we shall go next – It is quite impossible to take Kate to Spain.' Cobden was proved mistaken.'If I go there I must take the mail to Madrid.'

When they reached Cauterets, Cobden took the waters at the pump room of the principal establishment, and recorded in his diary that the water was 'upward of 100°F.' From there they went on horseback to Lac de Gaube. It seems that gallant Kate was living up to her husband's hope that she was 'going to be vigorous'. By 17 September they were at Bagnères-de-Bignorre, where Cobden took a bath 'the natural spring so hot I could hardly bear it – Tasted the water – a chalybeate, not resembling the flavor of the other springs which tasted of rotten eggs – '

On 23 September Kate herself was writing, as she did regularly during their long tour, to her niece Marian Lewis. In a lengthy, crossed letter, from Pau, Basses Pyrennées: '...I am amused at the Boy's saying that he was "happy enough" – and dear Baby by all accounts thrives famously. We are expecting Mr and Mrs Schwabe here tomorrow and they will stay with us for some time, that is a month or so perhaps. We have had the most delightful weather and consequently our excursions amongst the mountains have been extremely pleasant. We have made the acquaintance of some very agreeable French people – One young lady is to visit me on my return to England CA Cobden.'

Cobden records in his diary for Saturday, 26 September: 'Mr and Mrs Schwabe reached us.' Schwabe, like Cobden, was a calico printer, his wife an educationalist and an energetic letter-writer. It is thanks to her correspondence with friends in England; afterwards published as *Reminiscences of Richard Cobden*, that we owe much of the colour we share of the tour of Spain.

On 26 September Cobden wrote to Frederick, and after dealing with matters relating to their business tells him 'We have been a fortnight in the mountains a great deal of the time on horseback and far away from post offices...Kate is quite well again, as you may suppose by her having been 10 miles in one day on horseback...I expect Schwabe and his wife here this evening, we shall then decide what our future plans are to be. We had given up the idea of taking the ladies to Spain – but since we have been here, we learn that they may travel pretty comfortably in the mail or stage coach...My wife joins in kind regards to our circle.'

On 1 October the party were in Bayonne, where all the talk was of the Duke de Montpensier who had arrived that day on his way to Madrid to be married to the Spanish princess. The Cobden-Schwabe quartette had arrived in the town on 30 September in a carriage and four and had been mistaken for the Prince and his party. People in the streets stared and some shouted *Vive le Prince*! to their amusement, although we are told they bowed with dignity in response. On 7 October they were themselves on their way to the capital by mail coach. En route they stopped at Burgos, the ancient capital of Castille, at 5 o'clock in the morning, and as Cobden recorded in his diary '...ran into the old cathedral whilst the mail changed horses – almost dark, yet the doors open, and the people entering with their little lanterns for their matins.' From Burgos the Madrid coach was accompanied by a soldier with four loaded guns for their protection against bandits.

Madrid (9 October) was pronounced 'a modern bustling city with good streets and *trottoirs*. At present it is filled with crowds from all parts, anxious to see the bull fights which are to come off next week – ' On the morning of 10 October they did the Prado, and the Botanical Gardens in the afternoon, joined by the French writer Alexander Dumas, who was in the capital to report on the marriage. The double marriage of the Queen of Spain with her cousin, Don Francisco, and that of the Duke of Montpensier with her sister, took place the following day. The Spanish Prime Minister, Mr Istariz, to whom Cobden had a letter of introduction, sent the party four tickets of admission to witness the ceremony. Kate and Mrs Schwabe had to appear *en toilette d'Espagne* in black veils. They drove to the church at eleven o'clock and had two hours to wait 'in excellent seats, not twenty yards from the Queen and all the bridal party' before the ceremony took place.

On 16 October they went to a bullfight. Kate and Mrs Schwabe left, disgusted, after half-an-hour, but as Cobden told Frederick on 17 October: '...I sat it out, determined to see the whole of the atrocity. Indeed nobody can fully understand the Spanish character without seeing their national pasttime – Sufficient to say that this scene, presided over by the young Queen a week [?four days] after her marriage, would have revolted the lowest rabble in England. So long as public opinion, backed by the clergy and the women, sanctions such exhibitions, so long will blood flow at every political crisis....' He then switches to pleasanter matters: 'You will probably have seen some account of our free-trade meeting – the first ever known in Madrid...We have been all very busy here – Political economy, fetes and the galleries have kept us in one incessant occupation. The picture galleries I prefer to any I ever saw – Here is Murillo in his glory, and in my opinion he is the Shakespeare of artists. We have dined twice with Bulwer [Lytton] who is in wretched health.' What he went on to tell his brother about the English Minister will never be known, for the next two lines of his letter have been inked out, presumably by some member of the Cobden family.

On 21 October, in spite of his 'wretched health', Bulwer again entertained Cobden and his party to dinner. Kate and Julie had planned a quiet evening writing letters, but Bulwer invited them to his box at the theatre where the Queen and Royal Family were to be present. Cobden and Schwabe were placed in another box, and the ladies had excellent seats opposite the Queen and her Consort and the Duke and Duchess of Montpensier, and noted that the Queen was wearing '...white satin made in a blouse high up to the neck, and a net cap with a rose on one side. She wore scarcely any ornaments, but still looked very nice. The Duchess of Montpensier was dressed in pink satin, made high up to the neck, and had a very simple cap on her head. The entertainment at the theatre consisted merely of a ballet, which was, however, well performed, and the Queen seemed particularly to enjoy it.'

The energetic travellers were sightseeing again on Monday. Cobden, with his unfailing talent for making friends, had made a good impression on a certain wealthy Spaniard, Mr Salamanca, whom he had met at Bulwer's, and this worthy put his house and servants at Aranjuez at his disposal. After many days in hotels this seemed, according to Julie Schwabe, 'like Fairy-land.' When they arrived on 23 October, she wrote to a friend that they found a 'luxurious *déjeuner-a-la-fourchette* awaiting us, and at seven o'clock a dinner, with all sorts of wine, was prepared. We have constantly two or three men-servants at our command, and yesterday evening there were at least twenty five rooms lighted for us.' Whilst the ladies were revelling in the absent Mr Salamanca's hospitality, Cobden, in sombre mood, was writing to Bright, deeply concerned about the worsening of relations between England and France.'...God grant that something may soon be done to bring Englishmen and Frenchmen into closer contact and dependence upon each other, for I more and more feel how impossible it is to secure the peace of the world, and guarantee us against all the burdens which our present warlike attitude entails upon us by any means excepting a free commercial intercourse between all nations.' Wherever he was Cobden never lost touch with his aims, and peace was always one of these, but it was 1860 before he was able to make his unique contribution to the betterment of relations between Britain and the France of Napoleon III.

By 9 in the morning of 24 October they were on the diligence which passed through Aranjuez en route for Seville, their brief stay in fairyland over, and facing four nights of road travel. The climate of Seville, according to Cobden, was 'lovely', and he wrote to Frederick 'sitting in a room looking upon a court where oranges are hanging in the open air.' He wrote again from Cadiz on 6 November: '...even in pleasure loving Seville I found some men who are interesting themselves after their fashion, in the Free-trade question...Here at Cadiz I find a banquet arranged for me at the Casino [the merchants' club] for the day after tomorrow, without consulting me on the subject. Then the multitude of callers occupy my time in receiving and paying visits, and prevent me enjoying the view of those curiosities which all visitors must see. However, I hope I am doing some good in indoctrinating individuals.' At this banquet, according to Julie Schwabe, Cobden's health was drunk 'no less than four times...'

They left Cadiz for Gibraltar on 15 November, after visiting Xerez where the ladies were presented, not with bottles of sherry, but with 'pink and white roses and fine azaleas', and saw over wine vaults and a vineyard.

As soon as Cobden's arrival in Gibraltar was known there was the now usual spate of callers, and it was not until after the first English post had been dispatched on 16 November that their sightseeing could begin. Accompanied by the Military Secretary, Captain Walker, and Mr Costello, the Attorney-General, they went, the men on horseback, the ladies on donkeys, to the highest point of the Rock, about 1,500 feet above the sea, to enjoy the view. Next day, again accompanied by Captain Walker, they went to Europa Point and other tourist sights, including the apes ('large monkeys,' as Mrs Schwabe called them). On 18 November, hearing that the quarantine had been raised at Malaga and that the steamer *Barcino* was leaving that evening the party decided to join it and after paying a few hurried visits, packed their boxes and went on board at 5.30.

Miss Eveleigh, the Quaker lady who had charge of young Richard, reported regularly to the news hungry and always anxious Kate. On 20 November: 'Marian [Lewis] comes every week to see Richard...he has just commenced writing in a copybook instead of on a slate. I wish you could have seen his fine animated face this morning when he brought me his first production on paper the dear child seemed to consider it a great achievement and certainly it was very nicely done; he hopes soon to be able to write a letter to Papa and Mama this seems the height of his ambition wilt thou tell Mr Cobden that Richard is not kept at all close to school hours like the rest who are older.' She signs herself 'thy sincere friend'.

The party hired a coach for a week, and leaving Malaga at six o'clock, drawn by five horses, covered thirteen leagues on the first day of their journey up to Granada. According to Julie Schwabe, although the views were fine, as the route led over a mountain 6,000 feet high, the roads were 'simply awful', and the Posadas, or wayside inns, so bad that the travellers had to bring their own meals with them.

Meanwhile, the people of Malaga had decided to organise a dinner in Cobden's honour. According to Mrs Schwabe, Cobden was not over pleased by this news and wished to go on with their tour.'Mr Cobden,' she told a friend in one of her frequent letters, 'left England in order to be quiet, but not to meet with so many public dinners.' But was this, in fact, true? Cobden had taken pains to provide himself with introductions in every major city they visited, obviously with the idea of making new acquaintances and learning all he could about the region.

By mid-December they were thankfully back in France, after being fêted in Barcelona, and travelling all night by diligence ('We were all shaken on the Spanish roads for the last time').'The following afternoon the snowy mountains of the Pyrenées began to appear. Some of the little brooks had floating ice, and for the first time the landscape bore the stamp of winter. On Sunday evening at nine o'clock we arrived at Perpignan, and found everything prepared for our reception by our servants...' Cobden wrote in his journal from Perpignan on 14 and 15 December: 'Luxuriated in the comforts of a French inn. I felt almost ready to hug the furniture, kiss the white tablecloth, and shake hands with the waiters, so attractive did they all look after my Spanish discomforts! Sat indoors and wrote letters. Walked only once into the town, an irregular, confined and ugly fortified place. The only annoyance I experienced was from the military music and the parading and drilling of the troops.'

Kate wrote to Dick on 15 December, telling him the Schwabes were leaving them for England next day, and would bring him a small piece of the bark of a cork tree, stripped off for him by his father. After taking leave of the Schwabes (who were bound for Toulouse) in Narbonne, the Cobdens left at the same hour for Montpelier. Cobden wrote in his diary: 'Our road lay along a rich and populous but uninteresting country, through Beziers, and for some distance close to the Mediterranean. The people were busy in the fields, cutting off the long dry shoots of the vines with pruning shears, and leaving nothing but the stumps. When within ten miles of Montpellier, snow began to fall and it continued during the rest of the journey.'

Kate wrote to brother Hugh from Marseilles on 24 December: 'My dearest Brother, At this distance from home I always feel very anxious for news from my friends – John told me in his last letter that all our family were quite well, most earnestly do I hope that you may long continue so, each and all – I have hitherto had very comfortable tidings too of my dear children – notwithstanding the separation from them diminishes greatly the pleasure of my travels – however I have the comfort to find that my husband's health and spirits improve by the succession and variety of our journeys – I shall enclose this to John so as to save writing to him a separate letter and I shall hope to hear from either you or him very soon. We are delighted at being once more in France, it is wonderful how high this country has risen in our estimation since our two months sojourn in Spain – Here we have, at all events, good roads, good oil and good wine – the hotels are excellent, particularly on this route, the one at Montpellier having stirred them up right and left – it was lately established, and is one of the best, if not the best we have ever been at – We went to see its kitchen and there found the *'chef de cuisine'* in the midst of his pots and pans dressed in garments as white as the driven snow and stylishly made – he had in all probability been to Paris to learn his "profession". He walked round and pointed and explained to us, the various uses of the coppers, stoves and steamers around him with as much grace of manner, and feeling of superiority, as one might expect to find in a druggist in his laboratory. – We spent three days most pleasantly at Montpellier where we became acquainted with two or three very delighted [*sic*] families – We have very comfortable apartments and are likely to remain here for the next four or five days, before we start for Genoa. When at Paris I had the worked braces which you sent me some time ago, finished with straps and buckles &c and when our friends Mr and Mrs Schwabe left us the other day, I took the opportunity of getting them to take them with them to forward them to you.'

'Would you wish me,' Kate continues, 'when in Germany to get you a light steel chain – I believe Berlin is famous for that kind of ornament...We see from the papers that the protectionists in France are getting quite savage, which proves that free trade principles are making progress and alarming the enemy, who in turn are trying to arouse all the old mean prejudices against England. "Perfide Albion" as they call her – who has sent her missionary in the person of Mr Cobden to betray "*La Belle France*" – However discussion will do good even if it does nothing else but turn the minds of the French people a little from war – there is an uneasy feeling amongst them and they fancy that they must go to war with some nation or other – they are a (?)restless set and learn but little wisdom from experience. Intellectually they are, my husband finds them, very superior to the Spaniards. He found it quite a relief to come in contact with their consuls or with a travelling Frenchman in Spain. And the former quite outdid our own consuls in showing us attentions at the different places we stopped at along the coast of the Mediterranean – We hope Mrs Williams is in good health and to whom we beg our united regards – Believe me to remain, Your affectionate and attached sister Kate Cobden.'

Kate's letter to Marian now assumes what may be called her governess style: '...I believe the higher classes in France are improving very much in their mode of education – home tuition and English literature are much encouraged and the frivolous immoral French novels are prohibited in all well regulated families, so I was told by a lady who certainly personified to me the perfection of what a well educated lady ought to be.'

By 5 January 1847 the Cobdens had reached Nice, from where

Kate writes an account of their travels to their friend Mrs Elizabeth Woolley, who was still living in Manchester: '...We have had colds slightly and it is surprising that we have escaped so well, as the weather has been for the last month extremely severe for this latitude. We have often sighed for the snug and comfortable hearths of old England whilst we are warming one side of these wood fires, at the same time as the other is half freezing. I took to wearing my cloak within doors and by that means managed to keep myself all right...this Winter is quite an exception to the general rule...and we have sufficient proof by the deplorable state of the orange groves – the frost has made the leaves appear as if they were singed – however hopes are entertained that the trees are not so far damaged as to prevent their recovery next year. The oranges for exportation had been gathered before the frost set in...The place itself presents no attractions – the situation is fine and there are some very pretty excursions in the neighbourhood but this weather is too unfavourable to tempt us out of the main road...'

Several of Kate's letters at this time contain similarities and one suspects that she made rough copies of some of them to save herself the effort of composing each one afresh. She must have envied Cobden's unfailing fluency in letter writing.

John Williams' letter of 6 January 1847 states that young Richard 'must be feeling rather neglected alone in School but it is the best for him for his friends would have overfed him and he would not know when to stop.' Marian is still writing regularly.'I am very glad,' Kate tells her on 12 January, 'to hear that my father's spirits are good as I am consequently in hope that the [timber] works have gone on pretty well during the severe weather.' She is keeping up her interest in the girl's schooling, and in this letter along with other advice, she tells her: 'I have no desire for you to do needlework and on no consideration should you allow it to interfere with your studies. At the same time if your governess wishes it as a change or as a little beneficial relaxation from the duties of the school then of course I have no objection and you can do that which you think proper – but do not get to stoop over it.' One might have though Kate was responsible for her niece's education, but it seems John Williams was paying the fees, for she asks: 'Do you think that your uncle John has attended to your school bill? If you cross your letter you can tell me whatever you please for your uncle never will read a crossed letter...You will have seen my dear Boy long ere this reaches you – Kiss him a thousand times for us and the same to dear baby.'

Kate is now reporting regularly to Mrs Schwabe on their almost royal progress through Europe. From Genoa she writes: 'Mr Cobden delivered the following speech at a dinner given him on Saturday, 16th inst. There were fifty-three persons present, the Consuls of England, France, Spain and Belgium, sitting side by side like lambs. The party consisted chiefly of merchants, but included about half a dozen marquises, descendants of ancient families...'

From Genoa on 18 January Kate writes to another woman friend about Cobden's improved health: 'I hope by the time we return home that he will have become so stout and strong that his old acquaintances will have some little difficulty in recognising his person.' She is still complaining of the cold '...Often we have sighed for the snug and comfortable hearths of old England whilst failing to keep more than one side of ourselves warm by these wood fires. The 'ill-fitting doors and windows admitting sufficient wind to make the other feel perishingly cold...' When next she writes to Marian it is from Rome on 27 January.'We arrived here last Friday from Genoa and have seen but few of the principal wonders of Rome – which are so numerous that they for some time create quite a confusion in one's mind – New or present Rome, is built on the slopes of three of the Northern of the seven hills of ancient Rome – and is the dirtiest town I take it in Christendom. The principal street is called the Corso, which divides modern Rome nearly in two equal parts, and is the only one which has a foot pavement – may be compared to Deansgate in Manchester – of late there has been a great deal of rain here, and a little while previous to our arrival here many of the streets were under water and the people had to go about in boats. The Tiber was unusually full and the water issued out of the sewers and inundated the town.

'We were last evening at a ball given [by] Il Principe et la Principessa Forloma(?) there are about one thousand persons present – and a whole palace thrown open for their reception – About one half if not more were English visitors – We were entertained with *Tableaux Vivants* and dancing – We left early but I believe a great many remained till 3 or 4 o'clock in the morning. I am obliged to hurry to the conclusion of this or I shall be too late for the steamer which leaves for England today – Pray write and tell your Mamma where we are and other particulars you know about us – the same to Grandpapa I do hope he continues well, I often fear lest this winter as [*sic*] been too trying for him – and lest the works have suffered from the frost – Let me hear how he is in spirits write all particularly to me soon I hope you have enjoyed your holiday I am getting on famously in French I have so much practice I hope you will be able to talk a little with me on my return – Give my kind love to all enquiring friends – and believe me ever Your's [*sic*] affectionately attached aunt Kate Cobden Tell your Mamma to be particular when she gives baby raisins to skin and stone them for her as I used to do.' The letter is addressed to Marian care of F. Cobden, Esq., Mosley Street, Manchester, Angleterre.

John Williams writes again to his sister from London on 1 February, describing, among other events, a breakfast with the Schwabes, at which a letter from Kate from Genoa had arrived during the meal 'which threw her into great glee – it was read for the benfit of the table and gave general satisfaction – so much for the letter...The conversation part of the business was entirely performed by Mrs Schwabe in addition to the other duties of supplying cups of Coffee, muffins, &c. – and she seemed so busy and earnest about it that she totally disregarded the use of her pocket handkerchief which from a cold she appeared to have, she stood occasionally in need of – however, she is I am sure a kind hearted body and I felt pleased with both.'

Kate did not always go with Cobden on his sightseeing tours. On 22 February he records in his diary: 'Walked with Mrs Jamesson (authoress of works on early painters, an agreeable woman, whose good-nature and sense prevent her from displaying the unpleasant qualities of too many literary ladies) into the Sistine Chapel, to see Michael Angelo's frescoes; the *Last Judgment* at one end, and the whole of the ceiling from his pencil. It is a deplorable misapplication of the time and talent of a man of genius to devote years to the painting of the ceiling of a chapel, at which one can only look by an effort that costs too much inconvenience to the neck to leave the mind at ease to enjoy the pleasure of the painting...with all the enthusiasm of my fair companion, I could not feel much gratification at this celebrated work of art.'

22 February was also the day of his audience with the Pope.'At 7 same day was presented to the Pope in his private cabinet, where I found him in a white flannel friar's dress, sitting at a small writing-desk surrounded with papers. The approach to this little room was through several lofty and spacious apartments. The curtained doors and the long flowing robes of the attendants reminded me, oddly enough, of my interview with Mehemet Ali at Cairo. Pius IX received me with a hearty and unaffected expression of pleasure at meeting one who had been concerned in a great and good work in

England; commended my perseverance and the means by which the principle of Free Trade had been made to triumph; and he remarked that England was the only country where such triumphs were achieved by years of legal and moral exertion...' Before his audience ended Cobden tackled the Pontiff on the question of Spanish bull-fights.'I called his attention to the practice in Spain of having bull-fights in honour of the saints and virgins [*sic*] on the fête days, and gave him an extract from a Madrid paper, giving an account of a bull-fight there in honour of its patroness the Virgin. After a little conversation upon the cruelty and demoralization of these spectacles, he thanked me for having drawn his attention to it, and promised to give instructions upon the subject to an envoy whom he was about to send to Spain. He concluded by another complimentary phrase or two, and we left.' The 'we' suggests that Kate shared the audience, and certainly she had expected to, but she was not present on this occasion, and the 'we' probably denotes an interpreter. Cobden's summing up of Pius was: 'I was impressed with the notion that he is sincere, kind-hearted, and good, and that he is possessed of strong common sense and sound understanding. He did not strike me as a man of commanding genius.'

On 9 March Kate wrote to Marian saying: 'Our Southward course will terminate here and after we have made the excursions of the neighbourhood we propose to return to Rome again at Easter more for the sake of seeing St. Peter's illuminated than for the ceremonies of the church, of which one sees quite enough in the first example or two – Our stay here will be about a fortnight longer and the same at Rome where I expect to be introduced to the Pope – Your uncle had an interview when we were there the other day, with that wonder of the age, a reforming Pope! All the good he had previously heard of him, was only the more confirmed upon a nearer approach – He found him simple, but elegant and dignified in his manners, sincere and earnest to do good, with perhaps more commonsense than genius about him. The doubt is whether he will have sufficient sternness(?) of character to clear out the Augean stables his predecessors left him. One fears about [him] that he is too benevolent for the task – It is contrary when a man is removed from office in the Roman stables to promote him to a Cardinal – The late governor of Rome was nearly being an exception to that but, from his being so decidedly disliked that his Holiness at first to exalt(?) him, but afterwards gave way on the governor and his friends pleading and crying before him – Notwithstanding this and similar instances of those who have known him all his lifetime, say that he has, when he sees necessity sufficient endurance for a martyr – We have been seeing enough to become acquainted with parties who have known him from his youth up and all emphatically state that a better man does not exist – and even those who do not believe in Miracles imagine they see the working of Providence in his elevation.'

Kate, after giving her niece a detailed description of the career of Pius IX and of the method of 'electing a successor to the Chair of St Peter', tells her that 'What struck us most in Rome and its neighbourhood (the Coliseum we were prepared for) were the Aqueducts which stretch in solemn and noiseless grandeur across the Campagna. And then there is more of utility associated with them than with any of the other Antiquities one sees around. The great paintings are but few in the Eternal City, and those are scattered amongst the different palaces. We have yet to see the finest gallery in Italy – that of Florence – the statues in Rome are numerous and beautiful enough to satisfy the taste of any one in that line.' That the Cobdens were probably at Albano is suggested by a scrap, with no address or date, a draft perhaps of a letter to Marian from Kate: 'We rest here today and part of tomorrow – till our Courier will have returned from Rome, whither he is gone to try and procure apartments for us. On our arrival here this morning we heard that every place was so full there that we had but [little] chance of finding a hole to shelter ourselves in... we thought it better to remain at this beautiful spot and explore the neighbourhood – Accordingly we mounted some donkeys and rode for four or five hours along the far famed banks of the Lake of Albana the day was delightful and the loveliness and serenity of the scene were such as pen cannot well describe – Tomorrow we ascend again it's [*sic*] woody hills to visit the portion on which stands the Castle Gondolfo – The Pope's only country residence, which together with two or three convents which crown opposite heights, adds a picturesque feature to the landscape.'

On 12 March Kate writes to Marian from Naples.'Today we were to have gone to Pompeii and the Minister of the Interior had promised us a special excavation – Now it is postponed till next Monday in the hopes that the weather may clear up before then. We are likely to have a great retinue on the occasion as several of our acquaintances here, hearing of the favour that is to be shown us, have begged to be of our party. We are in the same fix with respect to Vesuvius – waiting the permission of wind and rain to have a near view of the great fire which is in greater activity at present than it has been for several years past. During the day time when uncapped by the clouds smoke only is to be seen – but at night an immense volume of fire bursts forth every two or three minutes and a stream of lava occasionally rolls down the side...'

From Naples in March Kate wrote to Dick about their ascent of Mount Vesuvius: 'When we were up on Monday last, showers of tremendous stones came rolling down its sides, vomitted [*sic*] forth by the crater every four or five minutes – Mamma was carried up by six men taking hold of the poles and the chair. Papa was dragged up taking hold of a leather strap around a man's waist – and another man pushing him behind – Notwithstanding all that assistance he was very tired by the time we reached the top. One goes half a step back for every one that is taken, and ankle deep in cinders, which combined with the very steep path renders the ascent most fatiguing and difficult. One comes down in full fun(?), for a tumble on the ashes does not hurt scarcely at all. We took our lunch on the top of Vesuvius in quite a warm nook – A little further on, the lava came rolling down in a great burning stream oozed forth from a fiery cavern – '

On 17 March Kate continues this letter: 'To-day we start for Salerno from whence we shall proceed tomorrow for Paestum – where there are most interesting and very ancient ruins. On Monday last according to agreement we visited Pompeii, and were accompanied by 30 or 40 people who were attracted by the excavation which was to be given in honour of your uncle.' On 24 March Kate tells Marian: 'On our return to Rome I expect to find a few lines from you again – Tomorrow we shall take our departure from here [Naples] and in all probability shall reach the Eternal City the beginning of next week. We purpose remaining a day or two on the road at Albano for the sake of a little quiet rest. I had a little letter from the boy enclosed in one from Miss Eveleigh the other day. We have not yet seen anything of Mrs Fiers [née Sarah Cobden] or her husband, though they expected to be at Naples about the 20th inst...I send this in the Ambassador's bag to your Uncle John in London who will be kind enough to forward it to you. We shall stay a week at Rome and then go on to Florence where we shall stay a week or nine days.'

On 12 April Kate wrote to Marian from Rome telling her that 'Tomorrow we start on our way to Florence by way of Perugia and today we are finishing our farewell calls here and making a few purchases of things peculiar to the place and presently we intend to have our last visit to the Capitol in order to see the bronze wolf and the paintings, which we had not time to examine on a former occasion.' Kate found the bronze wolf interesting only on account of its great antiquity.'I leave Rome,' she tells Marian, 'in the earnest hope of being one day able to revisit it, for though our stay has been seven weeks, yet I do not feel satisfied with what we have seen for where there is such a profusion, objects ought to be seen more than once or twice in order to make a lasting and distinct impression upon the memory. All who have once been to the Eternal City wish to come again, the reason, I believe, it works upon the affections in such a way is on account of the easy access to all the places which contain what is great in art – One feels almost that they belong to oneself, and has no other desire but to see them where they are.'

Unknown to Cobden, his arrival in Florence was assiduously monitored by the Italian Police as evidenced by the following extracts, translated from the Buon Governo Secret Archives:

'We think it our duty to inform Your Lordship that a certain Cobden, an Englishman, took up his lodgings at the Hotel "della Isole Britanniche" the day before yesterday, and we are ready to receive those orders which may be thought opportune if he turns out to be Richard Cobden the Revolutionary chief. A. Minuti.'

'Mr Cobden who is staying at the "Isole Britanniche", is indeed the well known Englishman, who has started Free Trade in England and has been enthusiastically received in Rome, in Genova [*sic*] and in other places. Yesterday evening we heard that as soon as he arrived a dinner for 60 was ordered from Donnay. Therefore we must keep a very cautious but alert watch, and endeavour among other things to find out the eminent people who visit him, those who have planned and paid for the dinner, and those who will attend.'

'April 20th. The above mentioned banquet has not yet been held, but the writer Under-Inspector Minuti is endeavouring with great energy to put himself in the position of giving the most precise details of this dinner, which indeed will be offered to the foreigner of whom we speak, of the promoters and of all those who will be present...'

'...the well known journalist R. Cobden arrived at the "Isole Britanniche" on the 18th with his family. He is about fifty years of age, rather short and lively in all his movements...'

From Florence on 2 April Kate reported progress to Julie Schwabe.'I shall enclose this and some lines delivered at dinner at a gentleman's house in this neighbourhood in the little packet which I shall send through the Ambassador's bag to England. I do not attempt to translate the latter, as you are a better Italian scholar than I can pretend to be. A friend has promised to render the poetry into prose, in which you shall have both. The dinner was at Monsieur Fenzi's [Finzi?] country house, about six miles from hence, beautifully situated on one of the numerous hills, which rise in conical shape one above another around Florence. The grounds are very extensive, and better kept than any we have hitherto seen in Italy. There were upwards of thirty persons at dinner, after Signor Zannini delivered a poetical address to Mr Cobden, which drew tears from the eyes of the ladies, and made the men clench their teeth and look sternly at each other...Nothing can exceed the kindness and hospitality, both public and private, lavished upon Richard, who is astonished and pleased with the individual intellect of the Italian people.'

On 23 April Kate wrote to Mrs Schwabe from Florence: 'I have a little pamphlet for you, which contains a speech which Mr Cobden delivered at the Academy of Pontaniana, at Naples, of which he was elected a member. I do not know when it will reach you, but I shall get it sent through the Ambassador's bag from here to London, and get my brother to forward it from thence to you. I expect a paper daily to follow us from the Eternal City with an interesting account of our visit to Perugia; as soon as it arrives I shall send it through the post as usual. I assure you I never was more pleased with anything than the elegant and enthusiastic manner the inhabitants of that city welcomed my husband. The first evening they sent a full band of music to the inn to amuse us with several airs. Then a deputation from the *Societa Economica-Agrarian of Perugia* called and presented Mr Cobden with the diploma [and] a silver medal – constituting him an honorary member of that body. The following day we were taken, accompanied by a party of gentlemen, to see the curiosities of the town and neighbourhood. Then in the evening a large party assembled at the Casino of gentlemen and ladies and entertained us with music and singing; then an address was delivered by Signor Bartoli, complimentary to Mr Cobden. On the walls were painted some lines in praise of his Free Trade labours, and the same printed on white paper was handed round for the company. The one given to my husband was done in gold letters on blue silk, fringed with gold, in a crimson binding. I shall never forget the scene; it had nothing of "dull reality" about it. It is fortunate that my husband has not too high an opinion of himself, or else the Italians would have turned his head, so many attentions, both public and private, were showered upon him.' The Italian police reported on Cobden's arrival:

'April 24th. We have learnt from a reliable source that Marchese Ridolfi as President of the Georgofili Society will offer in his own palace on May 2d, a dinner to Lord *[sic]* Cobden, and that he has already sent definite invitations to their Excellencies the counsellors of our Ministry...'

'April 25th. It has been discovered that the dinner offered to Cobden in the Casino Borghesi, will be held next Thursday and that more than one hundred persons will take part. We know also that Donnay will prepare this dinner for 300 'Scudi', and that the contributors will pay L.30 each...'

John Williams, wrote to Kate on 29 April with news of their father, saying that the old man 'looks worse than I have ever remembered him.' But he has lighter items to give her: he has taken little Kate 'a very pretty doll, but when she took it to the fire to warm it the wax melted and completely destroyed it. She however, kept pulling it about as it was made so there was no great harm done.'

'April 29th. No special detail has been yet received about the well known dinner offered yesterday evening by Mr Raffaello Bonfil to Richard Cobden in the Villino Torrigiani, except that this dinner started at 6 o'clock p.m. and ended about 10, and apart from Mr Cobden and his wife there were present: The Minister of Prussia, Duke Falleran, Secretary of the English Minister, and General Adam who is also English. The other guests were 20 in number and among there were other ladies besides Mrs Cobden. Their names will be known in the course of the day...'

'April 30th. The dinner started at half past six p.m., and ended a little before ten, with great order and gaiety. Only the heat was somewhat disturbing because, besides the hundred persons sitting round the table, the galleries were full of ladies, who not only enjoyed the show of the banquet but also the music of the amateur band...'

Nothing is said about these ladies being offered anything to eat or drink.

'May 8th 1847. The writer relates in this report what has been told to him concerning the great meeting of the Georgofili Academy, which took place yesterday Sunday in the 'Buonmore' hall, in order to admit Mr Cobden as a member of the Academy itself...Mr Cobden answered with a learned and wise speech, perfectly suited for the circumstances, but uttered in bad French...A. Minuti.'

'We arrived here last night, and found the hotel very full,' Kate wrote to Julie Schwabe from Turin on 21 May, 'this being the time of year for strangers to return from the South of France. The English Minister here has already sent to engage us to dine with him to-day, and for two days next week. On Monday a public dinner is to be given to Richard; the one at Leghorn went off very satisfactorily. Richard is become such a Frenchman that he now delivers his speeches in the language without the least difficulty. There were fifty persons present, and as many more were disappointed in consequence of the room not being large enough; indeed such was the eagerness for admission that the number might have been doubled. There were men of almost every faith excepting the Mohammedan. On our arrival at Genoa we found that poor O'Connell had died the night before.'

The Irish politician Fergus O'Connell, known as 'The Liberator', had perfected the system of constitutional agitation by mass meetings, and was consequently admired by Cobden. He had come to Italy for health reasons.

'The following morning we called on his son, and saw his old servant, Diggins, who had lived about his person thirteen years, and who appeared deeply sorrowful at his loss. He told Richard privately it was not his master's wish to leave England for Rome, that he had been advised by others to undertake the journey, and that he would have gone to Derrynane in preference if his wishes had been consulted. Richard saw Dr Miley, his chaplain, a very gentlemanly man, who gave him a better account of O'Connell's intellect during his last illness than he was led to expect. He did not sink into the low state of debility which I had heard described; he suffered little pain, and he was hardly insensible to the last. Dr Duff, who assisted in the *post-mortem* examination, described the brain, which had softened, as the source of the disease. Richard received an invitation to attend the funeral ceremonies for O'Connell, but was, unfortunately, prevented.'

Still at Turin on 23 May, Kate writes again to Mrs Schwabe: 'We have not yet fixed on anything certain, and least of all on our journey to Russia. There is no foundation in Mr Cobden's having had any direct communication with the Emperor; but two or three persons who have been lately in his dominions have given it as their opinion that he would be very well received there. However, the probability is that Mr Cobden will leave that journey till a future year. The Free-traders of Geneva have sent him a most pressing invitation to visit them.'

When brother John writes again to Kate on 7 June he reports that 'Mr and Mrs Schwabe are in London and they have been very polite indeed to me which of course is on account of you both but I cannot bear to receive people's attention unless on my own account, they asked me there to a dinner party and I went and had plenty of good things – it was a very handsome affair indeed.'

On 24 June Kate writes to Mrs Schwabe from Venice about the public dinner to Cobden given there on the 21st.'It was given on an island just opposite our hotel, under an alcove of vines; the party consisted of upwards of seventy persons, the Count Pricili in the chair, the Podesta, or Mayor, by his side. My husband made a short speech in French without any preparation, therefore I am unable to give you a copy. After the dinner the company entered their gondolas, which were waiting, and, accompanied by an excellent band of music, proceeded in procession down the Grand Canal to the bridge of the Rialto. The music and the gay liveries of some of the boatmen soon attracted a great number of other gondolas. The sounds and sight brought everybody into the balconies. As they returned, the moon, which had risen, gave a fresh charm to the picturesque scene, which was sufficiently romantic to excite poetical emotions, my husband says, even in the mind of a political economist. It was of a nature to remind me of the day when the Doge went in state to marry the Adriatic.'

On 29 July, Kate wrote to Mrs Schwabe from Berlin: 'We are quite wrong in being in Germany at this time of the year, for everywhere we find all the respectable families gone off to their different baths. There is every probability of my being home in the course of a fortnight after the receipt of this, but Mr Cobden will not return with me, as he wishes to go as far as St. Petersburgh so as to make himself acquainted with the state of trade in the Baltic; he then will have completed his information in that respect all over Europe. He is now in excellent health, and therefore I tell him he can spare me very well, for it would really break my heart to turn my back again on my children.'

From Stettin on 7 August Cobden records in his diary: 'Took leave of Kate this morning at the Hamburgh railway, and then started for Stettin at seven, in company with Mr Swaine.' The diary does not tell us whether Kate had a companion on her long journey back to England.

On 12 August he writes to her from Konigsberg, hungry for news: 'I expect wonderful descriptions of the boy and girl. Give them kisses from me, and do not let them forget that they have a papa. You must explain to them where I am and how long it will take to come back again, and then show the boy the route upon the maps.' Young Richard was only six at the time.'Let me have a long letter crossed very closely...' Evidently Cobden did not share John Williams's dislike of crossed letters.'It is sad work travelling without anybody to look after my things. I feel quite reduced in the world.'

Writing to Kate from Moscow on 25 August, Cobden confesses 'I am now quite tired of this wandering life, and I feel that after I get back there will be no more long journeys for me. If we go from home again it must be to take up an abode for a time in some given place. *That* I hope we may yet be able to do, to vary our mode of life, and give some advantages to the health and improvement of the children. Your letter will I am sure give me much interesting news about the boy – After your first transports are over – (now you will say I am going to preach) let all your attention be given to secure his affectionate *esteem* for his mother. I mean that you should make him feel your debtor for every opening thought and every first step in knowledge, so that in afterlife when he becomes as I hope he will not only a good but a clever and a wise man he may say I owe all that I possess to the inspiration of a good mother. You see I am not selfish – I wish you to be recognised as the source from which his mental and moral superiority flows. I hope you will not be again separated from him until he becomes of that age when the boy begins to ape the man. *Then* he will be naturally more the companion of youths and men than of his mother; but the reverence which your superiority and amiable solicitude for his improvement now will always secure you that influence which a mother ought to have, but which she can possess only through these means. I really feel that I ought not to press upon you the duties of an instructress yet, for you will naturally feel entitled to revel for a while in the abandonment of the Mother love after so long a separation. I really wonder when I look back that you endured so well the long absence from the little ones.'

By the end of the month Cobden was frankly homesick. On 31 August, still in Moscow, he tells her: 'I am now turned with face homewards and every step will increase my anxiety to be with you.'

Whilst Cobden was in St Petersburgh he wrote to Bright wishing him every possible happiness now that he had re-married, and confesses his own home-sickness: 'I have exhausted my appetite for novel scenes, and am sighing for my family and fireside.' In spite of this Kate's eagerly awaited letters from Wales did not all find favour with the lonely Cobden. On 17 September he writes to her from St Petersburgh: 'I have received your two letters from Machynlleth. The first one found me here when I was a little out of sorts with my eyes and rather unstrung, and as it was a fortnight in coming, from the date of yours at Southport, I was, to confess, a little disappointed with its contents, as it did not go sufficiently into details, upon many little matters – but your second letter which I got two days ago was quite satisfactory – ' Poor Kate, she must sometimes have felt that she was back at school.'...and as I was then recovered in my nervous system with my eyes quite well, I was in good spirits again. There is something in the air or water, or the moral or intellectual atmosphere of this part of the world which had cast a sort of languor over my feelings from which I have hardly recovered. Not that I can complain of the want of kindness of everybody here. Nor do I think that my visit to Russia will be less useful than to other countries. On the contrary...

'Yesterday I called upon the Minister of Finance, and had a long private talk – He invited me to speak to him frankly [presumably in French]. I gave him a free-trade lecture for half an hour without interruption...But you will have begun to wonder when I am going to talk to you of matters nearer your heart. I have been quite delighted with all that you say of the dear children. The account you give of the boy is delightful. He has had an impulse given to his moral sentiments which will never lose its influence upon his character. I shall never regret the sacrifice we have made of his society which has given him the advantage of being trained for a year in the midst of children of his own age. What you say of the little girl amuses me. I think I can see her standing in the field at Esgair asking her nurse who you are, and doubting whether her own Mamma was friend or enemy! I long to see you all and to tell you the truth I feel so unsettled and homesick that I have abandoned the idea of seeing any other country. I shall go direct to Hamburgh by way of Lubeck on leaving St Petersburgh tomorrow week by the steamer. I feel as if I had not elasticity enough to excite my mind to an interest in Sweden or any other country...I have found an English servant here who wishes to return to England and have engaged him for the trip. He has been a steward on board ship, and will therefore be able to take care of me at sea. I have made up my mind to 4 days' martyrdom on the Baltic.'

But as he told Kate on 29 September from Lubeck, the man was not a success.'To add to the discomfort of my voyage I was without shaving or dressing materials. That stupid English servant that I engaged at St Petersburgh contrived to lose my large carpet bag containing razors, combs, and change of linen, &c, whilst coming down the river to Cronstadt at which place we embark on board the large steamers for Lubeck...This blundering booby has me sighing for the precision and carefulness of that sour-faced fellow who accompanied us on our journey and who never lost anything in a twelvemonth. The Lubeck people have sent a deputation inviting me to dine tomorrow. I shall try to escape it. You can't conceive how tired I am grown of these demonstrations. I seem like a watch run down, and which must be wound up again before it can be of any use. However I shall be obliged to attend the large dinner prepared for me at Hamburgh.'

But at last the dinners were ended, and he wrote to her from Hamburgh on 5 October: 'I am heartily glad that these banquets are all over...I shall be knocked up with the heavy feeding...I have had many kind enquiries after you from the Schwabes, Israels, and Solomons. They are very civil people...my bag has just turned up. It came by the steamer which started a few hours before us for Stettin, and has been forwarded to me by the Consul there. I have not yet received your letter which was sent to Copenhagen.'

On 11 October he writes to her from John Williams's office in Verulam Buildings, saying he is on his way to 'the Euston Station'. He is to stay at the Victoria Hotel, the hotel from where he wrote to Hugh Williams in 1840 soliciting her hand in marriage, although he does not refer to this fact. His stomach, he says, is a little out of order – so many good dinners.

The grand tour was over at last. In Cobden's absence one or two of his friends had wound up his failing business which meant, sadly, that much of the money he had received via the national testimonial disappeared paying off the many debts which it had incurred during his work for Repeal.

Towards the end of 1847 Cobden fell a victim to the influenza epidemic. He wrote to Kate from 85 Eaton Square, the home of the Molesworths: 'I am told there never were so many people ill in London at one time before and that there are more deaths than there were in the time of the cholera...' He is still laid up when he writes on 29 November: '...horrid influenza which is seizing every third person in London...But I am getting better – thanks to confinement to my bed and slops. I shall not go to the House, or be out at night, for a day or two. Lady Molesworth has been a very charming nurse.' But he feels 'too stupid and prostrate for anything.' He reports again to Kate on 1 December: 'I am getting on well – Lady Molesworth has caught it and I must now nurse her.' Later in the month he tells her that he is dreading his return to Manchester and wishes they 'could escape together to Hastings and Brighton instead'. Kate herself was ill by this time and his wish to escape with her must have been a tonic.

CHAPTER FIVE

Life in London

In 1848 Cobden decided to move his family to London. He had taken a liking to the Bayswater area, then being rapidly developed and which he considered high-standing and therefore healthy. New houses were going up in Westbourne Terrace and one of these was already complete and occupied by his friend Sir Joshua Walmsley.

As Cobden was engaged on his parliamentary work during the session much of the labour of the move from Manchester to London fell upon Kate. On 5 February she was staying with Dick at Cassino House where the boy was still in the care of Miss Elizabeth Eveleigh, now Mrs William Fell, at her nursery school.

On 9 February the house is the main subject of his letter: 'I have not yet taken the house in Westbourne Terrace, but I see no reasons to change my mind...I will take care to make all the inquiries you suggest in your letter before I conclude!' On 14 February he pleads for 'a little more news of what is doing in the wigwham [*sic*] – a sort of diary of the sayings and doings of the family party would be very acceptable.'

Kate obviously announced her intention of seeing the house for herself, for on 18 February he writes: 'My dearest Kate I hope you will take good care of yourself and your little beau – this is not very safe weather for travelling – I am glad you have made up your mind to come to town for a few days – Let me recommend next Wednesday in preference to Thursday because on the former day there is no evening meeting of the House, and I could meet you – I went over the house again yesterday and found that the upper rooms had been papered and almost everything is ready. The bedroom papers seem to be good, and I think you will like them – There is nothing doing for the drawing room until you come – The landlord has let all his houses, so that those next to us will be occupied, before we get into ours which is pleasant.'

Kate's visit to London was seemingly postponed, for on 24 February he tells her: 'I shall be on the look out to receive you on the arrival of the train on Saturday to conduct you to Walmsleys. Our friend J.B. Smith is so much in love with the neighbourhood that he has written down to his wife to come up to look at another house. Nothing is being talked about to-day but the *émeutes* in Paris. From the last accounts it seems that Louis Philippe has been obliged to give way and change his ministry owing to the troops and the national guards having shown signs of fraternizing with the people. By-and-by the governments will discover that it is no use to keep large standing armies, as they cannot depend on them at a pinch. You are right in saying that the income tax has brought people to their senses. It is disgusting to see the same men who clamoured for armaments, now refusing to pay for them...last evening I dined, much against my wish, with a party at Mrs Drummond's [daughter-in-law of his Edinburgh admirer] ...I am more and more averse to these dinner parties – I always feel quite stupid and sleepy after an 8 o'clk dinner – the glare of the lamps on the table almost mesmerises me.'

On 8 March he tells Kate: 'We are a little anxious up here lest there should be riots in the north. We hear bad accounts from Glasgow, but I suppose they are exaggerated. I hope we shall have no imitations of the French fashions in this respect.' On 10 March he tells her: 'We were very late in the House again last night. Disraeli was very amusing for two hours, talking about everything but the question.' According to Morley, Disraeli had laughed at Cobden and Bright as representatives of Peace and Plenty in the face of a starving people and a world in arms.

Apparently their friend Mrs Schwabe has had a daughter, for on 11 March Cobden writes: 'I breakfasted this morning with the Schwabes – they are very well – She is looking better than ever – I saw the little girl which appears a small one – She was profuse in her kind inquiries after you.' On 14 March: 'On getting back yesterday I found such a mass of letters that, what with them and the committee I had to attend, and callers, and my speech last evening, I thought you would excuse my writing to you. I am more harassed than ever. The committees are very important (I mean upon army, navy and ordnance expenditure, and upon the Bank of England), and occupy my time more than the House. I gave them some home truths last evening, but we were a poor minority...There are many men on our side upon whom I relied, who went over to the Government, very much to my disgust. Don't be alarmed. I am not going to set up any new league. It is a mistake of the newspaper.'

Bad weather had further lowered his spirits when he writes on 18 March: 'We have had incessant rain here for several days...To-day, however, it is a fine clear day, and I am going with Porter the author of *Porter's Progress of the Nation* at 4 o'clock down to Wimbledon to stay till Monday. This week's work has nearly knocked me up. They talk of a ten hours bill in Paris. I wish we had a twelve hours bill, for I am at it from nine in the morning till midnight. We had a debate last evening upon the question of applying the income tax to Ireland, but I was shut out of the division, the door being closed in my face just as I was entering, otherwise I should have voted for the measure. The news from Paris is more and more exciting. There seems to be a sort of reaction of the moderate party against the violent men. The Bank of France has suspended speci payments, which will lead to much mischief and confusion. I fear we have not seen the worst.'

Next day he tells her he has sent her a *Times* containing a report of his speech in the Debate on the Navy Estimates the previous evening: 'Be good enough to return it to me after you have read it, as I shall want to correct it for Hansard, and have another copy. We were a miserable minority. The blue jackets and red coats were down upon me fiercely, as if I had been attacking them sword in hand. It reminded me of the old times when we were just beginning the Anti-Corn-Law battle in the House. We get astounding news from the continent; a fresh revolution or a dethronement by every post.' He shows his usual concern about Kate's health: 'Take care of yourself I pray – do not fatigue yourself by standing about too much. A little *walking* exercise is good, but it must be followed by rest – I hope to hear better accounts of you tomorrow.'

On 20 March he was able to tell her that Ponsford, their new landlord, expects to let the Smiths have the next door house, and assures her that he had said 'the smoky chimney shall be cured'.

On 4 April the new house is again uppermost in his mind: 'Will you let me know,' he asks Kate, 'which rooms you would like to have bars to the windows to prevent the children from falling out – I find that Sir Joshua Walmsley's sideboard is 11 feet long. I will try to learn some particulars about the proper packing of your delicate china.'

When he writes to her on 10 April he has been staying with friends in Surrey: 'We have been all in excitement here with the Chartist meeting at Kennington Common, which after all has gone off very quietly, and does not appear to have been so numerously attended as was expected. In my opinion the Government and the newspapers have made far too much fuss about it. From all that I can learn there were not so many as 40,000 persons present, and they dispersed quietly. I do not think I shall be able to go north with you before next Monday week.'

While Cobden had been negotiating for the Westbourne Terrace

House, efforts were also being made to dispose of their Victoria Park property. 'I am glad to hear from Fred,' he tells Kate on 2 May, 'that Mrs. Kennedy has made up her mind to take ours – It will be something off ones mind – By the way, the back premises of Walmsley's house have been whitewashed which gives a much more cheerful aspect to the back rooms behind the dining room...' On 11 May he reports again: 'I will have the paper done for the drawing room, the same pattern as Thos. Smiths – if I like it tomorrow when I am going to dine with him – You are quite right in having the same carpet as in Manchester – for we should not find a prettier one – the colour of Smith's paper is gold and neutral or cream colour – that will I suppose do with the furniture?'

The question of how to remove their belongings from Manchester to London by canal now occupies Cobden's attention: 'J.B. Smith tells me he has spoken about a boat for which he is to pay so much per cwt – they will not let out the boat entire – This will suit us quite as well as the other way. They are getting on fast with the house – In a week it will be as clean as a new pin – ' On 13 May he tells her: '...I am looking forward with great anxiety to your arrival in town, but I hope you will take care and not over fatigue yourself in the labours of removal. Today in looking at Walmsley's drawing room, we almost persuaded ourselves that it would be better to have a plain colour a little deeper than any pattern; that is provided there are pictures on the walls – Now I think we ought to cover our drawing room with the best of the plates of the Dresden pictures, neatly framed – If you think it would be well to try this, it could be altered if you like afterwards, and in the meantime we could have a little extra outlay from Ponsford upon something else – It is only an idea that has occurred and you must do as you think best.

'You will hear that all the papers are down upon me again. In making a few remarks about the Alien Bill, I said that the "best way to repeal republicanism was to curtail some of the barbarous splendour of the Monarchy which went to the aggrandizement of the aristocracy..." Whenever I speak I am sure to upset the fat in the fire. My few words drew up Lord John [Russell] as usual, and he was followed by Bright with a capital speech.' He is in hopes of being able to leave town on Wednesday morning. 'It is not a trifle that shall prevent me, for I am very anxious to be with you for a few days.' In this letter he goes on to describe yet another party which Kate was not able to share. 'I dined at the Molesworths, and met a party – the Bancrofts, Lady Lovelace (Byron's Ada), Macaulay, etc. After dinner there was a soiree, and little Lady

Morgan and many others were there.' Perhaps Cobden sensed that Kate might not have cared for his singing of Lady Molesworth's praises when she had nursed him through his influenza the previous autumn, for this time his hostess comes in for unflattering comment: 'You should have seen Lady Molesworth with her pink satin dress standing out as if she had hoops, and all covered to the bottom with lace flounces. She was so formidable in size that she spread over an entire sofa.'

On 16 May: '...I have not seen Walmsley since I received your letter this morning; and therefore have not been able to ascertain the length of the stair carpet – but the two drawing rooms took together 146 yards of carpeting – I agree with you about the papering of the drawing room, and will venture upon a pattern which I think will please – at all events I think it better to have everything done out of hand before you come up – they are now gilding the ceilings of the drawing room...' Next day he tells her: 'Lady Walmsley has very expressly invited you to join me as soon as you find it convenient to come up – I spoke about our taking lodgings but they both only laughed at it – In fact, my stay is not very troublesome to them for I have only dined with them once – Sir Joshua and I leave Westbourne Terrace generally before 12 o'clk and we do not return ordinarily till midnight.'

Arrangements for shipping their furniture had been completed at this stage, for on 16 May he tells Kate: 'I have written to Fred to ask him to procure the money necessary to make your preparations,' and asks, 'Has he been to inquire about the boat? It will be necessary to give notice when it will be wanted. Tell Orme to let the boatmen know that there are no wine or spirits and then they will not be tempted to rummage the cargo for drink...Is Fred sending off the writing table that was in Mosley St. and the maps and books, &c.'

Although Cobden writes to Frederick on 6 June telling him that the house in Westbourne Terrace would very soon be in order, two months later Kate was still living in Manchester, for it was there, on 6 August, that another daughter was born. She was named Ellen Millicent Ashburner, but was known to the family as Nelly.

A month after Nelly's birth Cobden took a furnished house – Staunton Lodge – at Hayling Island, at a rental of £2.12.6d a week for six weeks. This involved him in some expense and on 11 September he writes to Frederick to acknowledge £100 which he has sent him: '...so many people are sending in their bills that I shall want more money. We shall go down to Hayling on Wednesday morning (the children and servants will go tomorrow).' Frederick himself is to join the family there later.

On 16 September Cobden wrote from Hayling to Bright: 'I have come here with my wife and children to be out of the world in this corner of the island, where we are five miles from a butcher's shop, or a doctor, and where there are no politicians.' He was still there when he wrote again to Bright on 24 October.'Tomorrow we leave this place for London. I have been living the life of a family Robinson Crusoe for the last six weeks...We think we have all derived great benefit from the sea breezes.'

Meanwhile, judging by a receipted account, the Grand Junction Canal Company had carried their furniture and belongings form Manchester to London, charging for this service the sum of £45.3.7d. On 13 October there is a handwritten letter from the Company requesting settlement of the account, so presumably after their stay on Hayling Island the Cobden family returned to London and life in Westbourne Terrace.

November 1849 saw the birth of Kate's fifth child. He was named William, after Cobden's father, and was sickly from the first. Cobden told Henry Ashworth on 13 December: 'My wife is quite well. The little one is I hope better, but I am not quite confident of its safety.' During that winter he was away much of the time, speaking in different parts of the country, but by 19 February he was in London with Kate when he wrote to tell Frederick 'Our poor little baby has this morning been released from its sufferings. It would be selfish and cruel to wish that its life had been prolonged, for it has been in a constant state of suffering – Will you let Charles, the Sales, and Sarah, and Mary know. Kate is bearing up as well as could be expected – but it is a terrible trial for her.' Later he tells his brother: '...we men know nothing of the feelings of a mother towards an infant child – We shall bury the poor little dear in Kensal Green cemetery on Saturday...'

While Kate was at Westbourne Terrace hoping vainly for an improvement in the baby's health Cobden wrote to her regularly about his doings. On 18 December he tells her: 'I have received your despatches; don't trouble yourself to send the proofs of the speeches. I am staying with Mrs Carbutt, who has taken me from Mr. Schofield and Mr. Marshall. In fact, judging by the competition that there was for me, I am rather at a premium. The meeting this evening promises to be a very full and influential one. I wish it was over, for I am sorely perplexed at these demonstrations, for want of something fresh to say.' Next day he reports: 'We had a most thoroughly successful meeting last evening, and I spoke with tolerably good effect, but I am not sure that I shall not appear in the reports to have been rather tough with the landlords. At all events, I expect the Protectionists will raise a fierce howl at me.'

Early in 1851 Katie and Nelly were sent to stay with the Schwabes in Manchester, as Kate was expecting another child. Nelly seems to have charmed everyone: 'She continues to be the general favourite,' wrote Mrs Schwabe: 'She is a true treasure.' 'Your beloved ones are quite well,' she wrote to Kate on 25 April: '...We have decided on all the little ones remaining here for the present; Mr Schwabe thinks they will all be very happy. Then we shall all go together to Wales later in the Summer.' But the Cobdens had other plans for their children.

Kate developed a severe attack of rheumatism near the time of her confinement, and wrote to Dick that she 'needed two persons to turn her in bed'. When she writes on 27 April, however, Mrs Schwabe makes no mention of the rheumatic attack: 'I am delighted to hear that you keep pretty well, and feel much obliged to the little stranger that *he* or *she* postponed the arrival till I am there to receive the little pet. Tuesday evening I hope to be on the spot, and then I say the sooner the better.'

Four days before the birth Cobden wrote a bracing note to Kate from Dunford*: I am delighted to hear better accounts of your health – keep up your spirits – Recollect that not more than 1 in 700 confinements need any other help than that which Dame Nature affords gratis.'

Emma Jane Catherine, to be known as Jane or Janie, was born at Westbourne Terrace on 28 April 1851 and proved to be the most enduring of all Kate's offspring, living well into her nineties. The following day Cobden writes urgently to Frederick asking for £20 by return', and tells him, 'Kate and the little girl are doing well.'

Kate's health appears to have improved after the birth of Jane, for a few months later Cobden tells Joseph Sturge: 'My wife has grown quite fat and has lost her rheumatism entirely – Her baby, now six months old, is ready to be matched for health, strength, weight and appetite with any child in the Queen's dominions. It has had no other food from the day of its birth than that which it derived from its mother's breast, and my wife has not touched anything stronger than water. Yet the old fashioned notion still prevails that mothers whilst nursing ought to drink beer or wine...'

On 26 March 1853 a fourth daughter was born at Westbourne Terrace. Cobden wrote to Dick with the news on 28 March: 'I write to say that you have another little sister who was born on Saturday

* See Chapter Six

last. Your Mamma has been suffering from a severe cold and troublesome cough.' This new little sister she described to Dick on 12 April as 'a very small but a pretty little creature.' The baby was named Julia Sarah Anne, always to be known as Anne or Annie.

While Kate was in London awaiting the birth Cobden paid a visit to Bognor, where Katie and Nelly were now at Mrs Gardener's school at Dome House, and writes to her on 16 March: 'I arrived here safely yesterday evening, and found the dear little ones waiting for me. Nelly was the first to get into my arms exclaiming "you'll stay a *'foatnight'* won't you"...I was dragged off to the bedroom that I might open my carpet bag, and let them draw out all the oranges, cakes &c, which were duly unfolded and piled up on a chair. This morning they were in my bedroom as soon as I was up. Today we have been altogether to Bognor Church where Nelly behaved very well. All the way home she was running after pebbles which she asked me to throw for her...'

Whilst Kate was still at Westbourne Terrace she received a letter from Cobden dated 28 July, written from Dunford: 'My dearest Kate – Frederick has brought me a note which he has just received from Charles [their youngest brother] containing the shocking announcement of the death of our friend Schwabe – I can hardly realize to my mind the truth of this awful calamity. – The note says he died of scarlet fever, which may account for the suddenness of the event. I really can think of nothing else, and can hardly dare to realize the effects of this blow upon our dear friend Mrs Schwabe. I am afraid her reason may suffer another eclipse. What can we do for the poor soul? If it were your case she would have been at your side – But what can you do for her with your baby? I really do not know what service you could render her.'

Cobden travelled to Manchester to attend Schwabe's funeral, and writes to Kate from Broughton on 31 July: '...On my arrival here on friday night I found a note from Miss Brendon, asking me to go to Crumpsal by nine o'clk, which I accordingly did to see poor Mrs Schwabe before the funeral...she received me with her usual animation, without in fact offering either in her appearance or manner the slightest traces of the calamity she had suffered...I found her under a great religious excitement...It was with difficulty that I could get away from her – she held me by the hands, and when the servants came to the door to call me she would run across the room and tell them to go away, and in fact it was only when all the party were waiting to start that I could get away to take my place as one of the pall-bearers...'

At this stage in their marriage the roles of husband and wife were reversed, and Kate bore what Priscilla McLaren obviously felt should have been the man's share in the work: 'What a good wife thou must be to be able to set Mr Cobden free at such a busy time! I should have required my husband to have helped me!' she had told Kate earlier.

In a letter of 21 August to Bright Cobden says 'By the way, I must give you a piece of intelligence which may be useful. We have found a way of moving our furniture which causes us as little trouble as if we were merely transferring a portmanteau of clothes to the railway. The "Pantechnicon" manager walks into the house, a self-possessed cool fellow who will answer no questions, and scarcely look at you, till he has walked into every room from the cellar to the attics. Having done so, his only question is "Where do you want to move to?" Upon being answered "to Midhurst" he adds "that's 50 miles...my charge is £70." So for £70 he takes possession of the house and undertakes to transfer all its contents from the door of one residence to that of the other without shifting the furniture from his vans. It was a load off my wife's shoulders. Besides, as we are not ready for the furniture at Dunford; in our case he carried everything to the "Pantechnicon" and charges for rent £10 for the first month and £2 a month afterwards. If we had had to pack for ourselves the *cases* would have cost nearly £70.

'My wife goes to Bognor on the Sussex Coast where all our little girls will remain. They are with a lady, an old friend of ours, who was once better off, who has an establishment for very young girls. If you know anybody who wishes to place such little ones in good keeping, in the mildest climate and quietest spot in England, pray recommend my friend Mrs Gardener...Our house here will not be ready till Xmas.'

'I hope you will be able to come away tomorrow,' Cobden tells Kate on 1 September: 'Depend on it – whatever may ail the baby, there is nothing like a change to country air to set her right.'

Before she finally left her London home, Kate was asked by Cobden to have visiting cards printed with the Dunford address, as they would never move again until they went to their 'narrow home'.

CHAPTER SIX

Dunford: 'We shall shine in roses'

It was Frederick, not Cobden, who first thought of buying Dunford, the old farmhouse at Heyshott, near Midhurst, where their father William Cobden had raised his large family. As early as 1840 while Cobden and Kate were on their marriage journey he had written to his elder brother from Frankfurt on 22 July with his reaction to the idea: '...this topic of settling down in quiet after the labors [*sic*] of life, reminds me of the subject of Dunford about which you wrote me in Paris. If you would like to possess the old roof-tree and see a good opportunity of buying it, I have no objection to your doing so at any time. The money that will be necessary for such a purchase you can take from the business without any serious thought to our capital. But I must bargain with you that you will not let it be a bribe to induce you to join the Corn Law people. Take care that you pay such a moderate price only as shall give you a profit after we have carried the total and immediate repeal, and when Mr Benjamin Smith is President of the Board of Trade!'

The project seems to have been lost sight of in the excitement of the Corn Law 'agitation', and it was not until some years later that the small property was purchased after the payment of the national testimonial and the settlement of Cobden's outstanding debts. After close scrutiny of the lengthy correspondence between the two brothers it is plain to see that Cobden was carried away by the architect he chose and under whose influence the thatched farmhouse became a Victorian villa – some would say – of suburban rather than rural character, Weynert & Ashdown were a firm of London architects, with offices in Charing Cross, and it would appear that Cobden was 'taken for a ride'.

'Everything looks very *small* in comparison with my memory of the place,' he told Kate after a visit to his birthplace in the autumn of 1848: 'I send a rose leaf from the tree growing on the house where I was born.' This is now mounted between two sheets of transparent plastic in the volume containing his original letter in the British Library.

Cobden was once challenged at a meeting by a member of his audience who asked how he had acquired his property: 'I am indebted for it to the bounty of my countrymen,' was his reply.'It was the scene of my birth and my infancy; it was the property of my ancestors; and it is by the munificence of my countrymen that this small estate, which had been alienated from my father by necessity, has again come into my hands, and enabled me to light up afresh the hearth of my father where I spent my childhood. I say that no warrior duke who owns a vast domain by the votes of Imperial Parliament, holds his property by a more honourable title than I possess mine.' According to Morley, Cobden's reply resulted in 'boisterous cheering' from the crowd.

During the summer holidays of 1849 Cobden writes more and more frequently to Frederick about Dunford. On 8 September, from Eastbourne: 'Have you done anything about the poor people in the Dunford house? The subject has often been on my mind, and I should not be surprised at any moment to hear of Cholera or fever breaking out there – At all events the way in which they are crowded is disgraceful, and we are responsible for it.' Kate has been to see the house and Cobden reports to Frederick: 'My wife seems to have caught your fancy for the old place, and thinks it might serve for a summer retreat for us. But the first thing to be thought of is another retreat for at least two of the three families now pigging together there.' Adding: 'Kate thinks you ought not to have any more trees planted near the house, – it is already sufficiently crowded.'

By 13 September he has had further thoughts about the rehousing of the two families.'I don't think it will be necessary to remove all the poor people from the house at Dunford. The poor woman Tiller must of course go [she was to become their cook] and the younger Elcombs large family must be otherwise provided for. Kate and I think that it will be no inconvenience to us if the older Elcomb and his wife and younger daughter occupy the part at the back north end.' This letter contains detailed plans for the manning of the estate, and the building of cottages for the inhabitants: Cobden is obviously anxious to involve Frederick in the work, and offers him a room whenever he wishes to go there, another in Westbourne Terrace, and 'a home in Manchester'. Frederick accepted the task of supervising the work, and by 17 December Cobden is writing to him about the local builder's extravagant proposals about restoring what was still the cottage: 'I'm afraid Grist is treating you *en grand seigneur* in his estimate of the cottage.' Again on 3 January 1850: 'I cant help fearing that Grist will be dealing with us, as so many others have done, as very rich and liberal people, and that we shall have to pay more than outside prices for Cottages and everything else – you must prevent it...'

When Cobden wrote to Henry Ashworth about his plans on 7 October 1850 the farmhouse was still 'sheltering labouring families', for whom alternative accommodation had to be found-.'...with the aid of the whitewasher and carpenter we have made a comfortable weather-proof retreat for Summer: and are surrounded with pleasant woods, and within a couple of miles of the summit of the South Down hills, where we have the finest air and some of the prettiest views in England...'

On 21 October Cobden gives instructions about planting, transplanting and turfing. On 3 November he writes about the man responsible for this work: 'In your dealings with Alman, don't forget that he is interested in the suggestions – remember too that every attempt to introduce ornamental shrubs or artificial arrangements into the grounds round Dunford would be in regular Cockney taste and I should certainly root them up – Let us have consistency throughout, and therefore I am for wild evergreens rather than rhododendrons or even laurels – '

Recovered from another attack of influenza in the spring of 1851 (this time presumably suffered at home and without Lady Molesworth's help in nursing him back to health) Cobden joined Frederick at Dunford for a few weeks, and on 22 April he tells Kate: 'I left Chichester with Elcomb yesterday in the midst of rain, and it has been raining ever since. I can hardly see the trees on the side of the hill leading up to Walker's, [a farm on the estate, later to be known as The Hurst] and the Downs are quite lost in the thick mist. I am of course a prisoner, which is very disagreeable. Yesterday, whilst at Chichester, I was very extravagant in the purchase of a great number of roses in pots, which I expect to arrive today, and I shall have them taken out of the pots and placed in the garden. They are all of the autumn perpetual kinds. I intend to have a bed of them on the rising ground just at the end of the house, and also have a bed in the front of the house. We shall shine in roses. The hollies and evergreens are still looking rather sorry and downcast. But, probably, with dry warm weather we shall soon see an improvement. The temperature is mild, and the wheats are looking vigorous. The nightingale and the cuckoo are already heard in the hanger, and the foliage of the woods is assuming a lively hue. I long for the time when we can be here with the children in the autumn. You will enjoy it beyond measure.'

On 9 June Cobden is again at Dunford, and writes to Frederick to report progress: '...Old Mr Alman has managed the flowers and creepers, and the alteration of the green plot to perfection.' He adds a typical news item about one of the numerous dogs the Cobdens like to have about them: "Vick" is in the family way by Grist's white terrier.'

At the end of June Cobden spent an idyllic few days during Dick's summer holiday at Dunford, and on 3 August tells Kate (still at Westbourne Terrace) 'We have been here just 24 hours, and your hopeful son has made the most of his time...I need hardly say that the mumps are quite forgotten. The country is very inviting.' While waiting for Kate to join them, Cobden wrote to Archibald Prentice: '...I have run away from town, and here I am in a quiet nook in the midst of cornfields, looking at the scenery which first met my infant eyes – occupying the old farm house in which I was born, (the roof unaltered) and sleeping in the very room that witnessed my birth – Now, if you want to see a new phase of English life – the purely peasant existence of the least advanced part of the South of England, – come and see me, and I will give you a shakedown somewhere, and a hearty welcome, and lead you to pleasant walks, and crystal fountains, and we will ramble on the South Downs, and talk about the League...'

'...The children are racing about the garden without their bonnets, which I suppose is more than they could do with you in Lancashire,' Cobden wrote to Frederick from Dunford on 4 November 1851.'I have been today to Midhurst to appeal against an absurd assessment of Dunford for the house tax at £40 per ann. – I was kept waiting for my turn in the stone passage at the Eagle for nearly 3 hours with a crowd of malcontents including old Gadd, the Bex miller, and other equally amiable company, (always excepting your friend Miss Turner, one of the victims, who inquired for you) amongst whom were a couple of radical free traders who nearly baited old Gadd to death. The Commissioners, who were Captain Shirley, Mr Fisher, and Mrs Carnegie from Fareham, were very civil and asked me to name my own amount, and I proposed £20 as the outside, which they agreed to, and complimented me as being the only person they had had before them who was willing to pay any tax at all. – The work about the house, gates, approaches, fences, &c are being brought to a close, and right well do Tiller and Quinnell do their parts. – Tomorrow I shall put in some standard roses which Mr Allman [*sic*] will bring and have the garden cleared of decayed rubbish – '

Frederick wrote regularly to Kate reporting progress on the building work. On 25 April he tells her: 'I have rather a strong muster of men and boys on the ground every day, – what with bricklayers carpenters and our labourers digging at the back, there are upwards of twenty. We have got the roof on over the end of the house the dining room portion of it, and shall begin tiling it tomorrow. Yesterday we had a narrow escape from an accident, which could have terribly spoilt the beauty of our woods in front; in the afternoon a fire broke out in the dry peat and moss, on this side, – but below the saw pit – caused I believe by ashes from a tobacco pipe, some of the men having been strolling about there during their dinner hour; it spread most rapidly, but fortunately there was plenty of men within call and after a sharp scuffle with shovels and watering pots we put it out, it has made an ugly black patch of half an acre; had it happened in the night, or when no assistance could be procured nearer than the village, I believe more than half our fir woods would have been destroyed; nearly the whole of what was Dunford Common having a peaty surface, is now of the consistence of *German tinder*, and takes fire as easily. I shall not feel at ease about it till we have some rain. Lord Egremont has had some bad fires in his plantations, but these are supposed to have been maliciously caused by fellows who have been punished for poaching or petty depredations.'

Frederick must have been absent from Dunford in August 1852 for on the 29th Cobden wrote telling him: 'I have been obliged to stir up all parties about the work in the house. There was every prospect of our having the workmen about us till Christmas.' In October Kate was writing to invite Frederick to dine with her at Westbourne Terrace, bringing her the dimensions of the new rooms, as she wished to judge the pieces of furniture from the London house which will fit into their new home.'The gardener is now forming the kitchen garden and a very good one it will be I hope by and by. The cucumber, melon and vegetable marrow beds are likewise in a state of formation.' On 17 February: 'The front part of the house is now complete or next thing to it. Now the work people will commence on the butler's pantry [there is no record that the Cobdens ever employed such a dignitary] and the bathroom above – '

Cobden himself was attending to the installation of the bath, for he writes to Kate from the House of Commons on 16 March telling her of his discussions with Weynert the architect about this important feature: '...he thinks that a mahogany rim would be better than marble which he says is sometimes objected to as being chilling for invalids.'

The year 1853 started for the Cobdens – six in number now – with a holiday together at Dunford. By March it seems that Cobden had been persuaded into pulling down the old 'cottage'.'Your Papa,' Kate tells Dick, 'is going down to Dunford on Saturday next, where the architect Mr Weynert will meet him to settle about commencing the new building...'

On 19 August: 'The house is still in a very unfinished state,' Cobden tells Dick, 'and it will take many months before it is quite finished.' Again to Dick on 2 September 1853: '...The rain fell all day yesterday, and the brook was so swollen that Mr Weynert found much difficulty in getting over the bridge. – We are getting on but slowly with the house. Yesterday the slate cistern was hoisted to the top of the tower. – The bottom slab weighed 8cwt, and it was a very difficult job to get it to its lofty resting place. Your Mamma is coming down here tomorrow. She will remain here for two days, and then go over to Bognor where she will remain until the house is finished.'

On 20 October 1853 Kate writes to Dick from Bognor: 'I hear from Dunford that they are progressing with the building – the front bedrooms are nearly finished, but the late rains have been very much against the out of doors work – the roofing at the end of the house &c. I shall be glad when it will be ready for us to commence the furnishing part – It will be I am sure a long while before we shall feel thoroughly comfortable there.'

Cobden tells Moffatt on 12 November 1853: 'Now to descend to the humble level of domestic matters. You addressed your letter to Westbourne Terrace. Did I not tell you that we were able to give up that house, and that I was building a permanent home for my family here? The house is not yet finished. – Heaven knows only when a country builder will complete his undertaking. – Meanwhile my wife and children are at Bognor, and I oscilate between the two homes. She brings me in a carriage as far as the Duke of Richmond's park, and then I trudge across Goodwood Downs to this wild spot enjoying the walk even more than in Hyde Park or Pall Mall. Although the house is not finished the stables are roofed in, and I must tell you that we have a couple of stalls especially for yourself, and a friend, or a groom, so that you may be able to bring your horses here during the Goodwood race week, and ride over the Downs to the Course in an independent way. You have laid many pleasant plans for me in your time, and I intend to be "revenged" as the French say some day on you in this wild country. – My wife wants to know whether your sisters are in this neighbourhood. – ' Perhaps Kate was already feeling apprehensive about their lack of friends in Sussex?

On 9 December Dick gets a disappointment when Kate writes to him that 'It will be impossible for you to have Chatterton down to see you the beginning of the holidays as we shall have no place whatever for him to stay in. The servants will have even to sleep out of the house as the new bedrooms will not be fit for anyone to sleep in...You will go to Dunford before I [*sic*] and your sisters shall but I will not say a word about it to them so when we go over they will be so surprised to find you there to welcome them.'

By the end of the year Cobden was able to tell Hargreaves: 'We have been building a house here, and are taking possession next week. But the workmen have still full possession, and from the cellar to the attics nothing seems finished. I dread the discomfort that awaits my wife for the next two months. However, she and the children are fond of the country and as spring advances they will feel recompensed for present inconvenience. – ' But he still needed a base in London during the parliamentary sessions.'For myself I must look out for lodgings. I should not wish to be further from the House than Brook St. If you hear of anything likely to suit, be good enough to think of me. – I shall need two sitting rooms and a good bedroom. – I must be so comfortable that my wife can pay me a visit.'

Writing again from Bognor on 17 December Cobden tells Frederick 'Kate says you had better lay in a stock of meat for the family for the latter part of next and beginning of the following week. We shall not go to the Rhoades [relatives in Chichester] on Christmas Day, but to the Watkins [cousins] on New Years day. A stone of beef and mutton may be ordered at both Whites and Hales. She thinks you had better lose no time in ordering some beef for Xmas day and she will write further particulars about the rest. I suppose you will secure a good turkey...I shall come over on Monday by omnibus – so let Quinnell meet me at the corner. I quite agree with you that the lives of the blackbirds should be preserved.'

An unlikely observer of the home life of the Cobdens was a young Midhurst girl named Elizabeth (Lizzie) Clare. It was in 1854 that this very junior member joined the domestic staff at Dunford. She was to remain with the family for more than sixty years. As an elderly woman, probably at the suggestion of one of the Cobden daughters, she wrote what is called her 'Autobiography', consisting of hand-written notes in an exercise book, full of rather original spelling but radiating love for her mistress:

'The first time I saw dear Mrs Cobden was when I was about nine years old. I whent to Dunford House with my dear Mother to ask Mrs Cobden if she would give the washing to her, and she very kindly did. I was delighted to see such a beautiful lady. I little thought what a friend she was going to be to me. After some time three of my sisters, whent in service to Mrs and Mr Cobden at Dunford-house. They were there a few years, one day Mrs Cobden called on my Mother at the old corner house, and I was not very well So Mrs Cobden kindly told my mother, she thought a change would do me good in the country. So I was to go to Dunford the next day. Their were four young ladys, Miss Katie the eldest, Miss Ellen the next, Miss Janie, the next, Miss Annie the Baby, was about a year old. So the first thing I did in the morning, was to take Miss Baby, as Miss Annie was called, up and down the drive in her perambulator till the breakfast was ready. After I was there a few weeks, I was to remain, and be under the Nurse.'

As late as 11 January 1854 Cobden told Ashworth: 'We have taken possession of an unfurnished house and are suffering all the discomforts of noise, dust and open doors and windows. But we are bearing it with as much patience as we can, and are trying to console ourselves by drawing bills upon the future stock of enjoyment.'

With a Paxton-designed conservatory limpeted on to the sunny side of the house, Dunford, when completed, would not have looked out of place in a London suburb at that time. On 17 March 1854 Cobden told Frederick that he thought Weynert's estimate for putting up this obligatory Victorian addition 'very high' and begged him to 'profit by the advice of Alman to get your conservatory cheaper.'

As late as March 1855 there were still domestic problems. On 19 March Cobden tells Frederick: I have seen Weynert, and sent him to see Benham about the boiler. – It is a most disgusting business to have your house put into disorder again, for God knows how long a time, owing to the neglect of these people. I have not yet paid Benhams bill and shall not do so till I get this matter righted...'

Even as late as the autumn of 1855, when the Cobdens had a visit from W.S. Lindsay, MP and his wife, life was far from comfortable at Dunford. Lindsay describes their visit in *Incidents in the Life of Richard Cobden*: '...On my way from London by road to Portsmouth, we rested at Midhurst for a night, and spent the following day with RC at Dunford. Here, about a mile and a half from Midhurst, he had just completed the erection of a house of a more ornamental character in its outwards appearance than I would have expected of him. It stood on the site of his father's farmhouse, and in the very centre of Toryism. If ever the adage held good of a man being no prophet in his own country, it seemed to be so in his case, for the world-wide name and fame of Richard Cobden did not appear to be nigh so familiar to the people at the hotel where we had taken up our quarters as that of either of the two Tory lords or the Tory Squire who between them owned all the land in the neighbourhood of Midhurst.'

In the end, it seemed that the boots at the hotel directed the Lindsays to Dunford: 'Cobden had only half expected me. I had merely intimated, when we parted in London, that I might look him up, as Midhurst was on our road to Portsmouth, but I had not named any time, in case it might put him about, as I knew that his house was hardly fit to receive himself and family, much less visitors. Things were just as I had anticipated – only one sitting-room had by that time been furnished, and in it I found him and his wife seated before a rousing fire, which was kept up more for the purpose of drying the damp plaster and paint, than for warmth for themselves, as the weather was still fine. Their son, Richard, who was the eldest in the family and their only son, then a boy between thirteen or fourteen years of age, was away at school in Germany, and the four girls had all been despatched to bed on my appearance.

'His home, the design and completion of which I daresay he had left entirely to an architect, was built, as I have said, on the site of the one which his father had occupied. It stood in a basin, closely surrounded by hills or "downs"...He had a large stock of poultry, and pigs of the black Hampshire breed...After an early dinner we started for the downs...We continued our chat during tea, which was Cobden's favourite meal. Late dinners and "dining out" he invariably avoided when he could conveniently do so, and preferred the old homely style of a light dinner at one o'clock and a substantial tea at six or seven. He was temperate in all things, very simple in his habits, and easily satisfied.'

The effort involved in the rebuilding of Dunford had been costly in every sense of the word, and sadly their 'future stock of enjoyment' was to prove a delusion for Kate. By the spring of 1856 it had become a haunted place for her and was never to realise its early promise.

CHAPTER SEVEN

Commissioner's Wife

The first Great Exhibition held in Hyde Park in 1851 meant Cobden and Kate, in their separate spheres, were involved in a great deal of extra activity – some of it not to their taste. In 1850 Cobden, his political star still in the ascendant, had been appointed as one of twenty-four Commissioners invited by the Prince Consort, President of the Society of Arts, to organise the undertaking, when it became clear this was beyond the scope of the Society acting on its own. The aim of the Exhibition was to promote peace between the participating nations, and this fact no doubt weighed with Cobden when he accepted the Prince's invitation.

At this stage Kate was obviously delighted to be able to tell Mrs Schwabe of the honour her husband had received, and to give her advance information: 'Do you take much interest in the Exposition of Arts and Manufactures which is to take place in 1851 in London. We are likely to be pretty much in the thick of it, for Mr. Cobden is appointed one of the Commissioners...and the Duke of Richmond [Cobden's aristocratic neighbour at Goodwood] is one of his colleagues!!! I am told that several lists of names were submitted to the Prince, and that Mr. Cobden's name appeared in them all.'

The Exhibition project was to suffer a serious setback in the summer of 1850. On Saturday 29 June Cobden found himself sitting in committee with Sir Robert Peel. The meeting continued until two o'clock in the afternoon. Four hours later Peel was thrown from his horse on Constitution Hill. Cobden wrote to Kate with the news that same day: '...The accounts of poor Peel's health are very unsatisfactory. I fear very much the worst. It would be a great national calamity to lose him, and with him we should lose the best safeguard, if not the only one amongst statesmen against a reaction at headquarters from Free-Trade to Protection.' Peel died later that day. Cobden felt his death acutely, both at a personal level and because he, like the Prince Consort and the Commissioners, realised that without his support, the vote in the Lower House on the following Monday might go against them. As the Prince wrote to Stockmar, (Baron Christian Friedrich, mentor of the Prince Consort), on 3 July: 'We are in deep grief; added to which, I cannot conceal from you that we are on the point of having to abandon the Exhibition altogether. We have announced our intention to do so, if on the day the vast building ought to be begun the site is taken from us.' Peel, in favour of the Hyde Park site, may by his untimely death have influenced the vote, for he was to have taken charge of the business in the House.

On 4 July Cobden wrote to Kate: 'You will have seen the sad news of Sir R. Peel's death. I have not been able to think of anything since. Poor soul. His health has been sacrificed by his sufferings in the cause of Free Trade, and he may be said to have been a victim to the best act of his political life.' Cobden might have been writing his own obituary.'I should not like to be in the position of those who by their unsparing hostility inflicted martyrdom upon him.'

In addition to attendance at frequent committee meetings, Cobden was involved in the social functions connected with the Exhibition. In October he went to York to attend the dinner of the Mayors to Prince Albert and the Royal Commissioners. On the last day of 1850 the first preview of the Crystal Palace was held for Members of the Society of Arts and their friends. A month later the building was handed over to the Commissioners, and twelve days later exhibits were already being brought in. Although Kate was expecting a child in the spring of 1851 she apparently went to another of the previews, for Mrs Schwabe, writing enthusiastically on 19 April tells her: '...I cannot resist telling you myself what joy the sight of you and the Chrystal [*sic*] Palace gave me! I scarcely knew what was the most brilliant. your dear face or the Palace.' Kate and Nelly were staying with the Schwabes at Crumpsall House, Cheetham Hill, Manchester, and it seems Katie had caught Exhibition fever, for she is reported as having invited everybody to stay with her mother whilst it was on: 'She says there is plenty of room.' This was unfortunately only too true, as Kate was to discover to her cost.

Cobden was among those taking part in the immensely long procession which followed the Queen, Prince Albert, several of the royal children and dignitaries of all sorts, although he had refused to wear a Court suit, when the Exhibition was opened to the public on 1 May 1851.

There were many times during Kate's marriage in which she played the waiting role. Now their roles were reversed and it was Cobden who was waiting for Kate. The fact that she was now mistress of a large London house meant a stream of visitors during the months the Crystal Palace remained open. Many of these were house guests who became a trial for her and a source of irritation for Cobden. After the birth of a third daughter – Jane – on 28 April she was tied to Westbourne Terrace, and unable to share the delights of Dunford with Cobden, Dick and Nelly.

By 7 August Kate had still not joined Cobden at Dunford: 'My dearest Kate I am sincerely sorry that you should lose one day in getting away from London, and notwithstanding what you now say I do hope you'll contrive to get away by the middle of next week. – I should not scruple to begin clearing the drawing-room, and leaving your visitors to content themselves with the little library...'

On 8 August Cobden vents his feelings in a letter to Prentice: 'I got your letter just as I was getting ready to escape from the most irksome ordeal that ever man was exposed to! – The Session has been a disgusting ordeal, but to have in addition all one's constituents (and there are 36,000) in London, all wanting to have orders for the gallery, or something else done for them, was enough to drive the most disciplined temper to madness: so to avoid such a crisis I have run away from town...'

Another week goes by and still no Kate. Meanwhile, Dick's holidays are over and he should be back at school. He is not: he is at Westbourne Terrace with his mother, as there has been a hitch over his return to Worksop. Although Cobden when he writes to Kate on 14 August says he is grieved at her 'being subjected to all these troubles single-handed,' he deals with Dick's problem in bracing fashion: 'There is no difficulty in sending the boy to Worksop – go to the London and North Western station half an hour before the train starts – ask to see the Secretary or Station Master. – Tell him whom [*sic*] you are, and that you wish the boy to be put under the charge of the Guard, and it will be arranged for you without difficulty – You can explain that the master has by mistake gone without him – Griffiths must be a goose!' He calls the Exhibition a 'plague': 'I am really sorry you should be again delayed, but there is always the consolation that the plague you have undergone will not be a returning evil. Nelly is well and is learning the names of the flowers in order that she may tell them to her dear Mamma.'

By 23 August, when Cobden writes to Bright, Kate has evidently reached Dunford: 'We are settled in this quiet out-of-the world nook, very much to the relief and satisfaction of my wife, whose indoor duties in Westbourne Terrace, consequent upon the *Exhibition invasion*, had almost exhausted her strength and hospitality. – It is quite as well for those whose residences are in Cockneydom that Crystal Palaces are not to be annual affairs...'

While Cobden and Kate were 'getting rid of the effects of the London season,' he used the parliamentary recess to go through his old League correspondence, as he told Henry Ashworth on 14 September: '...I have brought all my old letters down here, *by the canal boat*, [on the Manchester Ship Canal] and have been looking them over, in the open air, under an old yew tree. The workings of the League agitation have been all revived in my mind again-...Bushel after bushel of letters are turned out and almost without exception they are upon the business of the League. I really was not aware until I took this review of the period from 1838 to 1846 how completely I had isolated my mind upon the one topic...The greater part of my letters are of course destined for the fire...'

The Dunford idyll ended, and Cobden was back in town that autumn. His letters to Kate were inevitably full of news about the Exhibition, which, after being open to the public for 141 days, was about to close. Although he had found his duties in the Royal Commission burdensome, and had complained to Prentice that it had been 'the most irksome ordeal that ever man was exposed to,' it is clear that he, like the British public, had succumbed to the fascination of the Crystal Palace. On 11 October, the day when the vast galleries were closed, he wrote to Frederick: 'I have just seen the last of the Exhibition – I am writing in one of the Commissioners Rooms – We have had *God Save the Queen*, and three times three, and now all the bells in the place are ringing the people out as fast as they can but they don't seem to like to go – In fact its a dying out of a great and pregnant event, and nobody seems to be free from regrets.'

Next day he tells Kate: 'I am writing again from the exhibitiion. It is ¼ past 5 – We have just had the last of this great and glorious work – At 5 o'clock exactly the organs struck up *God Save the Queen*! The crowd joined in the chorus, all uncovered. Not very good time was kept, but the effect was grand and imposing. I came to see the Exhibition last night at 11 o'clock with Mr. and Mrs Smith [their neighbours in Westbourne Terrace]. The effect whilst dimly lighted with a few lamps and the moon shining upon its solitude was very solemn, and striking.'

The closing ceemony on 15 October was not a State occasion and the Queen did not attend. Victoria wrote in her diary that day that it grieved her not to be present, but she thought Albert was right: 'I could hardly have been there as a spectator.'

It would seem from the records that she did not miss a great deal, for in contrast to the festive atmosphere at the opening on 1 May this seems to have been a rather stodgy affair, with the Prince

I. Richard Cobden, a portrait by George Patten, 1849.

II. Catherine Anne (Kate) Cobden, an unfinished portrait by Cittadini, *c*1849.

III. Dunford near Midhurst, the birthplace of Richard Cobden, before its transformation.

IV. Cobden's parents, William and Millicent Cobden.

V. Richard Brooks (Dick) Cobden.

VI. The Free Trade Bazaar held at Covent Garden in the spring of 1845. From the *Illustrated London News*.

VII. Dunford House, after extensive rebuilding.

VIII. Richard Cobden, *c*1860, a photograph taken in Paris.

Sarah & Priscilla will write to you I hope one or the other daily – Expect a long letter from the former tomorrow. They will have much news to tell you – I hope you will write to them whenever you have leisure But they will not expect you to tax yourself with writing to us all There is a little pocket book with a cover of beads, which I bought in Berlin last year, & which was intended for my intended, long before I knew the object. It is now packed up in wadding ready to be sent to my darling Kate. Sarah begs her kindest love as well as Priscilla. I have taken a kiss from Baby for you. Give my regards to your brothers It shall not be many many days before I see them & you again. Present my kindest love to Mary who I hope will remain till the last moment with you

Believe me, my sweetest Kate

Yours affectionately attached

Richard

write, write, write

L1

IX. Part of a letter from from Cobden to Kate.

X. The funeral of Richard Cobden, April 1865, as depicted in the *Illustrated London News*. The scene is that on the Cocking Causeway.

XI. Kate Cobden in widowhood.

and the Commissioners hearing a lengthy report from Lord Canning, chairman of the judges, or jurors, who had been selected to award the many medals to the exhibitors, which method had been announced as early as March 1850, as being preferable to monetary awards; and the bestowing of various honours. To make matters even less festive, the royal diarist reports that it was '...a very wet day'.

On 16 October the removal of goods began, an operation lasting over three weeks. By 11 November the great Crystal Palace stood empty.

The Exhibition had certainly given a boost to trade, and to the Prince's popularity with the poeple, but sadly it did not ensure peace: within three years the Crimean War broke out – with disastrous effect upon the Cobdens – and many of the participating countries were involved in what has elsewhere been described as 'a generation of wars'.

CHAPTER EIGHT

Dick: 'An Angel to lead...'

'We have arranged to send Richard to Dr Heldenmaier's school at Worksop,' Cobden told Frederick at the start of 1850. 'It is a well-conducted establishment, on the Pestalozzi plan, combining the training of a home, with good practical and modern tuition.' He delivered his son personally into the worthy German's hands, and reported to Kate from Sheffield on 22 January: '...He could scarcely find time to say goodbye to me – I feel quite happy about him as you may do – ' The boy was only eight years old at this time, but apparently no tears were shed.

'I had a letter from your dear Papa this morning,' Kate writes to Dick two days later, 'telling me he had left you very comfortably settled at school. I have no doubt you will be very happy there, and that we shall find you greatly improved when we next meet. Your sister Kate was talking a good deal about you to-day – she is always very fond of you when you are away...'

Dick was not to enjoy his five years at Worksop, and the tone of his parents' letters shows he was not a very satisfactory pupil. Their letters are full of complaint, criticism and exhortation; poor Dick seems unable to please anyone.'Sixpence a week is as much as your Papa and I think we can afford and I am sure you will be content with that when you know that we are not rich...Your dear Papa and I have had a talk about sending you *The Illustrated London News*, and *Punch* and we fear that your having them will interfere very much with your school duties – and I daresay that Doctor Heldenmaier will tell you the same thing.' In the same letter of 4 March 1850 there is more exhortation: 'If you are not able to wear your hat again, what will you do of a Sunday as I fear your caps are too shabby to put on for best. If you do not wear your hat, pray take care of it, and bring it home with you as I shall be able to make some use of it.' Later that month there is actually a promise of a treat in store: she tells him of an invitation to Twickenham 'to have a strawberry feast in the season for them and that will be when you are home for the Midsummer holidays.'

Heldenmaier's first half yearly report on Dick's progress reached Cobden in mid June, and included among other comments: 'Rather inclined to be idle in his lessons, but not in the playground, and if driven will resist to the last, but is very susceptible of kindness and can be easily managed with a little tact...He is not the most orderly, punctual, cleanly pupil. Great hopes may be entertained of a boy of his disposition.' Cobden's first bill for his son's education for the half-year ending June 1850 amounted to £52.9.1d.

On 13 June Kate told Dick: 'Your dear Papa wrote yesterday to Dr Heldenmaier to say that you were to come home on 19th with some other Boys. The Dr will supply you with the necessary sum of money to defray the expenses of your journey home. I hope my dear child you will be very careful when at the railway Station not to go too near the trains nor the engines. And when in the carriage be sure not to lean out of the windows for bear in mind that an accident may happen in one instant...Your little Sister Ellen's eyes brighten up when she is told that her Brother Richard will be soon at home...I am sorry to hear that you have lost your glass seal as it had belonged to your Papa for many years before you had it.' Dick had apparently expressed a wish to see Grandfather Williams in Wales during the Summer holiday, but Kate feels this to be tactless for she tells him: 'I will not say a word about Wales to your Papa till you have been with us some little time or he would feel hurt at your thinking of leaving us immediately.'

'You must keep some of the half sovereigns to spend in the Town on the Doctor's birthday,' Kate advises him on 5 September 1850.'I am sure I shall not be able to send you any more then. I am obliged to be very sparing with money now, as I have many bills to pay...Ellen is very fond of having my broach [*sic*] with your likeness to sleep with her, She calls it her "dear brother Rittard". We are going to have a dog here by and bye to guard the house. Let me know what his name is to be.'

In October 1850 Cobden went to visit his son and on 25 October he reports to Kate: 'I was rather an unexpected guest last evening at Worksop – for the boy had read my letter promising "tomorrow" without remembering that it was written the day before – I arrived therefore a day before I was looked for. I found Richard looking quite well and with renewed good manners. He had dined when I reached [word missing], but I found him quite ready for another dinner at the hotel with me at 5 o'clock.

Heldenmaier wrote to Kate about Dick's approaching Christmas holidays on 9 December 1850: 'Dear Madam I am glad to say that your son is quite well in body and pretty well in mind...our approaching Vacation begins on the 18th inst and ends on the 22nd of Jany next...I shall send you per Richard a Memoir of

Pestalozzi.' Dick had incurred a debt that half, and this news produced a stern letter from Cobden on 12 December: 'Lose not a moment in paying your debt which grieves me to think that you have been obliged to incur. Pray for the future make up your mind to be more prudent.' On 15 December Heldenmaier wrote to Cobden: '...your son's conduct and diligence is satisfactory and improving...He likes to play the "first fiddle" amongst the little ones, and is fond of being with older pupils...and it may be said of him that he is an angel to lead but...'

On 26 February his mother tells him: 'Your note reached me as your Papa and I had sat down to breakfast yesterday morning – We were indeed much concerned to hear that you had lost your hat in the train. And how came you not to mention it immediately on your return to school. You seem my dear boy to forget that these things cost money. I have by this same post written to Mrs Heldenmaier, and begged that she would have the kindness to write to the Railway Station respecting the hat. Your papa thinks that there is still a chance of its being there amongst "lost articles" – But had you named it, directly it happened, it would in all probability have been returned to you without any difficulty.' (This letter is incomplete, and was possibly one of Kate's discarded, but undestroyed, draft efforts.)

On 16 May 1852 Kate wrote to tell Dick that Grandfather Williams had died aged 80, and that his father was going to Wales to attend the funeral. She asks the boy: 'Can you have a little crape put around your cap?' In an undated reply Dick tells his mother: 'I am very sorry to hear of my dear grandfather's death – it is such a time since I saw him that I should not know him to face but I can remember how kind he was to me. I wish you had let me go and see him last holidays. I shall not feel any pleasure in visiting Wales next holidays.'

The Cobdens were obliged to make a second journey to Wales that summer. On 5 July Cobden tells Dick, from Dylife Mine near Machynlleth, that Aunt Pugh is ill and not expected to recover.'It is a long and tedious journey, and I am very sorry your Mamma is obliged to come so far; But she cannot refuse the wish, perhaps the last wish of her sister Mrs Pugh.'

On 11 August 1852 Dick went back to Worksop. Cobden, in London, reports to Kate: '...The boy went off yesterday in very good spirits – He was so absorbed in the interest of *Uncle Tom's Cabin*, an American work of great merit, that he could hardly sleep for fear of losing the pleasure it gave him: and as he had half the book still to read he would not have time to think of the journey or its destination. – He asked me what pocket money I intended to give him, and on my proposing half a sovereign he seemed well satisfied, and proposed that I should keep it and send it to him when he wrote for it in a post office order. – He put this on the plea that he might lose it – but he probably was thinking that it would fall into Madame's hands on his arrival.'

Kate had also read *Uncle Tom's Cabin* and wrote to Dick about it: 'What a beautiful book *Uncle Tom's Cabin* is – I have read it with great interest and so has your papa. The characters in the book are drawn with great force and with wonderful talent. It is really perfectly horrible that any country under the face of the sun can permit such laws to exist as allow children and parents to be separated.'

The book had also impressed Cobden greatly, as he tells Joseph Sturge on 26 August 1852: 'You have of course read *Uncle Tom's Cabin*, it will do more than ten thousand sermons or speeches to shake the foundations of that horrid "institution" of the United States. This is only the first gentle appeal to the hearts of Americans. By and by, in the fulness of time, some great genius like Isaiah himself will arise whose voice like an Archangel's tones will ring the death knell of that gigantic iniquity. In the meantime honor immortal honor, to the noble woman who penned *Uncle Tom's Cabin*! Have you the privilege of *knowing her*?'

The following year the Cobdens had a visit from the author, Mrs Harriet Beecher Stowe, who came to breakfast at Westbourne Terrace on 23 May 1853, and wrote an account of the meeting (in *Sunny Memories of Foreign Lands*). She described Cobden as 'A man of slender frame, rather under than over the middle size, with great ease of manner, and flexibility of movement, and the most frank, fascinating smile. His appearance is a sufficient account of his popularity, for he seems to be one of those men who carry about them an atmosphere of vivacity and social exhilaration.'

On 18 August 1852, Kate to Dick: 'I have consulted with your father with regard to your having beer, he says that he has no objection to your drinking it in moderation, particularly if the water is bad. Bear in mind that we drink nothing but water at home but then we get good water to be sure. Your Papa will consent to your leaving off dancing for the present, on condition that you will in the course of another year or two take to it again kindly.'

His father wrote to tell him, on 24 September, that his conduct paper has been received. He has not succeeded well in history or biography, 'both of which are very interesting and useful studies,'

Cobden assures him.'I hope you will be more successful next time. The way to succeed is to read with close attention; to discard for the time from your mind all other thoughts; and to concentrate all your powers on the task before you. You asked me to give you a book for your French Master. I have just been reading a small volume which I think will be interesting to him. It is a work lately published, written by Victor Hugo, called *Napoleon le Petit*.

Dick's efforts as a correspondent disappointed his parents. Cobden writes to him severely on 8 October 1852: 'Your Mamma has written two letters to you to which she has received no answer. I hope you will always reply to her letters, for it gives her much pleasure to hear from you.'

Cobden paid Dick another visit on 29 October, 1852, and reported to Kate the following day.'After taking a dinner with Mrs Heldenmaier, I sallied out with Dick, but the weather was so wet we could not walk far. I therefore brought him to the hotel, and invited a party of his Lancashire school fellows to tea with us – There was a goodly consumption of sausages, pork pies and fried ham, and buttered toast to begin with – Then followed marmalade, greengage jam, and current [*sic*] jelly, with plum cake toasted and buttered without end. Nothing so common as bread and butter was looked at even – Certainly none of my visitors were likely to want a good meal, and yet they devoured as much as if they had been brought up in a Heyshott cottage – After tea, and before they returned home, they all sallied out in the street, and invaded a sweetmeat shop, where their pockets were stuffed with acid drops, bulls eyes, sugar barley, &c. But the favourite article was "butter scotch" which tasted like toffy [*sic*] with an extra quality of butter. I took them home at 9, and remained to supper with the masters. Dick and I are now at the Inn again – He has just been tapping a cocoa nut [*sic*] and swallowing the milk...He's looking healthy, but still like an over restless fidgety spirit – in fact he appears to be scarcely ever out of mischief...'

Now that the Christmas holidays are again approaching, Kate writes to Dick on 22 November 1852: '...Your bedroom is being got ready. You will find it very comfortable for you will have a table with books on it, and drawers to keep your curiosities in...'

On 15 February 1853, she was able for once to praise the boy: 'The post has brought me the most beautiful Valentine from Worksop I ever saw – I shall ever treasure it for the sake of the donor.' She tells him the Valentines for his sisters had been redirected to Bognor, where Katie and Nelly were by now at school at Dome House. She prompts him to thank his uncle John Williams for a visit he has paid to him: 'It is an attention he will have been expecting from you.'

In a letter to his mother that month Dick had put a P.S.'If the French were to come Papa would look rather out.' She hastens to reassure him.'You need not fear, your Papa knew too well what he was about when he entered into that engagement about the French. He knows that they will never invade England.'

On 19 August 1853 she is fussed about his wardrobe: '...The list I sent you to school was perfectly correct according to the clothes you took from here. Can you have left them at your Uncle John's lodgings – write to him without a moment's loss of time – It is a most serious loss. Why you had 6 coloured shirts alone – and I recollect putting together 2 new white ones that had never been with you before!...You do not know how this loss presses upon my spirits. I cannot at times help shedding tears about it.'

Cobden's letter to Dick of 10 September is a severe one: 'I received your last letter just as I was leaving Dunford to come to Bognor for a few days. Let me first of all correct a mistake you have fallen into about my remarks with reference to your leaving school. I did *not* fix a time when you should go to the continent to learn German and French. That must depend upon the progress you make at Dr Heldenmaiers. Your anxiety to leave your present school made you put an erroneous interpretation upon my remarks. I have not yet made up my mind when you will go to the continent, but it will not certainly be this year, I am very sorry to hear you complain of your School. Recollect that the character of Dr Heldenmaier's school is very well established. Hundreds of young men who are reputable and thriving members of society, have been educated at his school. If *you* do not make good progress there, it will be attributed to your fault. Your character for life will be injured. It will be in vain for you to complain of the school Dr Heldenmaier can appeal to thirty years of success in his profession and to the hundreds of men who have been educated by him, and who speak well of his school.'

By 31 October things seem to be on a happier footing between mother and son, for she tells him: 'I shall send off your parcel either today or tomorrow. It will contain your great coat and two trousers and a shooting coat...I have packed some sweets into the pockets which I hope you will receive in good order. I am sorry to say that the toffe [*sic*] we have made at home is full of small tin particles which came off from the bottom of the saucepan in which it was made. You must be careful in eating it and tell any boy to whom you give any, to be the same as perhaps the tin might have some injurious effect upon you.' In this letter Cobden is not referred to as 'your Father' but 'Papa' once more, so Kate seems to have softened towards her troublesome son. But by 2 November Dick is in her bad books again: 'It is very strange that you have not acknowledged the 10/- which your Papa sent to you some little time since.'

When Dick was at Dunford for the Christmas holidays that year Cobden tells Kate (in Bognor with the girls) that he has taken to riding Jack, the pony: '...I must tell you that having been "clipt" the poney [*sic*] is so completely altered that I should not have known it – In fact, it is a beautiful little slim-legged thing. Dick has a surprise in store for you – he is going to ask how you like his *new* poney, and you must of course be quite satisfied that we have been going to some extravagance for another and you must ask for Jack.' But it seems that Dick misused the animal, and when Kate writes to him at school after the holiday she has serious news to impart: 'You had no sooner left than George came in and told us that Jack's *tongue* was nearly cut in two. The poor creature refuses to eat, and no one knows what the consequence will be if inflammation sets in. It may be that he will have to be shot. And this will be all owing to your racing and constantly tugging and pulling the poor thing up all of a sudden with a lead bit in its mouth. It is a sad grief to me that you are so lacking in care and reflection.' Happily for the boy, Jack recovered and was on active service at Dunford for many years.

On 14 September 1854 a financial cause for complaint: 'To our surprise the enclosed little bill was sent in a few days ago. It is not under any circumstances well that you should get articles on credit at any time. And I hope in future you will do all in your power to avoid it. Your Father wishes to know if the bill be quite correct before he pays it. Have you found your dress boots yet?'

Before he came home for the Christmas holidays, young Dick committed a more serious offence. He had broken bounds and had 'gone into the town against orders'. Cobden told Kate on 1 December 'When I was at school it was a flogging and no mistake.' His mother writes to him on 9 December: 'These constant complaints are very trying to us particularly as we never get any encouraging news from you about your progress in any branch of studies. I really have often very anxious thoughts as to what will become of you. You were wrong in going into the Town at all and you were wrong in undertaking to get sweets for the other Boys, but having once undertaken it and having promised not to tell of the other Boys you had no right to divulge their names. You see how the first wrong step complicated all that follows it.'

'I am sorry to hear you have written to Quinnell to ask him to gather birds eggs for you,' Kate writes to Dick on 2 March 1855.'I am so fond of having the dear little birds about our woods and once these horrid boys about here know that the nests may be taken they will overrun our woods – Will your write again to Quinnell and tell him not to destroy the poor birds nests about the woods except they be jays and hawks. If he finds anything curious he might just take out one egg or so without destroying the nest.'

On 8 May Kate tells Dick: 'Your portmanteau will be sent off tomorrow morning by the Midhurst coach...and I hope you will get it on Friday safely. I now enclose the key of it. You will find some eatables some of which are home manufactured. It is so very seldom I have the opportunity of sending to you, that for once in a way Mr. Ellenberger will not, I am sure object to your receiving the articles now sent as a little remembrance of your home – If they say nothing tell them so – and that I hope they will allow you to accept them – I have with pleasure packed up the portmanteau in the fond hope that you are trying your best to give your Masters satisfaction now in your studies.'

Kate's hopes were indeed fond, for Mr Ellenberger did object, and wrote a stiff letter to Cobden on 10 May: 'My dear Sir – Your Son has received a portmanteau, containing some clothes, and several pounds of cakes, two bottles of syrup, two jars of potted tongues and almonds in abundance. These are unwelcome in my establishment, and you will oblige me by saying how we are to dispose of them. The best plan would perhaps be to send them back again. Waiting for your answer I remain, my dear Sir, yours very truly J.S. Ellenberger.'

On 14 May Kate writes again to Dick: 'Your Papa received a note from him asking what was to be done with the Eatables contained in the Portmanteau – you will have heard by this that they are to be sold and the money given to you. At least I believe so.' That 'At least I believe so' suggests she had got into trouble for breaking the school rules, and that he, no doubt nettled by Ellenberger's letter, had not consulted her upon his decision as to what should be done with the 'eatables'.'However,' Kate continues, '...I hope you will, my dear Boy, submit to Mr. Ellenberger's decision without a murmur – bear in mind that he has a right to establish any rules he pleases at his own school. Be very careful to give satisfaction in your studies – the consequences will be serious to you if you do not. Your dear Papa left us early this morning. We were all up at 5 o'clock in order that he and your uncle might have a comfortable breakfast before starting.'

Nothing had yet been decided about Dick's future when Cobden wrote to Kate on 6 June: 'Let me know by return what you think. He is more important than any political question.' And two days later: '...I am not making satisfactory progress respecting his future destination...'

At this time his parents had not been told officially that Dr. Heldenmaier was giving up the school: 'We have received no circular from the Dr. which we consider strange and we should not have known a word about his intention to give up the school at Midsummer had not your Papa accidentally heard of it through Mr. Thomasson of Bolton the other day when we met him at dinner at our friends the Hargreaves in London.'

Heldenmaier's reason for retirement, they later learnt, was that he had been 'overtaken by old age'.

Cobden sought the advice of his friend Chevalier Bunsen, as to what he should do with Dick and received his reply from Charlottenburg on 30 June:

'My dear Mr Cobden I thank you sincerely for having believed me when I told you, it would give me great pleasure to assist you in choosing a place for your son's education, and I am happy to say that I have since become acquainted with an Institution such as you require, and with a man such as you graphically designate in your letter. The *Institution* is the *Real Schule* (or College of practical knowledge) and *the man* is Mr. Bender, the Director. The School has 45 to 50 pupils, but Mr. Bender's Brother (one of the Professors) takes 3 or 4 pupils into his house, for boarding and private tutorship, and one place is vacant. You pay(?) about 37L the year, per quarter in advance. Bedclothes, Linen, Fork, Knife and spoon, must be brought or bought – All expenses included except for instrumental music, and for the pedestrian tours which the Teachers and Pupils make every Summer to the Mountains of Tyrol or Switzerland. The system of instruction is excellent; exactly what you want. Greek is begun only at 15, and only taught for practical purposes, unless specially wished. Gymnastics, Bathing &c, form an integral part of the education. The situation is beautiful – The new term begins 15 Oct. Your son had better come as soon as possible, say beginning of August, after Parliament is over, to learn sufficient German for attending at the lessons &c. I hope you will bring him over, and if you send him, *send* him to me. In haste Ever yours faithfully Bunsen.'

Cobden lost no time in agreeing to Bunsen's choice of a school, and received a further letter, this time from Bender on 21 July:

'Your son is to have his lodging and eating in the house of Mr Lambelet, but to attend the lectures and lessons in our school as all other scholars in our house. As long as your son wants private lessons he shall have some in addition to the instruction in the school. A seperate [*sic*] sleeping room is at present not vacant but the Lambelets can perhaps arrange one later...We are very glad of your intention to bring your son at the beginning of next month and we hope you will find our Weinheim well situated at the renowned Bergstrasse. I remain Sir Your obedt humble servant Henry Bender per H.B.C. Bender.'

By 22 June Dick was at Dunford, free of his English boarding-school for good. Cobden paid what was owing to Heldenmaier and Ellenberger and had a reply on 30 July: 'My dear Sir I have had due notice of your remittance for which I offer my best thanks. I trust your plan with regard to your boy will be successful. Age will bring on reflexion and a reform in his ideas and disposition will take place, which will be rather the result of his own deliberations, than the effect of foreign interference. I shall always take a deep interest in Richard and I hope he will write one day to let me know how he gets on. Thanking you again for your kindness. Believe me my dear Sir Yours very sincerely J.S. Ellenberger.'

Before leaving England for Germany Cobden and Dick paid a visit to uncle John Williams in London, and on 14 August Cobden wrote to Kate from the Reform Club: 'I have not seen Dick but we are to dine together at your brother's at 5, and if you dont hear to the contrary you will conclude that it is all right – we shall go tomorrow at 1 and proceed over to Calais by the ½ past 4 Steamer which will arrive at Calais soon after 6, and we shall make our way straight to Cologne and then up the Rhine to Mayence...'

Father and son both reported progress to Kate: '...The weather was very calm and we escaped seasickness. In fact Richard seemed rather to long for a breeze that he might prove his seamanship and was very much amused at a poor gentleman suffering from seasickness. However he had his taste partially indulged when we came to land, for as the tide was out, and the vessel could not approach the shore, we were obliged to be landed in boats which was a very disagreeable process in passing over the swell upon the bar...We found Calais very gay, the streets full of people in their holiday dresses, and the fronts of the houses and public buildings hung with flags, in honor [*sic*] of the anniversary of the birth of the 1st Napoleon.'

Dick reported to his mother three days after leaving England: 'We have reached Verviers safely after being cooped up 12 hours yesterday in the railway. We started from Calais at ¼ to 8 in the morning and got out here about 9 o'clock. The heat was so very great and I had a headache most of the way. Verviers is between Liege and Aix la Chapelle and I daresay you can find it on the map. We start soon for Cologne and we shall be there in 4 or 5 hours. The sea was very smooth but the vessel being narrow rolled a good deal and papa and I had to stay in one place. Neither of us were seasick. I don't like the french. I like the Belgians best. The Guards [on the trains] have bugles instead of whistles. I will write you a long letter when I get to Heidelberg, and Kate [Katie] also. I am going to breakfast now, and then I shall walk about and see the place till the train is ready. The stairs are polished and have no carpets on them and I fell down a small flight last night. They use sand instead of blotting paper.'

Cobden wrote to Kate on 25 August from Mannheim: 'Heidelberg is an interesting old place shut in by the hills all wooded and crowned with the perpetual old ruins of castles which we see everywhere in Germany. Dick and I made an excursion to the top of the highest hill for the sake of the view, and the donkey on which I rode in coming put his head between his knees and threw me over his head very much to Dick's amusement, but I have some of the scars and wounds, which the fall gave me still visible...Yesterday we left Baden-Baden for Weinheim where we arrived about 2, ordered dinner for 5 at the little comfortable hotel and then proceeded to the school where we spent the afternoon and then after dinner joined them again till 9 o'clock. I saw them in school at study – at Gymnastics in the playground, and took supper with them. This morning I went to see Madame Lambelet. She has a little baby about a month old, and I was introduced to it lying bound like a mummy upon a little ornamental cushion. The house...is some distance from the school – It is a very old fashioned place with a tower and a room at the top which will serve for a museum for Dick. The boys rise at 5, take some bread and milk at 7, dine at 12, have a huge bit of bread and some fruit at 4, and sup off meat, &c at ½ past 7. The only faults I should find that they eat too often and get too much meat – ...Richard will of course be chiefly employed for some months in learning German, but he will necessarily be learning French at the same time as Mr. Lambelet can have no other way of communicating with him. I could not imagine a place where there is greater kindness on all sides than is shewn to the boys...

'Dick parted with me much better than I expected. If there was a tear he turned away and hid it. In fact, he will be as happy as it is possible for others to make him, and I have put him in every way on his mettle to gain a good report from the excellent people about him. I am glad that M. Lambelet has won his admiration in every way. He is a powerful young man, full of energy, which he shows in his mode of teaching and in beating all the boys at every kind of sport and exercise...You may suppose how much he excites Dick's admiration...I have been glad to find that the boys are only allowed a certain pocket money all alike. It is about 2d a week of our money. In fact fruit is so very cheap and they get such an abundance of it that there is little to be done with pocket money. I shall leave this [place] tomorrow morning by the steamer for Cologne, and shall go straight home as fast as the terribly hot weather will allow. I have not enjoyed myself much owing to my eyes which have troubled me.'

Dick wrote to his mother on 27 August telling her he liked Weinheim much better than Worksop: 'Papa left me last Saturday. I will write a long letter next Sunday and will take a week over it and describe you everything in Germany that is different to English things. I hope you are all quite well at Dunford, and give my love to all my sisters. We have a beautiful bath here, and I shall learn to swim well before I come home again. I went to a protestant church yesterday, but could not understand a word. I hope you will both write to me often – Direct to Mr. Bender Weinheim Heidelberg – Germany. It is very hot today and has been so ever since I have been here. The boys are allowed to have animals, and some have donkeys, and some pigeons, and some have fowls.'

Dick disliked sauerkraut, German blotting paper, asked for a sponge and complained about having to sleep on a straw-filled mattress, which complaint produced a bracing reply from his mother on 6 September: '...as for the beds being straw, why it is all the more wholesome as it is renewed every year. I never slept on any other beds whilst travelling on the Continent, and I recollect very well examining one, at one of the first Hotels in the South of France, and finding the hole you speak of in one side where the servants put in their hands in order shake the bed well up. You must my dear Boy try and not find causes of complaint, but bear in mind that you are at Weinheim for the sole purpose of improving yourself, and you doing *that* will be the sole condition on which your Papa will allow me and some of your sisters to visit you next Summer...'

By 13 November Dick was writing to Kate to let her know she will soon be receiving a list of all the things he wants for Christmas presents – this is a custom of the school. He is concerned as to whether they have 'had a character from Mr. Bender yet? When you do will you tell me what he says about me.' Cobden replied for Kate on 26 November: '...Your mamma hopes that you will be as moderate as possible in your wants so as to put it in her power to comply with your request as far as she can.' Kate sends a present, via Mrs Schwabe, for the Lambelet baby: '...hope the babys cap will be approved of. Should it be too large it must be drawn in by the strings inside. We shall miss you in decorating with Holly the rooms at Christmas. And we shall miss you too in many other ways dear Boy.' Her Christmas letter includes a cautionary note: 'I cannot allow the Christmas to pass over without writing a few lines to assure you how dearly you are cherished in the memories of all here,' she tells him on 20 December.'...be very gentlemanly when visiting Mrs Schwabe: all will be reported to old acquaintances in England.' Next day she gives him perhaps the best present he could have when she tells him that Mr Bender had given his father a good report of him.

After spending the holiday with Mrs Schwabe at Heidelberg, Dick returned to school in time for the New Year celebrations. When Dick wrote to his parents on 3 January 1856 he asks them: '...Is it true that Mr Ellison is a Jew a boy from frankfurt who is with us at Mr. Lambelet's says that he was at school with his son and that he knows very well that he is a Jew. The German schoolboys when they are angry with any one call him a jew and nothing puts them in a greater rage than to call them Jews. They cry against persons they see in the streets if he or she has the least resemblance to a Jew. In England the boys seldom if ever bothered a boy of about my age who was a jew, but here they are always teasing each other about it.'

Kate dealt with her son's first encounter with anti-Semitism in a lengthy letter on 21 January: 'Mr Ellison may have been a Jew for all we know – You know that we never trouble our heads about such matters in England – The Germans are as intolerant about the Jews as the Americans are about the poor Negroes. It is a great blot in the character of both Nations to be so intolerant. Dont you fall into that evil feeling – Should a boy say anything to you on the subject again tell him that God made both Jew and Christian – and that it is His Province to judge and not yours or his.'

Dick had his fifteenth birthday on 12 March, when Kate wrote wishing him: '...many many happy returns of this day. You will not receive this for some time but it will assure you of the fond hopes breathed here for your welfare on the anniversary of your birthday...Your Papa is coming home to-day for a fortnight for his

Easter holidays...I will wait patiently till Easter when I shall expect you to send a few lines to assure me that you have not forgotten me my beloved child. You are constantly in my thoughts and this world would have no charm for me without the fond hope of beholding you again before very long – it is the brightest hope I have.'

Back at school after the Easter holidays, spent with Mrs Schwabe at the Prince Charles Hotel in Heidelberg, Dick wrote a long and animated account of his holiday to his parents at the beginning of April: 'My dear Papa and Mama...Mrs Schwabe has 8 or 9 rooms in the Prince Carl Hotel and 2 servants and her butler. It is amusing to hear the Butler talk to the Germans – He has learnt a little German and so for about ever[y] half dozen English words he shoves in a German one and thus with the aid of signs he manages to make himself understood...Mrs Schwabes children had presents made them of such beautiful eggs at Easter. Some were as big as swans eggs and inside them were little pocket books beautiful little looking glasses &c in Ivory, nine pins, Jeu d hazard bracelets &c &c some of them had cost more than a pound.'

Kate had been reading Dick's letter aloud to the delight and amusement of the family circle at Dunford on the day when Cobden arrived home with the news that was to change her life.

CHAPTER NINE

The Crimean War

The Crimean War, when it started in the spring of 1854, had a disastrous effect on the careers of Cobden and Bright, and for a time the two men – national heroes since the successful Repeal of the Corn Laws – found themselves out in the cold, and the subject of bitter criticism, in Parliament and the press. Both men showed great courage in refusing to give up their anti-war principles.

For close on eight years Kate had been the wife of a popular, almost idolised, public man, but when his views regarding the war became known he was dragged off his pedestal and vilified in the press as a traitor. The reading of the newspapers must have been an ordeal to her, but at least she did not have to read of Cobden being burnt in effigy, as Bright was.

The Crystal Palace had by now been re-sited at Sydenham, and in spite of the war a splendid opening ceremony was staged, but Cobden was absent, as he tells Kate on 10 June 1854: 'I have been disappointed in going to the Crystal Palace. I went out at ½ past 9 to the Cab Stand, thinking ¼ of an hour ample for going to London Bridge but the cabman pleaded the police regulations for not being able to get there in time. So I decided not to go – after reading on the card of invitation which you sent me "Levee Dress", as I should have perhaps been the only one of the Commissioners again in a black coat – Everybody seems to have gone out of Town to Sydenham, and the streets are quite quiet – I will take care to meet the boy when he comes, and forward him in all haste, for he will I daresay be in a fever to get to Dunford.' Later he tells her 'I was after all very sorry I did not go to the opening of the Crystal Palace for I heard glorious accounts of the effect of the Music and the 1500 voices in the Choruses – Clara Novello's voice sounding distinctly over all – And now I find that several of the Ex Commissioners went in plain black...'

He was depressed in his letter to Frederick of 15 November: '...People now begin seriously to discuss the question whether our army will get away from the Crimea. It looks very likely when winter sets in to end with another Moscow.' Colonel Fitzmayer, who was with the Royal Artillery in the Crimea, kept Cobden posted throughout the war with what Cobden called 'regular news of your siege operations', and in return Kate supplied the Colonel with various newspaper and periodicals, including the *Athenaeum*.

Cobden wrote to Kate on 20 November: '...I was in the House last evening till 3 o'clk in the morning, got to bed at 4! and singularly enough did not get a wink of sleep. – Today I have been obliged to come down to a morning sitting in the House...'

On 13 December he tells her: 'I was quite knocked up and stupified [*sic*] in the House last evening and left before Disraeli or Lord John Russell spoke – I dont know what it was in the air that so affected me, but I went to sleep and found the greatest difficulty in so far rousing myself as to be able to make my exit. Layard said it must have been Chloroform put into the ventilators by the government to hocus us...Layard confirms Col Fitzmayer's report that the army has no confidence in Lord Raglan. But he tells me he is convinced the army will take Sebastopol.'

On 17 January 1855 he reports to her from Leeds: 'We have had a large meeting. – It was first called in the Music Hall, and adjourned to an open space in the Cloth Hall where we sat four hours in the open air through four snowstorms. – I was listened to throughout very fairly, and indeed the meeting acted nobly throughout. – But all the leading liberals took part against with the sole exception of the Quakers – The meeting was at the close very enthusiastic in their treatment of me – Indeed they were delighted with my courage...'

On 2 March he writes to her about the death of Tsar Nicholas I: 'I have an astonishing piece of news. – Lord Palmerston has just told me that the government has received intelligence of the death of the Emperor of Russia which took place this morning from apoplexy...I intend to come down to see you tomorrow. – I will bring some money with me. Send somebody to bring my carpet bag...'

On 16 April that year Londoners turned out in their thousands to see another Emperor, Prince Louis Napoleon III, and Cobden tells Kate: 'The Emperor of the French has just passed, and from all I can hear of those who saw the procession he was received with uproarious cheers by the people. The streets and houses and every available spot throughout the line of march were crowded with spectators.'

On 8 May the war is much on his mind: 'We have no further news. I have ceased to pay any further attention to rumours. The fact is both the French and English governments know what a mess they are in and would give anything not to have got into it – But now they are as afraid of making peace as going on with the war – the latter offers them a chance – the former would be their ruin.'

On 5 June Cobden made one of his most forceful speeches against the Ministerial policy and tells Kate about it in his letter of 6 June: 'The House was very full and sat and stood it out most attentively. Not one breath of disapprobation, and a fair share of support in the way of cheers. I was complimented by many members after it was over. Amongst others Lytton Bulwer walked across the House to offer his congratulations. All this is not fit to be repeated at your breakfast-table as coming from me. Sidney Herbert remarked that it carried him back again to my old Corn Law speeches: and Lord Elcho (formerly Mr. Charteris) has just come to whisper in my ear that he considers my speech better than Gladstone's. I have heard from several quarters that if I and Bright had not been so "wrong" on the war we should certainly have been forced into the Ministry. Two letters from Delane, the Editor of the *Times*, written to friends of his, but not intended for my eyes, have been put into my hands, in which this sentiment is expressed that Bright and I must have been Ministers if we had not shelved ourselves by our peace principles.'

Dick seems to have shared the general concern about the prospects of peace, for in an undated letter to him Kate writes: '...Plenipotentiaries of Austria are now sitting in Paris in order to negotiate if possible terms of Peace – It is supposed that all parties are so sick of the war that they would be glad to find a good excuse to back out of it. No one likes to confess that he has been in the wrong and that he has gained nothing by so much bloodshed and misery. I will let you know again how matters end at Paris...'

The Crimean War was brought to an end at the Congress of Paris in the spring of 1856, but by that time the Cobdens had no heart for joining in the peace celebrations.

CHAPTER TEN

'Domestic affliction'

On 7 April 1856 the main source of trouble for Cobden was the Dunford boiler. He wrote irritably to Kate from the House of Commons: 'Your account of the boiler is enough to drive me to despair! Chorley never told me that it would take 12 hours to heat the boiler – I never dreamed of it... To be always without hot water in your boiler during the day is out of the question...'

In spite of this trouble, the spring of 1856 was surely the happiest Kate had known for many years: Dunford was at last in order; the detested Crimean War had ended with the Treaty of Paris in March and she was not expecting a child, which freed her to join Cobden in a pleasant social round. But most important to both parents, Dick, at his German school, was showing signs of maturity after having been the cause of continual anxiety to them during his five years at Worksop. Then, out of a clear sky, the blow fell.

As he was to write later in a heartbroken letter to Moffatt, Cobden had invited Colonel Fitzmayer, newly returned from the Crimea, to breakfast with him at his lodgings on Thursday 10 April:

'When I came down from my sleeping room in Grosvenor Street I found him and the breakfast waiting. My letters were lying on the table, and I apologised for opening them before beginning our meal – and the third letter I opened informed me that my dear boy, who by the latest accounts was described as the healthiest and strongest in the school, was dead and in his grave. Chevalier Bunsen, having fixed on the school, at about 14 miles from his present residence, the master sending him a telegraphic message reckoned on him communicating with me. Bunsen on the other hand took it for granted that the master had telegraphed to me. The consequence was that I heard nothing till I heard all.'

Leaving Fitzmayer at Grosvenor Street, Cobden had headed at once for Dunford. He tells Moffatt that '...the journey to this place took me five hours, bearing a secret which I knew was worse than a sentence of death to my poor wife – for she would have gladly given her life a dozen times if it were possible to save him – I found her in the happiest spirits having just before been reading to my brother and the family circle a long letter from the dear boy written a few days previously, and when he was in the best possible state of health – I tried to *manage* my communication, but the dreadful journey had been too much for me, and I broke down instantly and was obliged to confess all.'

It was at dusk that Cobden arrived home and met Kate, unexpectedly, at the door.'She did not comprehend the loss but was only stunned,' Cobden goes on, 'and for twenty hours was actually lavishing attentions on me, and superintending her household as before. But need you wonder what has followed...'

According to Morley, when Kate grasped the truth of what had happened 'she sat for many days like a statue of marble, neither speaking nor seeming to hear; her eyes not even turning to notice her little girl whom they placed upon her knee, her hair blanching with the hours.'

It could not have been an easy matter for Bunsen to write to Cobden as he did from Charlottenburg on 8 April, marking his letter 'to be read alone': 'My dear and afflicted Friend – It is only at this moment, nearing the closing of the Post Office, that I received the detailed letter of Dr. Bender, which I had requested to have, upon the receipt of the dreadful telegram of Sunday night...The blow came quite unexpectedly only on the morning of Sunday. Dr. Bender had written a line to Mrs Schwabe (opened by Mrs Curtis) and to Madame Ellison, that he had fever, but hoped to give better news the next day. Alas! that next day never came, *at noon* of that same Sunday, Dr. Henry Bender, the highly esteemed physician of the institution, brother to the director, came to see him, and stopped with him *till half past three*. Richard upon enquiry answered, "I feel a little better". Whatever he said was most rational. No sudden danger was anticipated. However, Mr Lambelet, sat with him when Dr. Bender left him. At five o'clock the fever became most violent. Mr. Lambelet had great difficulty in keeping him in bed. The physician was immediately fetched: but cerebral apoplexy put a sudden end to the struggle. He expired without a struggle in a moment. All attempts to bring back life remained fruitless. He breathed his last and gave up his beautiful young life in the arms of Mr. Lambelet.

'No boy was beloved like him in the school, as I have seen myself, none deserved it more as we have all opportunity of observing when he spent his holidays in the vacation with dear Mrs Schwabe.

'The burial will take place tomorrow morning, according to the existing police regulations. I have advised Dr. Bender to have a lead coffin put over the other. Should you wish to remove the coffin all is prepared for that. I shall collect all traits relating to that lovely angel now with God. He alone can comfort you and all who weep for him. Nothing has been neglected here or been amiss. In haste with true regard and sincere attachment. Bunsen.'

Cobden replied on 11 April on writing paper with a deep black border: 'God help us to bear the blow which your letter inflicted on us. No earthly calamity could have fallen so heavily on us as the loss of that dear and affectionate boy, and it came so suddenly upon us – Fifteen years of hopes and dreams, all centred in him, to be thus in one day cast into the grave! We cannot even yet realise to ourselves the dreadful truth!'

As Cobden and Bender shared no common language, Cobden asked Bunsen to act for him, and gives instructions for bringing Dick's body back to England.

Julie Schwabe wrote from Heidelberg on 5 April: 'My dearest Friends – Tears I have plenty, but words few…' and went on to fill four closely written pages, assuring them that she is prepared to leave her children with her 'good old nurse' and come to Dunford for a week. Cobden took Mrs Schwabe up on her offer.

As soon as the news of Dick's death became known letters of condolence poured in, including one from Joseph Parkes, to which Cobden replied on 13 April: 'My dear Parkes – I cannot find the resolution to open the letters that come, – but your handwriting draws my wife and me, from the sense of common sorrow towards you and dear Mrs Parkes, you knew the greatness of our loss and the depth of our suffering, and yet our cases are not the same. You had a long and merciful warning, and though I could not wish that my poor boy should have for our sakes lingered for months on the brink of the grave, yet it would undoubtedly have lessened the force of the blow had we been permitted for days to have watched over his death-bed. – The only intelligence we received of his illness was that in the letter from Chevalier Bunsen of which I enclose, written two days after his death – we have never to this day received a line directly from the poor distracted masters of the school, but who, as we learn indirectly, have mourned for the dear boy as for their own child. Two days before his death he wrote us a long and manly letter which spread like sunshine on our domestic scene. – He was never better. God! what a mystery of mysteries is this life, that one so young and bright, around whom our hopes and dreams had been turning themselves for fifteen years, should have been struck down in a few hours and withered like a weed! I must not tell you and Mrs Parkes how my poor wife is prostrated. I have almost feared for her reason. I cannot say that I am better than a woman myself. God and time can alone lift us from the depths of our woe...'

Cobden realised that it would be impossible to leave Kate in her state of shock and asked his friend, J.B. Smith, to take the necessary steps to have him released from attendance at the House. The Notice of Motions for Tuesday 15 April reads: 'Leave of absence at half past Four o'clock. 1. Mr. John Benjamin Smith, – To Mr. Cobden, three weeks, domestic affliction'. In the event it was to be many months before Cobden returned to public life.

Bright wrote to him that day: 'My dear Cobden, When I heard you were not in the House owing to a domestic affliction, I felt great anxiety to know what blow had struck you, and where it had fallen. I did not picture to myself anything so severe and so near as that your poor Boy should be snatched away from you, and the more I consider the character of the trial which has overtaken you, the more I feel how unable I am to say or do anything that can in any way lessen its bitterness. Fifteen years ago you called upon me, in Leamington, when my poor wife lay dead in the room above; and I recollect well the manifestations of your sympathy, and the encouragement you gave me...I know that you will bear this great affliction as becomes you, but I scarcely dare imagine how it will be felt by her to whom it has not been permitted to solace the last moments of her beloved child. I wrote a few lines to Mrs Cobden as soon as I heard the sad intelligence. I hope they would not rudely break in upon her sorrow. I am much obliged to your Bror. Frederick for sending the copy of the Chevalier Bunsen's letter. I am sending it to my sister Priscilla, for no one out of your own house will grieve more truly than she will. My wife desires to join me in expressions of much sympathy. Believe me most truly yours, John Bright.'

Many years later Elizabeth Clare wrote about this period in the lives of her employers: 'Some years after I had been at Dunford, Master Richard Cobden Mr. Cobden's only son died. the news was quite sudden. He died at school in Germany – it was very sad times at Dunford then. Poor Mrs Cobden could not be comforted in any way. I remember the day, quite well – when his poor body, was brought in the Hearse to the front entrance at Dunford House. Poor Mrs Cobden walked through the day-nursery to look out of the window, for her to see just the end of his coffin. She was most sorrowful...'

Cobden wrote to Hugh Williams on 3 May: 'My dear Sir, You will I am sure be anxious to hear how we are, and especially whether your sister has in some measure recovered from the effects of her sudden terrible bereavement.' Here follows the account of Dick's death, then: '...up to this hour your poor sister has hardly realised it in her mind...Still she is exerting herself to the utmost – We have been a good deal in the open air. I have persuaded her to use her muscular powers as much as possible. Today we have been spudding weeds on the lawn, and she has for the first time used the knitting needles. It is impossible yet to induce her to use her pen. – by degrees she will I hope be weaned back to the outer world by her dear little children. But it will take a long time to restore her to her former state of mind – I cease to think of my own blighted dreams and hopes in the presence of her inexpressible sorrow.'

On 5 May Cobden wrote to his sister Priscilla Sale: '...it is not a subject admitting of consolation...But it will take a long time to restore my poor wife to her former health. Her spirits will never entirely recover from the deep shadow now cast upon them...his [Dick's] letters to us indicated a most remarkable change in the tone of his mind, being full of manly thoughtfulness, and indicating how rapidly the levity of the boy was giving way to the sedateness of the youth. The reports from the schoolmaster and from Chevalier Bunsen and all who know him were of an equally gratifying character. Alas, it was like decking out the victim that his sacrifice might be the more felt by us. Whilst we were thus living in an atmosphere of joy came the awful tidings. I know that his poor remains rest on the hill that overlooks us and all that he loved best, and yet the whole house and grounds seem alive with his agility and mirthfulness. – This is poor dear Kate's present state of mind. – She starts into tears, when we walk out, at the sound of the pony's steps or at a whistle in the woods thinking it must be he coming to meet us as of old. Sleep, which under no trials, never failed *me* long has almost deserted her. She has not passed a night since her bereavement without the aid of medicines, and I fear opiates however skilfully administered will have the effect of *wrecking* the nervous system...Dear Mrs Schwabe has left us. – She was necessary to poor dear Kate, because she alone could answer questions about the dear boy's last days. – But our noble-minded friend is too energetic for poor Kate. – who would not follow her advice in all things as she could have wished. But Mrs Schwabe's visit did good service, and I shall ever love her for coming 700 miles to offer consolation to us in the midst of so much affliction. – The only other person besides Mrs Schwabe that dear Kate has even expressed a wish to see is our sister Sarah.'

Henry Ashworth visited Dunford shortly after Dick's death and Cobden wrote him a progress report around 10 May: '...my poor wife is very much the same as when you saw her. – You rightly described her character in a few words when you were there. – She is all affection, and has withdrawn from all the attractions of fashionable life to live only for her family. – she has had no outer-world existence. – It would have been better for her peace of mind now if she had other cares and distractions. The...boy...was her first-born and favourite. – I am afraid he had engrossed the larger share of her heart. – He was for years almost her sole companion, when I was so much away from home on my League agitation.'

On 28 May Cobden reported to Mrs Schwabe on Kate's condition: 'My dear friend, – Since our visit to Chichester, which lasted a week, my dear wife is, I hope, better. She is exerting herself to the utmost to master her absorbing grief, and the dear little children have succeeded in engaging much of her attention. The difficulty in securing sleep still remains. If passing her time in the open air is calculated to promote sleep, she certainly does everything to secure it, for she is on the lawn or in the meadow all day when the weather permits. She carries a "spud" in her hand, with which she employs herself in digging up little weeds. It is impossible for any peasant's wife in the village to be more industrious. There is scarcely a weed to be found in our lawn or field. When in the house, she employs herself in knitting. She has also used her pen a little in copying. But hitherto she has not written any letters. When we get to London I hope to get her to correspond with her children. Still, she is in a prostrate condition. Your letter giving an account of your visit to Weinheim she read with much avidity. Nothing interests her so much as the facts connected with the later hours of her dear boy's existence. Letters of condolence, however beautifully expressed, fail to effect their object. If human sympathy could cope with such a visitation as hers, we should have been abundantly sustained, for we have had it most generously manifested from all quarters and ranks – from the prince to the blind and deaf paupers in our village; and we are grateful, for if it be still unavailing it is well-intentioned, and in offering their sympathy they do all that it is in their power to accomplish.'

He then confides to Mrs Schwabe the strangeness of Kate's mental state: 'But any *facts* respecting the last days of the poor boy tend to her relief in a peculiar way. I don't know whether you understand her state of mind, but I can hardly explain it in a better phrase than by saying that she seems to have been harbouring the suspicion that he did not die by fair and proper means, but that she has been somehow cheated out of her dear boy. This state of feeling arises solely from the suddenness with which the blow fell on her at the very moment when she had reason to suppose him in the strongest state of health. Had she stumbled over his corpse at her bedroom door it could not have been more cruelly sudden. This, and *not any mistrust of the good people among [whom] Richard was placed*, is the cause of the peculiar state of her mind. Any details which may be sent of his illness and death tend to remove this state of doubt and suspicion, and to familiarise her mind with the fact of his *inevitable death*. I have, I fear, been tedious, in this analysis of the state of my poor wife's mind, but you will not, I am sure, misunderstand me...'

Another private letter to Moffatt, written on 26 May in the midst of the 'peace rejoicings' marking the end of the Crimean War, talked of a possible visit to London with Kate when these were over. Cobden tells him: 'She constantly recurs to the disease of which he died and with *Grahams Domestic Medicine* in her hand, she holds an argument as it were with Death, and proves how such attacks are to be cured. The bible, and this medical work under the head of "Fever" are the only volumes she will look at.' Cobden is still deploring 'the most dreadful German *gaucherie* in the mode of announcing our bereavement.'

On 4 June Cobden writes sadly to Parkes: 'I cannot prove as good as my word by coming to town this week, but my poor wife will accompany me on Monday. She is as helpless as one of her young children, and requires as much forbearance and kindness. God knows how much the comfort and regularity of her domestic life have always been made subservient, willingly and meekly so, to my political engagements, without one atom of ambition to profit by the privileges which to some natures offer a kind of compensation for family discomfort. And, bearing this in view, I have from the moment that this terrible blow fell on us, determined to make every other claim on my time and attention subordinate (even to the giving up of my seat) to the task of mitigating her sufferings. No other human being but myself can afford her the slightest relief. I sometimes doubt whether for the next six months I shall be able to leave her for twenty-four hours together.'

But by Wednesday, as he wrote sadly to Moffatt: 'As I expected my poor wife is anxious to return home. She carries her heartache everywhere with her, and it really matters but little in what locality she finds herself. Still the change will I hope, be a step, though an imperceptible one, towards improvement.'

Brother-in-law Sale was among those begging Cobden to get Kate away from home.'If possible without the children. At home, with you and them around her, she has nothing to rouse or interest her but when separated from them, she will by degrees feel more interested about them and think less of the past – Why not take her to London or if she will not leave home, send the children away – Send them to us – We will do our best for them and she will soon want to see them and be always anxious writing to them and about them...'

Bright's sister, Priscilla, now Mrs Duncan McLaren, wrote to Kate from her home, Newington House, Edinburgh, on 21 July with condolences on Dick's death and referred to Cobden's return to public life: 'We read with deep interest and sympathy of the effort Mr. Cobden has made to enter once more upon his public duties. I have often dwelt with wondering interest upon the circumstances that both he and my Brother shd. have been brought into such close retirement at the very time they had been so longing for as affording opportunities for their great usefulness. However, I believe they were of more use than they were aware of at the time when they felt themselves as it were over shadowed by the late calamitous war.'

Back at Dunford, Cobden wrote to Bright on 22 July: 'My wife has accompanied me twice to London (for I could not leave her side for twelve hours) first to enable me to attend a couple of meetings of the Committee on Dues, and then to wind up at my lodgings for the close of the session...I have paid some visits to kind friends with my wife since my last letter and I hope she is gradually getting up from her great prostration...We were nearly a week at J.B. Smith's in Westbourne Terrace and made an excursion to Windsor, Ascot and Kew. We have also been on a visit to Moffatt's kind sisters near Guildford, and they took us several long drives – one day over the "Hogs Back", so much praised in Cobbett's rural rides, to Farnham – another to Henry Drummond's house as queer and eccentric as its owner, and of all places in the world, we went to Aldershot, where are being erected the most extensive, solid and costly barracks in the world.'

In August the family were at Bognor, from where Cobden reported to Frederick on 7 September: '...The children have improved vastly with their bathing and sea air. – We shall leave all the little ones in Brighton for a week or two [with the Ashburners] and then I hope they will be quite set up in health...Kate and I shall go to Ascot on Friday or Saturday.'

'I cannot tell you what we shall do with ourselves during the

Autumn,' Cobden told his sister, Priscilla Sale, writing from London on 22 July, 'for it must depend on poor Kate's health and spirits...Sometimes I am almost in despair.'

But a solution to this problem was not far off.

CHAPTER ELEVEN

Retreat to Glyn Garth

It was to Mrs Schwabe that Kate owed the start of her painfully slow recovery.

'...I have yielded to the energetic offers of my friend Mrs Schwabe and agreed to occupy her house Glyn Garth on the Menai Straits for some time,' Cobden told Hugh Williams on 25 September 1856. 'We shall go by Brighton (where we leave little Kate at school) and on Saturday evening I shall arrive I hope at our destination with the three youngest children – this remove to Wales will I hope tend to restore your sister a little from the depression in which I am sorry to say she still remains. – As we shall have no governesses with us, she will undertake I hope the instruction of the little ones for a few hours a day which will afford occupation to her mind. – It is this alone which can afford her relief. – time without mental labor [*sic*] will not give relief, and hitherto unfortunately she has not been able to find consolation from reading or writing...If you carry out your plan of going to Dylife could you not come round by Bangor and meet me? I am almost in despair about the mine and sometimes think the wisest plan for all parties would be to sell it. – We are in such an entanglement that when we think we have cleared ourselves we only find fresh meshes enveloping us.'

The Cobden family arrived at Glyn Garth on 27 September, and next day he tells Frederick: 'We got here safely yesterday after a marvellous journey so far as speed goes but a more expensive one than I expected. – Today we have found ourselves comfortably installed in this place which has accommodation enough for half a dozen families. – As an illustration of its size, there are *three* bathrooms with all accompanying equipment.

'We have made a great mistake in not having brought the laundry-maid instead of little Elizabeth Clare, but it never occurred to Kate till Clare suggested it – I have a letter from Bright to-day he is coming with his family for a month to Llangollen (the place Weynert is building) opposite the Strait, and I shall have some fishing with him. – Pray make good use of eyes and ears and tongue whilst we are away, so the people do not get into loose or wasteful ways. – Let your voice be heard both indoors and out, not only when great occasions arise, but occasionally in the way of caution and information. The servant class about you are like children and for their own sake as well as yours, let them feel that a superior intelligence is presiding over them...Let us know before you decide on going to Manchester, that Kate may send instructions as to the precautions to be taken when the house is left to the servants...'

Joseph Parkes to Cobden on 8 October: 'My dear Cobden. I drop you a note – not merely for "kind enquiries" but really anxious to learn whether (and as I hope is the fact) Mrs Cobden is regaining her health of Body and Mind. I trust that she is gradually resuming her interest in her many remaining blessings of this life. You must counsel her, that it is irreligious to allow the loss of one source of happiness and one grief to overpower her sense of her many remaining means of happiness. But such sudden and severe misfortunes, as hers and yours, do benumb the feelings and deaden the senses for a while...Still we ought ever to be alive to our Duties, and Time is usually an irresistible Consoler – Drop me a *few* lines; I do not need details, but I shall be most glad to hear – on *your* as well as on her own account – that she is gradually recovering her tone of cheerfulness and her *habits* of interest in her Children and Household cares.'

Cobden writes to him by return.'Your long letter – more interesting than a weeks series of the *Times* – has just reached me...My wife seemed to be falling into a settled torpor which alarmed me; and dreading the winter gloom and associations of home I came to a very sudden determination to try a great change. Putting my eldest girl to school at Brighton and parting with my governess I accepted Mrs Schwabe's offer of her house here and brought my wife and three little girls with the hope that change of scene and air, and the sound of her native Welsh tongue would restore her to a more cheerful state of mind. But above all I have relied on the mental occupation which she will have in attending according to agreement for a few hours daily to the education of the children. I am filling the office of writing master, and I hope a feeling of duty and responsibility will induce her to devote herself to a labour which alone can give her relief.'

Frederick it was who fulfilled the role of Cobden's confidant at this time and was expected to supervise the domestic staff at Dunford in Kate's absence: 'We wish you to speak to all the servants together, and explain to them the rule we wish them to observe – ' Cobden tells him on 22 October: 'One of them only is to go to Church or Chapel on every third sunday evening, taking it by turns, or agreeing among themselves if either of them goes out of his or her turn. Two of them must always be in the house – This is the rule we wish not to be departed from unless after an application to you and with your consent. – As there is now nobody but yourself in the house, and Emily can have nothing to do but what she can get through with ease in the morning, we expect her to turn her hand, during the rest of the day, with cheerfulness and willingness to the work of the kitchen and that she will assist Susan in the washing up, preparing the kitchen tea and supper – and in the work of the dairy. --

'I mentioned to you that accounts have reached us through Clare from her sister Charlotte that Susan Clare is dissatisfied with the way in which she is *put upon* and left to do all the work by Emily and that she is doubting whether she can continue at Dunford. – I have written the above at Kate's dictation, and we wish you to read it to them all in a distinct and emphatic way so that they will understand it. – Kate considers Susan Clare of more value than both the others, and especially more important at the present moment when everything is entrusted to her; but she is of a very quiet yielding nature, rather reserved, perhaps a little sullen with those about her. – George is a respectable, slow and trusty fellow, but not always the most agreeable to those he does not choose to be on good terms with. As for Emily although quick active and a good worker Kate considers her the most awkward temper she ever had about her. – It was only out of consideration for Robinson whose boy we were obliged to return on his hands that Kate kept Emily instead of Caroline who was a most excellent and amiable girl. Kate has her suspicions (but she does not know that they are well-founded) that probably Emily has heard of Caroline having got a place at higher wages (£4 advance) and may be plotting to leave – but if this should turn out to be so she will get no character for it would be an unpardonable thing if she were to misbehave whilst we are away. – When Kate returns she may go if she wishes to leave. – I have now told you exactly how the land lies, and you can deal better with these parties having heard all the particulars of their characters.'

Again on 25 October: 'I hope we are going on a little better here. Kate is some days better and others worse but I think on the whole she is improving. – Everybody around us is very civil. Colonel Pennant (Penryhan Castle) has just sent to offer me the use of his yacht and the key of his grounds and gardens – Mr and Mrs Darbyshire were here yesterday. – Bright and his wife the day before. Today we took an early dinner with the children at Lady

Williams and her two little girls next door to us. – I hope in time these little changes and visits will break in upon the moodiness of her feelings. – Will you say in your next for her information what quantity of butter you are churning weekly.'

Cobden took up Colonel Pennant's invitation to go out in his yacht, 'but were becalmed and had to be rowed back.'

The one bright subject of Cobden's letters at this time, when he was near the end of his tether, was his eldest daughter, Katie. When he writes to Frederick on 1 November he reports: '...We have very good accounts of little Katy. – She writes long letters which might have been written by a girl of 18, – Miss Jeaffreson speaks very highly of her...Some days Kate is much better than others...But I find this is a very mild relaxing climate. – The bay trees are as big as your largest hollies, and the fuschias [*sic*] grow as high as the roofs of the cottages. – It is milder than the Isle of Wight...How is your cough? Have you had any more attacks? – Kate says George ought to sleep in the room next to you.'

In December Cobden wrote again to Moffatt: 'It is very doubtful whether my wife is not worse than when you saw her. The maid-servant whom we brought from home is of opinion that she is worse, that she takes less notice of the children, and flies more to the solitude of her bedroom, and evinces less interest in what is going on in the nursery. The children are as lively as butterflies in the sun, and they cling about her, and do their best to engage her smiles but she seems to compress her lips, and thus to make a silent protest against being again cheated of her affections. The fact is, I only confess it to you and *her* relations, she has never submitted to the blow in a spirit of resignation, and therefore to this day she has not had the consolations of either religion or reason. She is fighting against her fate...She has naturally a defect in her temperament in the want of elasticity of spirit...This is now a real calamity to her and all about her.'

The Anglesey experiment was coming to an end. On 4 December Cobden tells Fred: 'We were thinking of having some more provisions forwarded, but have come to the conclusion not to do so. – We shall go on the 24th to the Darbishires to spend the Xmas week, and from there proceed homeward without returning to this [place]. – We think of stopping for a night or two at Sturges at Birmingham and either go thence by way of Oxford and Godalming and have Elcomes omnibus to meet us, or else go through London in a day to Chichester, and stop there all night at the Watkins and the Hayllers and come by a new omnibus next day to Dunford. – stopping at Birmingham will break the journey. I enclose £5. There has been a thaw here, but last night was a frost again. It will not last long I expect.'

Things seem to have deteriorated even further by 8 December, when Cobden's letter to Frederick begins angrily, goes on in desperation, but by the end shows his resilience of spirit: 'We are amazed at the Easebourne butchers bill being unpaid. – He is a struggling man and the £4 was of more importance to him – What difference on earth could it have made to us whether it was paid in Octr or Jany? – Why didn't you ask me for the money? Pray tell him that I didn't know it was unpaid.'

At the close of this letter Cobden's own 'elasticity of spirits' shows through: What say you to this? – The pigs are actually fed and fatted here at Glyn Garth without buying an ounce from the mill. – They never have meal of any kind – nothing but house stuff and potatoes. – and I can answer for it the ham and bacon are good.'

With the approach of Christmas it seems that in spite of her condition Kate was worrying about the villagers at Heyshott, for Cobden writes to Frederick on 12 December: 'I enclose ½ £10. Kate has had bad accounts of poor Mrs Powell. – I suppose half the people about you are nearly starving, but this poor woman Kate thinks has some claim on us. – She wishes you to inquire into her case, and says that Susan could make her some broth, and suggests that she should have a shillings worth of stuff from the butchers occasionally (or Mrs Clare would procure it for her) avowedly for making a mess with rice and vegetables for these poor people. – She supposes that Mrs Poat must also be in great want. – Let something of this sort be done with judgment and economy, and she says that if Mrs Powell be in a state to require a little wine you had better let her have some...It is very mild and relaxing here and not at all suited for Kate's case...'

Writing to him from Bonn on 10 December, Mrs Schwabe now ventured to give Cobden some forthright advice: '...I do beseech you without hesitation do not take Mrs Cobden home in this dismal season. – If public and private duties compel you to go to Dunford for a time, leave Mrs Cobden and the children at Glyn Garth till the days are longer and the sky brighter. Think of the long winter evenings, when you will be busy amongst your papers, the little ones in bed, and your wife alone with your excellent but silent brother – From what I saw at Dunford she has no congenial neighbours and at Glyn Garth I feel sure after you are gone the Misses Roberts and Darbyshire will take care that she is seldom or never alone and I can most likely arrange that Miss

Brendon spends a little time with your wife at Glyn Garth...

But this time Cobden did not take Mrs Schwabe's advice and after Christmas he wrote to Frederick with details of their intended movements: '...We shall go from this [Cobden then omitted the place name in his letter] tomorrow to Sturges, and have decided to return home on Friday – that is provided we can get from Birmingham to Godalming in a day which I suppose we shall be able to do.'

The family returned to Dunford in the first week of January 1857.

Later that month Cobden took Kate to Ben Rydding, a hydropathic establishment at Richmond in Yorkshire, leaving the children at Dunford in the care of Mrs Higgin. Cobden had little sympathy with what he called the 'hydropathic superstition' but he felt that 'the simple diet and regular hours are always in favour of health.' Kate's mental health was still causing him concern, as he admitted to Moffatt on 7 April: '...I hope my wife is better – Her brother who has been uninterruptedly with us for three months (I was obliged to resort to the aid of her two brothers) thinks her decidedly better. – I do not see so much change as I could wish.' He is obviously worried, too, about his own health: 'I find a retreat to this drowsy neighbourhood very necessary for my health. I overdid it in trying to canvass Huddersfield and Manchester at the same time, and was almost afraid my head was giving way. However, my old medicine, sleep, has nearly restored me. But I am determined to keep out of the ring for the present. It suits me on private and domestic grounds to have been beaten at Huddersfield (where my good friends ought not to have taken me), and although the dose is a little nauseous, the medicine will ultimately be of service to me. But I am persecuted with innumerable letters from kind people, who have taken the notion that I must require encouragement and condolence, etc.'

On 15 April Cobden wrote to Priscilla Sale about Frederick's deteriorating health: 'You will see by the enclosed letter from Reynolds that he has a bad opinion of poor Fred's case. I hope he may on further investigation be induced to modify his views. I have written to advise him to consult Sir James Clark, who from his intimacy with me is most likely to give extra attention to the case. But it is clear that Fred ought to have taken the advice of a competent person years ago. You had better not say anything to frighten him. I have not mentioned Reynolds' letter to him.'

On 9 June Frederick musters his strength to write to Priscilla: 'My dearest P...my journey to London was unsatisfactory, for the great authorities I consulted, evidently knew as little of my case as our country practitioner here; there is in fact nothing indicative of disease about me, other than the paralysed state of my legs, but the *case* all seem to be in ignorance of...I have very *good nursing*, enough people to attend to me, and when the weather is favourable, I go out in the pony chaise or a little hand carriage, I do not see *much* company as you may suppose, for I do not leave my room often except for the open air; I will not however fill my paper with but a dismal story. I hope now that I have written to hear from you again soon.'

Bright, who had suffered a serious breakdown, but was now recovering, was among the many friends enquiring about Cobden's domestic problems at this time. Cobden tells him on 10 June: '...the heavy cloud still hangs over my household. My wife's grief does not yield to time as I had hoped. An additional nightmare has befallen us in the serious illness of my brother who as you know has been my second half in all private affairs. He has for many years been a martyr of a nervous disorder which is little understood by the doctors and so to hide their ignorance they give it a grand name and call it *Neuralgia*. – the seat of his greatest sufferings is in his legs, and about three months ago their muscular power gradually began to give way. He went to London staid at my lodgings a week, and saw both Dr Reynolds and Sir James Clark, but he returned no better. Although his body is a mere wreck it is a consolation to us that his mind is quite unclouded...'

William Hargreaves to Cobden, 13 June 1857: 'My dear Sir, Having heard of your Brother's very serious indisposition we had anticipated the postponement of your intended visit to us. We shall hope to be more fortunate at some future time, when your Brother's sufferings may be diminished, if not entirely removed, of the last, however, judging from the tone of your letter, I fear you have poor expectations...My wife [Alice] desires me to acknowledge the receipt of Mrs Cobden's very welcome letter – doubly so, I assure you, that it breathes *a rather more hopeful tone*.'

At the end of 1857 Cobden was still reluctant to leave Kate and return to politics. He told Moffatt on 3 December: 'The truth is I cannot leave home for 48 hours and preserve that tranquility and elasticity of spirit which is necessary to success in public life – Under the circumstances I am therefore useless anywhere but in my family – There might have been a state of things – indeed there has been – when I sacrificed every domestic consideration for public duty – But there is now no motive or justification for my doing so – I cant see my way for accomplishing any good in the political arena.' The next year was to lower his spirits still further.

One of the people who interested themselves in Kate's recovery was Lady Hatherton, formerly Mrs Davenport, on whom the Cobdens had paid a call when Kate was staying at the Grosvenor Street lodgings and who, as she wrote to Dick afterwards, 'is a very amicable clever person'. Cobden's reply to her enquiring letter, on 12 February 1858, was a frank one: 'In reply to your kind inquiries my poor wife is better. – I wish I could say more. – But the truth is she was shattered by the opiates she flew to for oblivion. – If I had again to go through my terrible ordeal I would rather place her in a straight waistcoat than allow her to resort to any such expedients for relief. – If grief and sorrow are allowed their full sway they bring their own relief. – It is only when we gird against nature that our sufferings are strengthened and procrastinated – I am still hoping that her dear little girls will restore her to her former tranquility --

'Tell Lord Hatherton I am very busy farming – I am not a "bull frog", having only 120 acres – but I am copying him in miniature having my water wheel (3 horses) with chaff cutter, circular saw, pulper, mill, manure pump etc – I have been kept alive and in health by this occupation when I was fit for nothing else...I relax a good deal with pigs! Sheep look all the same, – but there is an individuality about pigs and we become quite acquainted. There is a cunning expression in their eye, when they are speculating whether you are about to give them a slice of turnip or carrot, that looks dreadfully human – '

In a long 'crossed' letter to an old school friend, Sarah Brook, in Wales on 26 February 1858, Kate tells her: 'Our Christmas was a perfectly quiet one – except that the Tiptearers [Christmas mummers] broke pretty frequently upon our silence.' The children too enjoyed all the gaiety that Midhurst afforded. Poor Mr Frederic is a great sufferer – Some of us have I dare say told you that he has not use over his legs – When the weather is very fine he is carried a little out of doors – The schoolroom is now his bedroom and his own room his sitting room – and George sleeps in the little room next in order to be within call at night...'

Cobden wrote to Bright on 31 March: '...Then age brings other claims and responsibilities...My conscience tells me that I have no right to disregard the duties of private life unless upon very strong proof that by sacrificing the interests of the few I can serve the more urgent cause of the many...You know what a state of hopelessness my household is in. Now if I could bring my wife and my brother up to London and could live there for six months whilst my little girls were here in the charge of a governess, it would suit me very well, for it would give me the opportunity of consulting a first-rate doctor for my brother and of finding distractions for my wife's mind that might be useful to her case. But I find it quite as much as I can manage to take lodgings for myself during the session. To transfer one's whole household to London must be very agreeable to those who have 5 or £6 ,000 a year. To me it is an impossibility...I am every day confirmed in the conviction that under present circumstances, I should not be justified in accepting a seat in Parliament...For the present I wish to be allowed to bury myself with my pigs and sheep here.'

April was again a month of bereavement for the family at Dunford, for Frederick's agonising illness came to an end when he died on the morning of 10 April, his death bringing relief to everyone. Cobden wrote the news to Bright the same day:

'It has mercifully pleased God to relieve my poor brother from his sufferings...He was calm and free from pain, but insensible, during the last twelve hours, which was almost our only consolation during the whole of his illness, for he suffered most awful pains for nearly a fortnight. Even now although the poor body has been at rest for many hours I still find his cries and groans sounding in my ears.

'We shall long feel the blank which the loss of this gentle and harmless and yet intelligent companion occasions. Owing to his timidity and shyness he was hardly known beyond his family circle. But although these qualities prevented him from doing battle with the world, he had acquirements which I often coveted. His memory was quite wonderful. He could take *Haydn's Dictionary of Dates* and correct its errors from his own mental storehouse, and when I found myself at a loss for a date or fact I consulted him as I would an Encyclopedia. There is no other way of reconciling us to the justice of an overruling God, when witnessing the torments which for years this harmless being has suffered, than in the belief of a future state, where all that we suffer here will be compensated to us, in a manner which to our faculties is quite incomprehensible. There is no other present refuge from doubt and despair but in the trust in God and the mistrust of our own powers.'

According to the death certificate of 13 April 1858 the cause of Frederick Cobden's death was 'disease of the spinal cord'.

On hearing the news Parkes wrote Cobden a sympathetic letter from 17 Wimpole Street on 26 April: 'As you have been long assured of my sympathy with you in all social griefs or troubles which may befal [*sic*] you I did not hasten to answer your kind note on the death of your Brother. Also, I heard that you were early coming to London. Not however hearing of your advent I drop you a line of commiseration on your sore loss, and know well your particular attachment to your brother and his high qualities. But Death was indeed a happy release from intense suffering and hopeless disease. You have really been severely disciplined by your recent domestic woes. I trust that no more are in store for you or yours. – I trust that you and Mrs Cobden will break the painful associations by leaving home for a short time.' Parkes was equally persuasive in his letter of 8 May: 'I hope you and Mrs Cobden will come and dine *above* with us – any day except next Thursday. Can you both do so, and we will have an hour's confab after dinner?...I should like to spend a morning with you in some sightseeing – such as the Prince Consort's new Palace of Arts at Kensington, and which I am ashamed to confess I have not visited.'

Bright had wished to attend Fred's funeral, but Cobden wrote dissuading him on health grounds on 15 April: 'It was very kind of you to think of coming, but if there were no other reason why you should not make the journey here to attend the funeral of my poor brother, the risk you would run in standing bareheaded in an exposed Church yard for half an hour in a cold east wind would be sufficient...'

'...I am sometimes in doubt whether I will resume a political career again,' Cobden confided to Bright at this unhappy stage of his life, on 17 October.'I am full of perplexities upon the subject, and they are not wholly of a private character. Looking at those public questions which I now regard as the most important, I feel myself in such complete disaccord with every political party, and with *nearly all mankind*, that unless I play the rogue and hold my tongue, or say what I don't believe, I could not find a plank to stand upon on any platform in the country. I consider that we as a nation are little better than brigands, murderers, and poisoners, in our dealings at this moment with half the population of the globe.'

That autumn Cobden learnt ot another family death, which was to add to his financial burden, and told Bright about this in a letter on 18 November: '...I have just heard of the death of my youngest (but one) brother who went to Australia nearly twenty years ago and from whom we scarcely ever got a letter. He has left 3 young boys – the mother is also dead – He died at Lolong near Sydney, and seems to have been greatly esteemed by his neighbours, according to the notice in the papers and the accounts of his funeral. But, he has not left a shilling, and his children are of course bequeathed to my care. The curious part in all these troubles of mine (and *you* can appreciate it) is that people everywhere assume that I am a very rich man, and in too many instances act accordingly.'

From the time of Frederick's death, although occasionally subject to fits of depression, Kate began to play a more active part in the marriage, and when the following year Cobden found the 'plank' he needed to give him the impetus to re-enter public life, she was to make a valuable contribution to his work.

CHAPTER TWELVE

Return to Public Life

Early in 1859 Cobden decided on a visit to the United States. As there was always what Morley calls 'ill-natured gossip about his affairs', he was quick to assure his friends this decision did not mean that he was unduly concerned about his investment in the Illinois Railway.

'Personal interests have brought me to the determination – though I have a strong desire on other grounds to see that country after an interval of 24 years,' he tells Henry Ashworth on 3 February, 'to witness its great progress and to judge of its prospects for the future. There is nothing, I must tell you, in my investments in that country to cause alarm or render my visit necessary. I have gradually yielded to some of my colleagues' and friends' wishes to go out with a view of infusing some new blood into the management of our affairs. But having decided to go this spring, I am starting speedily with the view of getting to Washington before the close of the short session of Congress as I wish to see how the politicians compare with animals of the same species at home.'

'I have actually taken my berth for the 12th, ' he tells Bright on 5 February. What would this mean for Kate? 'My wife will take the children to Paris and reside with an old friend of ours from Manchester, Mrs Woolley, who takes in boarders.' Elizabeth Woolley had been one of the 'Ladies of the Bazaar' in 1842, and whose circumstances had sadly deteriorated after the sudden death of her husband.'This will give Katie an opportunity of having good music masters, and all of them will learn French correctly without trouble.' But it was not only his wish that Katie should forward her musical education: Kate's health was his main concern.'I think the complete change, and throwing her on her own resources will also be of service to my wife. I shall not be many months absent. We shall let our house, if we find a customer to our mind, for the summer and autumn. But I shall not let any "fast" people into possession.'

Cobden sailed on the *Canada* on 12 February, and his first letter to Kate, when they were off Halifax, Nova Scotia, on 25 February, is full of the physical miseries he suffered on the voyage: '...I was very sick for a week. I never was so bad before – tell the dear children that poor papa could not hold up his head or shave himself for a week – Nor could he eat or drink anything excepting a little dry biscuit. He took a dislike to everything he tasted. Even tea caused quite a nausea which he has not yet got over...There is only one lady on board, Miss Muir, who was not so sick as myself...Tell the dear children also that our watches by the London time are 4¼ hours in advance of the time at Halifax – We are a quarter past 12 when the clocks here are 8 o'clock. You can explain to them how this is...Speculating on the chance of your not having left, I address this to Dunford...Young Higgin (at Liverpool) introduced me to the Manager of the Steam Boat Company who gave me the best cabin in the ship.'

On arriving in New York on 8 March he tells Kate: 'I went straight to Washington on arriving in the States to see the closing scene of the session...As yet I have had no time to look below the surface of things in connexion with the Illinois Company. But there is really nothing to discover in the matter. What is wanted is patience, and the power to wait which are very difficult things in my case...My thoughts are much with you and the dear children. – I feel great anxiety to know that you are settled and that the house at Dunford is let. We must do our best to live economically for the next year with as little appearance of penury as possible – Everything has gone as unluckily as possible with me. I sometimes feel almost unnerved great as is my energy and natural buoyancy...I shall be anxious to know that you are in Paris, and comfortably settled. Let the dear children be systematically taught French. It will give a good opportunity and save them much labor [*sic*] hereafter.'

On 30 April Cobden was in Washington staying at the White House. He tells Kate he has fallen out with Moffatt over advice Moffatt has given him on 'this Railroad business'. He has been staying with their friends the Gilpins in Philadelphia: 'Nothing could have been more warm and kind than their reception – They were anxious in their inquiries for you...Mrs Gilpin with every luxury about her had I found also her settled grief. She had in her bedroom, which she showed me, the portrait of her only son whom she lost when a youth. The Gilpins tried to keep me, and if I had been in spirits for visiting I could have enjoyed myself long under their hospitable roof. But I remained with them only 4 days when I came to Washington to take up my quarters for the same time under the roof of the President of the United States. this is a somewhat rare honor [*sic*] for an English traveller and under other circumstances I would have enjoyed myself much. Mr Buchanan the President is an old bachelor and his niece Miss Lane, whom I knew in London, does the honors [*sic*] of the Executive Mansion. Our hours are early, we breakfast at ½ past 7, and of course go to bed in corresponding time. I shall leave tomorrow and cross the Alleghany Mountains to Cincinnati in Ohio. Let the dear children see my route on the map.'

Far from being in Paris Kate was still at Dunford, corresponding with a new friend, Mrs Mary Leathley who lived with her son Dudley at Easebourne and was to become a loved friend of the family to whom she was known as 'Aunt Mary'. How the two women first met is not known, but it may have been through Nelly.

On 6 May Kate writes to her: 'Nelly returned last evening and is delighted to accept your kind invitation. But how will you manage all the children together! I shall send the young servant Elizabeth [Clare] with them, and you can discharge or keep her at your pleasure. Her mother lives at Midhurst and she will, if of no use to the children go and see her. They shall have their dinner at half past 12 o'clock and the little carriage shall be at the door to take them to you at one – then if you will be kind enough to let them have an early cup of tea I can send for them about 8 o'clock. They are looking forward with great pleasure to the visit...Our kind love to you and your dear Boy – I have hope of having a little chat with you before I go as our journey is again postponed for another week.' Kate gives no reason for this.

'...It is dreadful news the breaking out of war again in Europe,' Cobden writes from Chicago on 11 May, 'so like the exact repetition of what happened 60 years ago...If I were a younger man, and with my career undecided in life I would at once make up my mind to remain in the far West of America where life is easy and everything in the greatest abundance, and where at least people are exempt from the follies and crimes of the statesmen and rulers of the stupid and wicked old *world*...I hardly know whether this will find you in France, or whether the breaking out of war may keep you in England...And for God's sake do not spend a shilling that can be helped – this war makes that more necessary than ever – talk of these matters to nobody. I am worried at the idea of their having launched me for Rochdale. It is a most inconvenient step for me and I am praying that I may not be returned.' But returned he was.

He tells Kate on 1 June that he is going to Montreal, down the St. Lawrence River, then from Quebec by screwsteamer to Liverpool: 'This route gives me an opportunity of seeing the scenery of the St

Lawrence which is very fine, and it saves 500 miles of Ocean navigation by bringing you so much nearer to the Continent of Europe on leaving the mouth of the River' [and saving him many agonising hours of seasickness, which was an equally important consideration].'I expect to leave Quebec by the *Indian* Steamer on the 18th June certainly not later. If I have an average summer passage I shall be at Liverpool in from 10 to 12 days afterwards...'

Unsuspected by him, Cobden's parliamentary life was about to enter a new and important phase, and one in which Kate was to play an active part.

Kate finally made the break from Dunford, and writes to Mrs Leathley on 3 June from the Ashburners, Chichester Terrace, Brighton: 'Dearest Mrs Leathley, We performed our journey all right yesterday – I brought Dimmock on to Brighton as I felt a little nervous about looking after all the luggage – However I need not have done so, as we found ourselves met by Mr Ashburner – with arrangements most complete for our comfort.' Living up to her girlhood reputation as 'the late Miss Williams', Kate hadn't done her accounts before leaving Dunford, and had brought her books with her to finish before sailing: 'Dimmock remained the night and I am making use of him in sending back accounts properly arranged herewith for Dunford – which I failed in completing before I left – so now I feel all will be in right order there – I enter into these particulars knowing your most kind interest *in all that concerns me* due too, to you after all your assistance to have the satisfaction that I am comfortable on this head – I had all the kind hearts constantly before me during the night, that grouped around us on our departure from the old house yesterday morning Dear Betty with her bewildered look following me to every corner [Betty was a dog]. Tell Dudley that my darlings send much love to him and so they do to you as well – '

When Kate and the children reached Paris Mrs Woolley was still living at 36 Rue de Ponthieu, near the Champs Elysées, where Kate found the size of the rooms 'disappointing', as she wrote in an undated letter to Mrs Leathley: 'I consider them very small for French rooms – however they are all ensuite and the house is situated very openly consequently we are able to keep the rooms well ventilated.' The homely English cooking provided by Mrs Woolley was quite to her taste and 'better cooked than it would be in England under similar circumstances. Our rooms are most comfortably furnished – More English than French – but at this time of year we would have dispensed with furniture for the sake of space – I must keep the children out as much as possible.'

Landing at Liverpool on the 29th June, Cobden went to the Adelphi Hotel where he wrote to Kate in Paris to tell her of his arrival, after a good passage 'in spite of icebergs', and enclosing the diary of his travels for the children. It was not until the following day that she learned in a second letter, from Manchester, of the totally unexpected welcome he had received before he even disembarked: 'My dearest Kate – I had but a moment yesterday in Liverpool to apprise you of my safe arrival in England. As I came up the Mersey I little dreamed of the reception which awaited me. Crowds of friends were ready to greet and cheer me; and before I left the ship a packet of letters was put in my hand, containing one from Lord Palmerston, offering me a seat in the Cabinet as President of the Board of Trade, and another from Lord John Russell [the ex Prime Minister] 'urging me in the very strongest terms to accept it. There were letters form Moffatt, Gilpin, and a great many others, advising me not to refuse the offer.

'I was completely taken by surprise by all this, for I had heard nothing of the change of government, and was twenty-five days without having seen the latest news from England, namely eleven days' passage, and fourteen days which we were behind the news when I left Quebec.

'I went on shore and proceeded to the hotel, where my troubles began. More than a hundred of the leading men of Liverpool assembled in the large room to present me with an address, which was put into my hand by Mr William Brown...Afterwards Mr Robertson Gladstone, from the Financial Reform Association, Mr Rathbone, from the American Chamber of Commerce, and the President of the Peace Society, all presented addresses, to which I was obliged, without a moment's notice, and with my head still swimming with the motion of the sea, to deliver replies. It was really like killing one with kindness. I have come on here to see my friends, and hear what they have to say. A deputation from Rochdale is over also. And I have an address from a number of persons, including Bazley and H. Ashworth, wishing me to accept the offer of a seat in the Cabinet. Indeed, almost without exception, everybody, Radicals, peace men, and all, are trying to persuade me to it.

'Now it really seems to me that they must all have gone mad, for with my recorded opinions of Lord Palmerston's conduct during the last dozen years, *in which opinions I have experienced no change*, were I suddenly to jump at the offer of a place under him, I should ruin myself in my own self-respect, and ultimately lose the confidence of the very men who are in this moment of excitement urging me to enter his Cabinet. So great is the pressure put on me, that if it were Lord Granville, or even Lord John, at the head of affairs, I should be obliged, greatly against my will, to be a Right Honourable. But to take office now, without a single declaration of change of view regarding his public conduct, would be so monstrous a course that nothing on earth shall induce me to do it. I am going to town this afternoon, and shall forward him my answer on my arrival. I listen to all my friends and say nothing, but my mind is made up.'

When he reached London Cobden went almost at once to see Palmerston who vainly tried to persuade him to enter the Cabinet. He had already made up his list and had been keeping the Presidency of the Board of Trade for Cobden. At the end of what seems to have been a long and friendly interview Palmerston told him: 'Lady Palmerston receives tomorrow at 10.' Cobden accepted the invitation.

Cobden's refusal of Palmerston's offer disappointed many of his friends, both at home and in France. Chevalier (the French economist and defender of Free Trade) was particularly vexed: 'When a man has mixed himself up in public affairs,' he told him, 'with so much superiority and success as you have had, the public has a certain claim upon him, and the exercise of this claim is the demand that he shall take part in the government of the country.' As was to be expected, Bright approved of his friend's action.

When Cobden wrote an immensely long letter to his brother-in-law William Sale, a Manchester solicitor, on 4 July, describing the reasons for his rejection of office in Palmerston's Government, he complained of feeling ill: 'I never had before so much annoyance to my feelings as in this matter. To be pressed by nearly all my friends to take a course which I felt from the first moment to be impossible was a most painful ordeal to go through. I don't remember any political occurrence which ever before made me ill. This has really upset my physical health.'

Kate and Cobden were staying with the Paultons at Cleveland Square when she wrote to Mrs Leathley on 23 July: 'My dear Friend, I am here for about a fortnight or rather till Parliament closes – I should like so much to see you but there is little chance of my visiting the neighbourhood of Midhurst this time...Mr Cobden will return to Paris with me and it is probable that we shall remain the Winter there. The dear children of course were very unwilling to my leaving them, but Papa insisted upon my coming as he could not exist very long without me...Have you suffered much from the heat? Paris before I left seemed like one great furnace – but thank God the children except in discomfort felt no ill effects from it – the roses however had fled from Nelly Janie and Julia's [Anne's] cheeks in consequence. I continue to receive good accounts of their wellbeing – Mrs Woolley makes us all very comfortable and I prefer living with her in her quiet way than elsewhere in style – I can well perceive what a struggle she has had to go through but I trust the worst is over for her poor thing – I have already been able to effect some good for her in my visit to England by procuring her two boarders. I shall be glad to hear from you and ever believe that my best wishes attend you – I am your very affectionate friend C.A. Cobden.'

Kate was also in touch with Mrs Leathley about a story she (Kate) has written, when she writes from the Paultons on 22 August: 'Dearest Mrs Leathley, when you arrived on Saturday I was occupied in writing a note, which you will find enclosed, to Mr Darton. Its perusal will enlighten you as to the subject it treats upon, and why I address him anonymously. – Whilst I have been waiting for Monday's post, I have thought often of you, and have felt, as if I could trust you with my secret, and depend upon your candid advice. – If you think this little attempt of mine stupid, you will think no more about it, will you? And if worth attention, you will perhaps do me the great kindness of showing, the small portion herewith sent of the manuscript, of the *Tale of my Parish,* to Mr Darton, who for your sake, no doubt, will pass an opinion upon it – which I, as an anonymous writer, dare scarcely hope for. You will still, if you please, withhold my name – and ask the favour in the name of a friend of yours – Should the tale, be pronounced not worth publishing, of course I shall not waste my time any longer upon it – but employ it in other ways more profitably. The pictures in the tale are true, but the frames they are set in, are of my own imaginings and construction...' Then across the top of the sheet she writes: 'Perhaps such a simple and short thing as "A Tale of my Parish" will be even when concluded fitter for a periodical than a small book? – should it even be deemed worthy of publication.' On Thursday 28, still from Cleveland Square: '...I have a great desire to write a line to say that you have given me quite sufficient encouragement to try and proceed with my tale, so pray do not show it to Mr Dalton [*sic*]. In such matters you must be quite as good a judge as he is – If I feel in the humour I can amuse myself with writing it – and in any case it will interest the children – And when it is completed we can confer together and if you think it will be worth making up into a little book I can venture to see how far a sale will benefit old Alie. So my dear friend return it to me at Mrs Schwabe's Rhodes House Middleton Nr Manchester.' Kate wrote again to Mrs Leathley from Mrs Schwabe's on 20 September, whilst she and Cobden were involved in a round of calls, visits and dinner parties. Kate asks her friend to call at the Post Office to forward their mail, 'or desire the Post Office to do so.' '...I have not given my story a thought further – for you can scarcely imagine how occupied I have been seeing old friends – this has been pleasant, but the daily dinner parties I am sick off [*sic*]. Mrs Higgin was much pleased to hear of you.'

There ended Kate's brief flirtation with literary effort.

That Session the idea of a commercial treaty with France, inspired by Michel Chevalier, was in the air; and Bright, in the 1859 session, made a speech in the House asking why the government did not go to the French Emperor and try and persuade him to allow his people to trade freely with England. The French Ambassador, Count Persigny, had expressed a wish to Lord John Russell, as an earnest of the sincerity of the Emperor's desire for peace, for such a treaty. It was with these facts in mind that Cobden sought an interview with Gladstone. On 5 August he wrote a letter which was to have far-reaching effects on trade with France:

'My dear Gladstone, If I were to run over to Hawarden Castle on Monday morning next, to return on Tuesday, would you have an hour at your disposal for a little quiet talk? In that case, I shall avail myself of Sir Stephen Glynn's kind offer of hospitality for the night. The fact is I wish to have a little talk about the trade with France. My good friend, M. Chevalier insists very pertinaciously that the Emperor can't reduce his duties unless you help him by a corresponding movement. How you are to do so and fulfil Lord Clarence Paget's promise to keep up 50 Line of Battle ships, I don't know! My daughters are in Paris, and I shall spend a part of the winter there, and if I can be of any use to you in the way of inquiry I shall be glad. Oblige me with a line, and I remain truly yours, R. Cobden.' Cautious as to practical matters, even when writing to the Chancellor of the Exchequer, Cobden adds: 'If the proposed visit suits you, would you be good enough to direct me how to reach Hawarden from Chester?'

The meeting between the two men took place early in September. Cobden's 'modest proposal' (Morley's words) 'expanded into something more definite and more energetic'. Gladstone realised that if Cobden was given the informal authority of the British

Government this would enable him to use his well-known powers upon the Emperor and his Ministers and that between them they might work out a reform of great benefit to both countries. Cobden was not happy at the prospect of dealing with governments, of whom he held no very high opinion. As he wrote to Bright at the time: 'Governments seem as a rule to be standing conspiracies to rob and bamboozle people, and why should that of Louis Napoleon be an exception?' Back in London he learned that a Cabinet Council had been called and promptly called on Palmerston and Lord John Russell to discuss Chevalier's ideas. As so often in the past, it was to Bright that he confided: 'It is not easy to interest men whose foreign policy has been running in such different grooves, in questions of political economy and tariffs. But I spoke frankly to both of them as to the state of our relations with France, and disparaged the value of an alliance in China or any other pretended *entente cordiale*, whilst we were keeping up twenty-six millions of armaments, principally as a defence against France. From what I hear, the Cabinet is concerned with the mighty question whether France is to take a bit of territory from Morocco. We are, I suppose, to protest from Gibraltar against anything so shocking to us as picking and stealing our neighbours territory going on within view of that reputable possession of ours. We have taken a whole empire from a Mahometan [*sic*] sovereign in Asia, and we are horrified at France taking a province in the same latitude from a Mahometan sovereign in Africa...'

Shortly after this meeting with Gladstone, Cobden wrote a 'Private' letter to Gilpin from Sale's office at 29 Booth Street, Manchester, on 22 August: 'I had some idea of going straight to Paris, but have altered my mind, and my wife is coming down to join me here tonight and we shall pay some visits to our friends...I have some hopes of getting rid of all my land, etc, here, through the intervention of some rich friends who will disguise an act of friendship with the mark of business. People here are making money as fast as they can count it, and some of them are pleased to say that whilst I have been neglecting my own business I have been promoting theirs, etc, etc. This between ourselves.'

As early as 1835 Cobden had speculated in purchasing land in different parts of Manchester. Optimistically, he anticipated a demand for sites for factories, shops and houses once the Corn Laws had been repealed. Sadly, he had miscalculated, and for twenty-five years had been paying rent of a thousand pounds a year on what continued to be waste spaces between Oxford Street, Quay Street, Victoria Park and Rusholme. No sooner had the investment been made than he was to be strenuously involved as leader of the agitation which led to Repeal in 1846. By then the neglect of his personal affairs had crippled him financially. The national bounty of some £80,000 voted to him that year for his services in the cause of Free Trade had largely been absorbed in paying off debts incurred by his calico printing business, in investing in shares in the Illinois Central Railway, and in buying the Dunford farmhouse. In 1859 he badly needed fresh capital. His visit to America had convinced him the affairs of the railway company were sound enough but not likely to produce quick profits, so he applied for advice to one of his oldest Manchester friends – Thomas Thomasson. In doing this Cobden hoped that a few men who could afford to wait for a return on their money might buy the Manchester building land at his valuation, but investigation showed that nothing could be done with it. A group of his intimate friends then raised a private subscription which reached £40,000. He never knew the names of the ninety and more people who contributed to this rescue operation. He requested that the list should be given to him in a sealed envelope, and this was found in his desk by his executors after his death – the seal unbroken.

On 5 September Cobden confided to John Slagg, a Manchester merchant: 'My hair has been growing gray latterly with the thought of what is to become of my children. If I were to consult my duty to them, I should withdraw from Parliament, and accept some public employment by which I might earn £2,000 a year. The present Ministry have sounded me as to my willingness to take such an office. But I see the difficulty in justifying my withdrawal from Parliament at the present time…It is one of the miseries of a public man's life that he must be liable under such circumstances to have his private troubles gibbeted before the whole world.'

By 3 October Kate was back at the Paultons preparing to return to Paris with Cobden, when she writes to Mary Leathley on what might seem a trivial matter but which was always important in the lives of the Cobdens: the well-being of their pets, particularly Cobden's bird. She asks Mrs Leathley to have tea at Dunford and inspect the cage Mrs Tiller has for the 'little bird' to be sent to Paris in. Two days later she is with the Ashburners in Brighton, and Cobden writes from Dunford, where Colonel Holden had started on a furnished tenancy:

'My dearest Kate I hope you and your friend have reached Brighton safely. I find matters pretty straight here. 'The Colonel' seems to be a vigilant disciplinarian and keeps everybody and thing in order from men to dogs. Betty and Garth are not allowed to show their faces down the hill, and Quinnell was telling me with some little suppressed indignation that the Colonel takes to scolding the dogs when he is up at Walkers. 'They are at home you see, then, Sir' he said 'and he has no business to meddle with 'em".' The family censor has been at work here and a portion of the letter is cut out.'Mrs Holden has a little pet Maltese dog in the house. She has it generally in her arms. This little pet is subjected [*sic*] to cramp, and last evening when I was dining with them she was on the hearthrug rubbing the little beast out of one of its fits. By the way she has had a terrible fall from our black pony. She was cantering in the park when his fore-foot plunged into a rabbit hole, threw her off, fortunately on one side of her head and shoulder, and the pony threw a complete summerset on to his back with his heels up in the air, and resting on the pommel of the saddle which was broken. It was a mercy she was not killed. She was brought to the *Angel* much shaken, and Dr Ingram attended her. Her eyes have been affected, so that she cannot bear the light or any thing glistening – all the little engravings had to be removed from the bedroom wall. However she is well enough now to nurse her dog. Mrs Quinnell is very weak. I don't think she will live through the winter. I have asked colonel Holden to take a photograph of the family party up at Walkers. Quinnell, his mother, and Mrs Tiller, and the two dogs, which he has promised to do.'

It must have been with serious misgivings about his health that Kate said goodbye to the 55-year-old Cobden when he left Paris on 9 November at 8 in the morning for consultations with Gladstone in London.

He had faithfully written to Kate whilst in London, telling her on 12 November: '...When I got to Calais at 4 I found that the steamer did not leave till 8, and when the hour came the Captain was afraid to leave owing to the appearance of the weather so we had to stay the night. I was taken to the Hotel where I passed the night with our poor boy when I was last in Calais. I did not sleep 5 minutes. We started in the morning at 9, and had a good passage – I avoided actual sickness. when I reached London, I was not able to see or speak to Gilpin who was and is ill. I went to Mellors (15 Cleveland Square) and finding him still in the country, I took my portmanteau to W. Hargreaves...I hope to cross over from Newhaven to Dieppe on Thursday and reach you that night.'

In Paris at this time, learning French, was an English boy about eleven years old, Arthur Bigge, whose father, an MP, was known to Cobden. Young Arthur was often asked by Cobden to 'run down to the Embassy' with his letters for mailing in the Diplomatic Bag. When the treaty was ready for signature Cobden was confined to the house with a cold, so the document was brought to his room for him to sign. Cobden sent for Arthur and told him 'You won't know all about this treaty, Arthur, until you are older but remember you saw it signed.'

On 23 November Kate wrote a long, crossed, letter to Mrs Leathley which included the request: '...in the meantime dear Mrs Leathley, get for me a small pot of black currant preserve or jelly for Mrs Tiller to give to poor Mrs Quinnell [mother of the Dunford factotum, who was dying]. It is one of the drinks I am now making for Mr Cobden – who returned back to us on Thursday last so ill that he could not walk up the stairs – he has been confined to his room ever since and we have had one of the first medical men in Paris attending him. He was not well when he left for England and the London fog brought his complaint to a crisis. – congestion of the lungs – accompanied by fever – He is today for the first time decidedly better – but the Dr says he will have for the future have [*sic*] to observe the greatest care as he has a tendency to asthma. I had seen his suffering similarly before but in a very modified way – Mrs Woolley – whose husband died under similar symptoms was greatly alarmed and thought he could not have lived the night through. Thank God he is now out of all danger as far as we poor human beings can know – '

Cobden was well enough by 23 November to write – or perhaps dictate – a report to Palmerston. Next day Chevalier called, and again on 24 November; on 28 November Baron Bunsen called.

On 5 December Cobden received from an anonymous donor a box containing an overcoat lined with fur, accompanied by a letter in French, with homage, fearing the cold of the Parisian winter might harm his precious health. Cobden had no idea of the sender's identity. On his first day out, 8 December, he went for a drive in the Bois. The Journal reports he was feeling better, which was as well for he heard discouraging news on 12 December: the Emperor was less inclined for the Treaty. But two days later he was relieved of this anxiety, Chevalier presented the plan and it was approved by his majesty, and by 21 December Cobden had his next audience with Napoleon III.

From what Kate wrote on 19 December to her new friend Mrs Leathley it seems she had enlisted Kate's help in finding jobs as governesses for two young girls, the Wardroper sisters, whose solicitor father had fallen foul of the law: '...in Paris scarcely any families have governesses residing in their houses. Daily Governesses, and the "Cours" are the modes of education here – but places may be found at schools – and in the country. I suppose the poor girls would be satisfied to begin as Nursery Governesses – with a small salary – however I will try what can be had and then submit the matter to their approval afterwards – But I must know what they can and are willing to do first – I do hope I shall be able to do something for the poor amiable girls.'

Christmas is only a few days away: 'I hope my dear friend you will let Dudley tell them at Walkers when it would be most agreeable for you to have his Turkey killed it ought to be some little time before Christmas day – that it may be a little more tender – ' On Christmas Eve she writes again: 'I think it most kind of you to have written me such a long newsy letter as your last. I have just been reading it out to Mr Cobden, as the contents interested him. I feel it pretty well settled that we are to go South – and therefore I am anxious to have little Elizabeth Clare over to the children. Eliza has been a complete failure with them, but in other respects has conducted herself extremely well and has been a good needlewoman – but as far as the children went they might be logs of wood for all she cared. She is much please [*sic*] with Paris and intends to remain here, after us – I have an excellent situation for her in view – I only hope she will fulfil her duties there satisfactorily – they will be very light – sewing principally.'

Writing many years later Elizabeth Clare described her journey to Paris after Christmas 1859: 'Some months after that my sister Maryann left Mrs Cobden, and then Mrs Cobden whent [*sic*] to Paris with her four daughters, with a maid by the name of Eliza Littlefield and I had to go to my home to my Mother and my brother William. I was very unhappy to loose all my dear friends, dear Miss Nellie always used to write to me. After some time Mrs Cobden wrote for me to go to Paris. I was very pleased to go. So my old wooden box had to be packed and my dear brother William put a strong cord and wrapper on it.

'I left home one morning, by the Omnibus to Chichester. I met some friends of Mrs Cobden at Chichester station their name were Miss Haylers. Then I was to go by train to Brighton, to some friends of Mrs Cobden at Chichester Terrace. Their names were Mr and Mrs Ashburner. I whent with them to Newhaven, they took me to the boat, and put me in charge of the Captain, for Dieppe. I had no passport so I had to have my pockets and basket searched.

'When I got to Paris station it was about 12 o'clock at night. I was to wait until I saw some big doors open. So I did and their [*sic*] was

Eliza Mrs Cobden's maid and french cook, and Madame Schwabe carriage and Pr. of horses. Then my box was examined, and we drove to rue de berry. I think that was the name. dear Miss Nellie had waited up to see me. I think we talked nearly all night. I had left my basket and shawl, and a few shillings I had at the Station. Mrs Woolley very kindly took me to the station the next morning. all my things were safe their.'

At the start of 1860 Cobden, Kate, Katie and Elizabeth Clare were still at Mrs Woolley's, and in spite of Cobden's ill-health the family had plenty of opportunities to enjoy life. Cobden's letter to William Sale of 9 January confirms this: 'The children are all well and have been enjoying themselves this winter. We have had plenty of boxes for theatres given us, as well as other young people – Today they are acting a play, Katie, who has grown as tall as her Mother, is dressed as a housemaid, and she is at this moment dancing with young people in all sorts of disguises. Since I began this note I have been dragged away to take a partner in Roger de Coverley's dance – '

A witness to the Cobdens' life in Paris was Henrietta Corkran, a child at this time, who recalled in *Celebrities and I* Cobden during the Commercial Treaty negotiations: 'I recollect his joining us children in a game of Blind Man's Buff. He caught me so often that I accused him of seeing through the handkerchief tied round his eyes. He answered that as I happened to be the fattest little girl in the room, he managed to find me out. His voice was soft, the expression of his face kindly, his manner most sympathetic. He often spòke to us children, and would listen gravely, seriously and encouragingly to our talk. I was surprised to hear that he was a great politician, he was always so simple and charming. I remember Mr Cobden invited us and many other children, numbering about twenty, to visit the Chateau des Tuileries. He had received an order to inspect the splendid palace. We all mounted inside four fiacres,. When we arrived at the gates, Mr Cobden got out first, and had a talk with a big gardier [*sic*] in a cocked hat, and we had heard him remark – 'Though une famille Anglaise is often a very large one, this number was impossible"; he could not admit more than ten children. I can never forget Mr Cobden's abashed look. He was so sorry for those who could not be admitted. I was amongst the rejected, and to console me for my disappointment he sent me next day a big box of bon-bons' (which could not have helped to reduce her weight!).

Henrietta saw Kate as 'one of the prettiest women I have ever beheld, with beautiful brown eyes and prematurely white hair, which then looked powdered. She was like a pastel, so soft and yet vivid in colouring...'

Cobden was corresponding frequently with Hargreaves at this stage in the Treaty negotiations. On 11 January he writes to him: '...I am budding into official life at my old age' (he was only in his mid-fifties) 'in spite of myself. – Meantime, as I trust no one with any details, in order that secrecy may be kept, I am always at work writing or copying with no one but my wife and Katie to help me. And, odd enough, this is the case with the other side, where the copying is also done by the female members of the family of the *Minister*. However, all this must soon be at an end as everything must be settled one way or another before Parliament meets. The nervous excitement in which I have been kept (sinning as I do against Talleyrand's advice to a young diplomat is in being too much in earnest) by the daily doubt, rumour, and difficulties which have beset me has not been favourable to my health – It is the very state which my doctor told me to avoid and to keep my mind quiet. – I sometimes think it affects the action of my heart...I must again ask you to treat this as a confidential Communication, for I repeat until everything is signed and sealed here nothing is certain. And there are parties who look smilingly on my efforts who would not be altogether distressed if I failed altogether...'

On 13 January Cobden wrote a Private letter to Potter: 'My dear Sir, Since I walked with you on my native Downs, I have been very busy here at my old Manchester agitation, with only this difference that, instead of teaching pupils in large classes, I have been giving private lessons in Political Economy. – whether anything will be done by my imperial pupil remains to be seen – He gave me two audiences of an hour each, and is certainly a good listener...Everything depends on the will of the Emperor...'

On 23 January Cobden wrote to Hargreaves: '...I have today put my hand to the French Treaty which will, I hope and trust, prove the commencement of a new era in relations of France and England. – It has taken more time than I expected, when precisely three months since I had my first interview with the Emperor...I shall leave Paris tomorrow for the South of France for a month. I think of going to Cannes, but I have not yet quite determined. – I have nothing the matter with me but a bronchial affection, and I feel certain that if I could breathe a soft warm air and be quiet for a month I should be well...'

But there was a setback, as the diary for 28 January records: '...It was decided to have the Treaty wholly rewritten and that we should meet next day to sign it again.' On 29 January he can at last record: 'I trust this Treaty is now finally completed, and wants only the formal ratification of the two sovereigns to become the international law of France and England.'

Cobden was still in Paris when he writes to Hargreaves on 1 February: 'I expected to have been in Cannes long ago, but was detained first by Downing Street red tape, some verbal inaccuracies having been discovered in the Treaty, and then by my wife's indisposition in the form of a swollen face. But we hope positively to leave for Lyons tomorrow.' Alas, nothing like 'soft warm air' awaited them.

On 3 February the Cobdens left Paris for Lyons, where Arlès-Dufour, Cobden's silk-merchant friend, met them. Next day, according to Cobden's diary he 'went with Arlès-Dufour to see the industrial school, the *Martinière*...In the afternoon we accompanied Mr and Mrs Arlès-Dufour in a drive up the banks of the Saone which presented some beautiful scenery.' The following day, accompanied by Dufour, they went by train for Marseilles and Toulon.'It was keen frosty weather when we started,' Cobden records, 'and as our course lay south it was pleasant to feel the change of temperature with each degree of latitude we passed over...As we came near to Marseilles about 4 o'clock we found ourselves in a mild temperature and under a clear blue sky, such as we had not enjoyed for some months in Paris. The almond trees were in a few cases out in blossom, and the wild flowers in full bloom...Took another train and went forward to Toulon...On arriving at Toulon walked out on the quays, and found crowds of men of war French sailors, merry with wine, having been on shore on leave, and singing most boisterously in Groups.'

On 11 February Kate was ill again.'My wife is laid up with a terrible cold, and is being kindly nursed by Miss Schnell [old governess of Bright's daughter].' Cobden himself seems to have escaped with an attack of *herpes zoster*, for he writes to Bright: 'I have an eruption on my lip which is trying my temper sadly.'

Bunsen had written to Cobden that they were coming to Cannes on an auspicious day, '*the beginning of Spring*, and had assured them that nature was 'very regular in these parts'. But these hopes were dashed, and the Cobdens were to have bad weather for most of their stay in the south of France. The diary records 'days generally clouded, and the wind keen, with occasional rain. Nights very cold. Mountains covered with snow...The residents of the place shrug their shoulders and make excuses for the weather as something quite exceptional. I am only confirmed in opinion that if we would have a second summer in the twelve months, it cannot be insured in Europe. We must follow the example of the swallow, and migrate to Africa – And why should not those who are delicate in health enjoy equal privileges with the birds? Travelling is now so rapid by railway, that our English express trains, going at 40 miles an hour, will take only about six days to go the distance from the Pole to the Equator. It will therefore be easy to migrate to warm latitudes for the winter months.'

The Cobdens left Cannes on 22 March at 6 in the evening by Mail Coach for Toulon 'where we arrived at 7 in the morning: took the train to Marseilles, and thence proceeded...to Lyons where we slept at the Hotel de l'Univers; and the following morning started for Paris where we arrived the same evening at 7 o'clock and took up our quarters at Meurices' (Hotel Meurice, rue de Rivoli). From there Cobden wrote to William Hargreaves on 26 March telling him: 'We have arrived here from Cannes, and I find to my dismay about 100 letters waiting for me...My wife will remain here with the children, until I know more exactly what my movements will be...We have not been lucky in our weather at Cannes and our lodgings were not very pleasant, being situated in the little town so that we walked out of doors into all the dust of the highroad. – But our next neighbours being Baron Bunsen with his charming colloquial talents and genial character atoned for all. – We are better. – And are at all events consoled with the reflection that we escaped the severe winter which you seem to have had in London.'

Cobden was invited to stay with the Hargreaves in Craven Hill Gardens, and on 30 March tells his friend: 'I am not able at the time of writing to say at what hour the tidal train starts on Monday, *or when it arrives in* London. I shall however leave by it, and have only to beg that you will all take your rest at your usual hour and merely let your servant sit up for me. A cup of very weak tea and a piece of bread and butter are literally all that I shall take before my bed...I saw the Emperor this morning, and as I was taking my leave he asked me to accept a vase as a souvenir – I gave him your address, where I suppose something, I know not what, will be delivered. I hope it will be of little value – (My wife says *she* hopes quite the contrary!) – Whatever it is, I suppose I shall lose my character, and be charged with accepting a bribe. – However, it would have been churlish to have refused a piece of porcelain because it was offered by an Emperor...'

Louis Napoleon lost no time in dispatching his gift, for Cobden told Kate on 6 April: '...The vase has arrived, and is placed in Hargreaves drawing room. It is a huge cup of the shape of a vast goblet – with a stand of figures – not like anything I have seen. – I suppose it should have flowers in it. – Mrs Hargreaves values it at 200 guineas – Say nothing about it!'

In the same letter he tells Kate he is to be Chief Commissioner when it comes to arranging the details of the Commercial Treaty: '...reverting to Minister Plenipotentiary when signing the new treaty with Lord Cowley, as I had done the old one...It will involve a good deal of labor and much time – But I would not allow the matter to go out of my power. This will I suppose necessitate my being in Paris for at least a month or two, and I expect I shall have to return in ten days at the outside.'

Extracts from Cobden's diary, 1860:

Apr. 9.'Went in the morning by train to Petworth, and thence by carriage to Dunford, where I remained for a couple of days. Met Mr Brooks the house agent and arranged to resume possession of my house and release Colonel Holden the tenant from further responsibility, he paying £55. – Ordered from Mr Chorley a hot-water apparatus for heating the house to be completed by the end of May. Settled farming accounts with Mr Lunn and received from him a check for £150.'

On 12 April he went to Chichester to take luncheon with his relations, the Watkins, then to Brighton to stay at the Ashburners. He was up in London on the 13, 14 and 17 attending meetings at the Board of Trade.

Apr. 19 'Attended a meeting of the Committee of the Illinois Central Railway Company, at which it was agreed to dissolve the Committee. – Left London for Folkestone in the afternoon. – The railway company, by way of offering me a compliment, set apart a carriage exclusively to myself, and I was thus made a solitary prisoner during the whole journey much against my wish.'

After a night at the Pavilion Hotel at Folkestone he crossed to Boulogne. Apr. 20: '...Sick as usual. At the *Hotel des Bains* where I dined, whilst waiting for a train to Paris, I fell into conversation with a traveller in the Coffee room upon the subject of the recent prize fight between the English and American champions. – On the fact being mentioned that a subscription was being entered into for Sayers the English champion my companion remarked ' I can't see any sense in that, any more than in the subscription which it is proposed to raise for Cobden, merely because he has lost the money which was subscribed for him before.' – reached Paris at 11 p.m.'

There are few references to any private life in the diary at this busy time, until 9 May when there was a ball.'...Then to the ball at the Countess de Morny's where the numbers of handsome toilettes were more striking than the beauty of their wearers. M. de Lesseps in speaking of his project for the Suez canal says that 40 million francs are paid up, that he has upwards of 50,000 shareholders, that there are 800 Europeans at work on the undertaking, with an immense body of natives. He remarked that the opposition of the English government to his project had given it great popularity on the Continent.' On 10 May he had his first sitting with M. L'Aime, a sculptor, 'who took the bust of M. Michel Chevalier'. On 30 May 'Went with my children to see the performance at the Cirque, where there were some clever feats of horsemanship'.

14 June: 'Today a fête day at Paris – a holiday, a review, flags and illuminations. – The Emperor was well received by the populace on his way from the railroad to the Tuileries, and in going and coming to the Champs de Mars where he passed in review upwards of 50,000 troops and national guards.' Two days later he complains: 'The weather very boisterous wet and cold – I was glad to have a fire lighted in the *salon*.' On 22 June he records that he had met a party of eminent medical practitioners at dinner 'whom I endeavoured to enlist in opposition to the cruel practice of *vivisection* at the veterinary colleges of France. – But I am afraid I did not meet with much success.' By 1 July 'The weather was so chilly today that a greatcoat was quite agreeable.' On 3 July he 'Witnessed the funeral cortege of Prince Jerome, the last member of the family of the first Napoleon of whom he was the youngest brother. – The procession consisting chiefly of soldiers and national guards was nearly two hours passing the place where I stood, on the balcony of the Ministry of Finance. – There is nothing to me so wearisome and monotonous than a stream of troops carrying their muskets all in the same position. – Prince Napoleon the only surviving son of Jerome was the chief mourner. All the ministers of State were in the procession; and everybody including the archbishop and the chief mourner *walked* after the corpse – all excepting the cavalry – This is I think a more earnest mode of offering respect for the dead than following the corpse in carriages.'

On 12 July he records that he 'Wrote to Lord Palmerston to suggest that the rumoured intention of the government to propose a large addition to the expenditure for fortifications ought not to be carried out until at least after the terms of the Treaty were settled and published so that the public might know exactly what were the prospects of an extended commerce between the two countries.'

On 18 July he records that 'My wife and the three youngest children left Paris via Dieppe and Newhaven for Dunford.' Two days later he dined with 'M. Chevalier in company with Mr Lionel Lawson of the London *Telegraph* newspaper, – and afterwards went to the *Theatre Francais* where the acting and elocution were good but the performance too long.'

At 69 Champs Elysées Kate had been once again responsible for finding – and keeping – her own domestic staff. She complains to daughter Jane on 1 November 1860: '...On my return from you I did not take Sophy back – but the cook who followed was so cross that she made all the other servants constantly cry – and one day I was called out of the dining room and in the hall I found Marie from Mrs Woolley standing trembling and bathed in tears – the old cook had so frightened her when she passed through the kitchen. I then went and told the cook she must leave at once as I could not have my house disgraced by a person like her who could in no way control her passions. She was away in the course of an hour. And now I have a very quiet peacible [*sic*] woman but perhaps not so good a cook – I herewith enclose the key of the box which I shall send off tomorrow – I hope it will arrive safely – It has nothing in it but some winter clothing – My fond love to you and your sister and I am ever your affectionate and fond Mother C.A. Cobden.'

But the 'peacible woman' was not required for long: a fortnight later, on 14 November, Cobden tells Bright: 'We have given up our lodgings at 69 Champs Elysees and gone to an hotel in order to afford my wife a little leisure to wind up before we leave.'

The offices of the Commission were closed on 24 November, and on that day Bright came over to Paris, where he and Cobden had an audience with the Emperor on 27 November. Cobden admitted to Hargreaves: 'When I began last winter as a volunteer in the corps of diplomacy, I little dreamed what a year's work I was preparing for myself. Certainly mine has not been an idle life, but I never had so tough a task in hand as that which I have just finished. And much as my heart was in the work, I feel intensely satisfied that it is at an end. Nor do I think, if I must confess so much, that I could again go through the ordeal. It would not be easy to explain to you what it has been, but if I should again have the pleasure of toasting my knees by your fire, I could explain it in a few sittings.'

CHAPTER THIRTEEN

Second Honeymoon

On 9 December 1860 began what was to prove the Cobdens' second honeymoon. With their eldest daughter Katie they left Paris for a holiday in Algeria. Cobden dreaded the effects on his voice of a winter in the cold and fogs of London, and was anxious to escape to the milder climate of North Africa. Heat was essential, for he had been warned by Sir James Clark against the danger of public speaking if he were not to impair his vocal chords for ever. So, the treaty negotiations successfully concluded, in spite of invitations to meetings and banquets in his honour, he decided on a long break. He had been advised to stay away from England until after Easter, and as he felt there was nothing in the parliamentary programme to tempt him to return to the House, he agreed. The holiday was a successful one, and was to have one result which could hardly have been anticipated at the time.

At first the weather was against them, and they could not find a suitable house in Algiers, as Kate told Jane in her letter of 17 December: 'I cannot write you as long a letter as I could wish as we are still in an unsettled state. With our boxes unpacked and without any of our little conveniences about us. There are not many apartments to choose from, and we are late in the Season – so we find the best taken. So we are now just in a state of indessission [*sic*] whether to remain here or try our luck elsewhere.' It seems that although Thomas Cook had been in operation since 1841 it was not yet the custom for English travellers to use his expanding organisation to book in advance for accommodation abroad.'We have had very heavy rains the last two nights and today it has rained all day – I earnestly hope for your dear Papa's sake we shall soon have a change – or the benefit expected for his health will not be achieved – If the little dog be still with you – I hope he is cared for, and that he is by this time quite well – If not you must get Mrs Tiller to boil a sheep's head for him. When you go to London I hope you will make provision for all your pets to be well cared for. You must let me know how poor old Alie is in your next I thought the old man looked very ill and quite out of spirits when I was at home. I think he works too much in the wet. – I hope the pretty stools you and Julia [Anne] worked for me are well covered up and not much used, as I prize them very much – Give my kind love to Miss Hagemann [German governess]...My affectionate embraces to Nelly and Julia – And believe me my darling Jane your fond and attached Mother – C.A. Cobden.'

The Cobdens soon found an alternative to the Hotel d'Europe in the Maison Chauve. This house in Akha became their headquarters for much of their stay in North Africa, and on this, their last holiday abroad, Cobden and Kate at last found the sun and warmth that had eluded them in Cannes the previous winter, but while Cobden was obviously able to relax Kate did not discard her role of anxious mother, and on 8 January she wrote to Jane: 'I am now becoming very anxious to hear from some of you – I address this to Mrs Dimmock that she may give the piece of newspaper to her husband [the Dunford gardener] that he may see from the numerous accidents which occur how necessary it is to be watchful over the kitchen boilers...'

Again to Jane, from the Maison Chauve on 12 February: 'My sweet Janie, I was very grieved to hear of your being poorly and very anxious about you till Miss Hagemann's letter came this morning to tell me you were getting quite well again. I have no doubt you have been made very happy between Miss Hagemann's kind attentions and Elizabeth's [Clare] kind attendance upon you. And then I daresay, good Mrs Tiller took care that you had proper and good things for your cold to eat whilst you were so poorly. It is the greatest comfort to me to know you have such kind people about you...you must take care to keep yourselves warm with clothing and fires when necessary – '

By 21 February Cobden was able to tell Bright: '...I am every day stronger; and my mind is so much improved that whereas on my arrival I could hardly mount a three pair of stairs, I can now climb the Arab paths which ascend behind the City and walk at a stretch over the hills above the Fort of the Emperor, and down to the sea on the other side.' On 25 February he writes to Nelly, who was staying with the Ashburners: '...your mamma is so good a correspondent that she hardly gives me a chance of sending you a piece of news. The other night we were disturbed with jackals and hyenas; and I said to myself here is a nice subject for a page in my next letter to Nelly; and I thought how your imagination would be excited, until you would picture us in the centre of the Desert of Saharah, [*sic*] in the midst of lions and panthers – but the next day I found your Mamma very busy writing to you all about it...Katie takes long rides on horseback nearly every day. There is a terrace facing South East on which we pass much of our time. There is a table covered with newspapers and chairs; we receive our friends there, so that it is both newsroom and drawing-room. The view from this terrace is very beautiful. The foreground is covered with Moorish houses, all white, interspersed with gardens. Beyond is the plain of the Mitdje; bounded by the rugged mountains of Kabylia; and in the remote distance nearly 100 miles away rises the Atlas range covered with snow. On the right the scene is shut in by the hill which rises behind Algiers – Altogether it is a beautiful specimen of Swiss like scenery. Your Mamma has sent by a private hand some little pictures of native costumes.'

On 11 March they were invited to a boar hunt to be provided by an Arab Chief near l'Arbah, some twenty miles from Algiers. Cobden reported this in his letter to Jane on 14 March: 'My dearest Janie You must not think that I was not pleased with your present of a wiper for my rasor [*sic*]. I should have been pleased with anything, even the leaf of a flower, which showed that you were thinking of me, and which proved that you loved me. But your present is so very pretty that I ought to have thanked you for it long ago. Indeed it is so pretty that I do not like to spoil it by wiping my rasors upon it; and so I keep it to admire for my dear Janie's sake. I hope we shall soon return home. We are all very anxious to see you and dear baby, and Nelly. You will hardly know Katey again she is grown so much taller than when you saw her last. She rides almost every day on horseback. Last week she rode 20 miles, nearly twice as far as from Dunford to Chichester to see a boar hunt. We saw two wild boars after they were killed. Your Mamma and I went in a carriage. We were invited to dine under a beautiful tent in the open country by the Chief of the Arabs. We saw two sheep being roasted for us in the open air. They had their horns on. We were surrounded by hundreds of Arabs, a great many of them on fine horses, and your Mamma was half afraid that they would carry us off into the mountains or the desert. But they were very polite. The great chief who entertained us in the tent examined all the dishes before they were put before us, like a head cook, to see that everything was properly cooked...Remember me to Miss Hagemann very kindly.' This German governess seems to have been exceptionally well liked by all the Cobdens, and she and Kate became friends after she left their service.

The tone of all Cobden's letters was not always cheerful and positive at this time. He had obviously found leisure to take a look inwards at his prospects for the future: 'The truth must be told,' he wrote to his old friend Ashworth, 'though one does not like publicly to shelve oneself – my work is nearly done. I am nearly fifty-seven and not, like you, of a long-lived family. Since I passed my meridian a few years ago, I have found my powers sensibly waning and particularly those organs of the voice which I exercised so rudely whilst in their prime, and which were naturally but a weak inheritance from my father. If, however, I could pass the remainder of my days with only the labour of an average person of my years, I could, I dare say, nurse myself into a good old age. The question is whether I ought to content myself with a briefer span and the satisfaction of trying to do something a little beyond my strength? It is a nice question for casuists, for the home duties affecting one's young children intrude.'

But if Cobden felt himself to be on the shelf this was not the opinion of Prime Minister Palmerston.

After ten days 'upon the plain of the Mitidje' the party returned to Algiers and the Hotel d'Europe on 10 April. Awaiting Cobden was a letter from the Prime Minister:

'My dear Mr Cobden, – The Queen being desirous of marking the sense she entertains of the public service rendered during the long and laborious negotiations in which you were engaged on the subject of the Commercial Treaty with France, her Majesty has authorized me to offer you either to be created a Baronet, or to be made a Privy Councillor, whichever of the two would be most agreeable to you. – I am aware that you might not perhaps attach any great intrinsic value to distinctions of this kind, but as an acknowledgment of public services they would not fail to be appreciated...'

Cobden declined both offers on 13 April: 'My dear Lord Palmerston. I beg to acknowledge the receipt of your letter of the 26th March, which reached me yesterday only, on my return after an absence of ten days from Algiers. Whilst entertaining the same sentiments of gratitude towards the Queen which I could have felt if I had accepted the offer you have been so good as to make in her name, I must beg permission most respectfully to deny myself the honour which Her Majesty has graciously proposed to confer on me – An indisposition to accept a title being in my case rather an affair of feeling than of reason I will not dwell farther on the subject. With respect however to the particular occasion for which it is proposed to confer on me the distinction I may say that it would not be agreeable to me to accept a recompense in any form for my recent labours in Paris. The only reward I desire is to live to witness an improvement in the relations of the two great neighbouring nations which have been brought into more intimate connection by the Treaty of Commerce. I remain my dear Lord

Palmerston, Yours sincerely Richard Cobden.'

'The time is now passing very fast indeed for our return home,' Kate had written to Jane on 12 April.'In fact we count the days for our departure from Algiers. Papa has had an invitation to stop with a gentleman in France before we go to Paris so that visit will delay a little our return...' It was to be several weeks before she was reunited with her children in England.

They left Paris on 16 May, travelling in a carriage provided *gratis* by the directors of the French railways, for Dieppe. An official welcome had been planned at Dover, but Cobden landed at Newhaven. When Kate got to Dunford on 18 May she had a new and very personal pre-occupation: after nine years, and at the age of 46, she was once again expecting a child.

Cobden stayed with the Hargreaves at 34 Craven Hill Gardens on returning to England, and it was from there that he wrote to Kate on 28 May, 1861: 'My dearest Kate I was in the House last night for the first time and had an infinite shaking of hands with all sides – The debate was a wearisome one and lasted till past midnight. – I did not get home till ½ p 1., and this morning I found myself with a headache, and my neck feeling the effects.' And then he tells her something which, in her condition, must have alarmed her greatly: 'I doubt whether my parliamentary life will be prolonged many years, – I find myself less and less equal to it. – And I really see nothing at issue between the two contending political factions which is worth the sacrifice of my life or the loss of my health – '

In the same letter he tells her: 'Yesterday our friend Moffatt carried me off unexpectedly to dine with him, and I found the lady in great dismay when I arrived as she had only cold lamb and salad...Joe Parkes who visited them at their beautiful house in the country, where they have a park and pleasure grounds with 6 or 8 gardeners, says he was nearly starved.'

Cobden had evidently informed Sir James Clark about Kate's pregnancy, for Clark, who was with the Queen at Balmoral, had replied on 5 September: 'I am not much surprised at the expected appearance of an increase in your family, as I have known more than one instance of children appearing for the *first* time after 21 years of marriage! I hope every thing may go well and that it may be a boy. Mrs Cobden should be kept very quiet during her confinement...'

In the matter of where the baby was to be born Kate bowed to Cobden's wish that she should be confined at home at Dunford. She confides her doubts about this to Mrs Leathley from Dunford on 9 September: 'I should have followed out Mr Young's suggestion and have taken the apartment opposite his house. My inclination in favor [*sic*] of such an arrangement has given way to my husband's desire, that the event should take place here. And the great pleasure of having all my dear children around me, during my illness, reconciles me very much to the sacrifice.' Following the example of Queen Victoria it was now acceptable for women to have chloroform during labour, and Kate adds: 'I have arranged to have second advice from Chichester and chloriform [*sic*] if necessary.'

Cobden writes to Henry Ashworth on 16 September and tells him Kate 'is as active as is advisable under the circumstances and I hope all will be well within a few weeks.' But it seems Kate was 'out' in her dates and the child was not born until 5 November.

Kate gave birth for the eighth time within two months of her forty-sixth birthday. The child, another daughter, was named Lucy Elizabeth Margaret, but was known to her family as Maggie in the thirty years of her life. This was Kate's final confinement. The first name, Lucy, was no doubt intended as a compliment to George Moffatt's wife, who became her Godmother.

On 6 November Cobden was able to report to Thomas Potter: 'I was last night relieved from much anxiety by the birth of a daughter. – Some persons will say it ought to have been a boy. – But owing to the unusual delay of 3 days after the usual premonitory symptoms I was so anxious about the fate of the mother that I have not concerned myself about the sex of the child. Both are doing well.' To the Hargreaves he wrote: '...When I looked at my little girl and thought of the danger overhanging the mother it put all other thoughts but the interest in her life aside...Some persons will wish it had been a boy, but I am satisfied...'

With Kate nursing a new baby at Dunford there was no possibility of foreign travel for the Cobdens that winter of 1861–2, so instead of seeking lodgings in London for the Session when it opened, Cobden accepted the invitation of William and Martha Paulton to make his headquarters in Cleveland Square.

He told Bright on 23 January: 'I have been living for two or three months as I have not lived before for 25 years – seeing nobody but my family and then only for meals, and then living apart up stairs in a room facing the South and only going out in the middle of the day when it is fine. The consequence is that I hardly talk as much in a week as I often did in a day, and I am perfectly well, – I have no cough, or asthma, and the stiffness in the neck is completely gone. How I shall stand night work is another question...'

Maggie was growing fast, and Kate seemingly blooming once more by now. Cobden told Moffatt on 26 January: '...My wife is looking younger than ever and the baby is such a Brobdignag that her socks are an inch longer than those of any children of her age. What more could I say?'

Installed at Cleveland Square Cobden writes to Kate on 8 February: 'I went down to the House of Commons the first day, and found the same unpleasant symptoms again in my head. It is very strange that nobody else seems to be affected as I am by the air of that place. I shall not go often if I find the same symptoms continue...Mrs Schwabe is going to Florence to live for 3 years to retrench...'

'I fear dear friend', Martha Paulton writes to Kate that month, 'that Mr Cobden won't be induced to try a Respirator – he thinks a handkerchief better. William has long since given his up, thinking it injurious, and puts his cloak up (when the air is too sharp)...Mr Cobden was quite hoarse the first day he came – he said with talking in the railway with someone he met...the first mild morning seemed to relieve him immediately...as he is careful – comes home to tea if out in the afternoon, I trust he will not suffer very much during the remnant of the winter...I'm so glad Baby has weaned herself so nicely and saved you all the worry of the usual process – depend upon it you have had quite sufficient drain and will be stronger now without her – does she sleep with you still or beside you in a cot or with Elizabeth? and how are your spirits? Is it still as difficult to be cheerful and to banish the one absorbing regret or has the new tie and the necessity of attending to it helped a little *onward*? You are too nervous and anxious my dear friend – if you *could* but *drift*, as easygoing people do, and let the future take care of itself (making the best of the present and taking care of number one)! I heard...Paulton say 20,000 were settled on you and the children, but you have been worried and anxious so long that the habit is formed...'

On 27 March Cobden writes to Kate: 'My dearest Kate I am very sorry as we all are to hear of your bad cold. There is but one remedy I think – to take to bed and get into a strong perspiration...Katy [who was also at the Paultons] is going tonight to hear Dickens, and seems in high spirits about it – '

He wrote to Tom Potter on 15 May on Athenaeum paper: 'My wife and Katie are settling in Blandford Square where I expect to join them in a few days. On 8 June he writes Kate from Dunford, where he was finding it difficult to get to know his latest daughter: 'I found baby looking pale yesterday – She has been troubled with her teeth. she did not know me and was a little frightened at first. – And when I tried to kiss her she turned away and looked quite puzzled – she made wry faces as I looked at her, very much as if she had been eating mustard. – when I whistled and snapped my fingers she turned inquiringly to Clare as much as to say – 'do I know him?' But when I tried to take her in my arms she cried and again made her mustard faces. So we parted last night. – Today she is looking brighter and her cheeks have a little colour. – we have got on better together. When I took her on my knee and began to jump her she seemed to recognise an old friend, and she began to laugh and crow, and we have been allies ever since.' Two days later he tells Kate: 'Baby and I do not get on so well as I could wish. It is clear that her teeth keep her in such a state of discomfort as to make my rough nursing rather too much for her. But she has ceased to pull faces at me. She is a fine child.'

Tom Potter had invited the Cobdens and Katie to Scotland, but as late as 7 August when he wrote to Bright about the project, Kate, who complained that Cobden never made up his mind to a journey until the last moment, was still on tenterhooks: 'My wife and I,' he tells Bright, 'are all but decided to go to the Highlands. If so, we shall take Lancashire on our return...I have never seen the classical scenery of the Highlands – was never on the Caledonian Canal, or Loch Catrine, or at the Trossachs.' That day he also wrote to Hargreaves: 'I feel that the air of the Highlands would be good medicine for me, and I should like to set my mind free from politics for a time, which nothing but new scenes and associations will do...'

But before going North there was Maggie's christening to be planned. Unlike her older sisters Maggie was christened within a year of her birth, and as in 1859 when he baptised the second, third and fourth girls, the Rev. Caleb Collins performed the ceremony at the local church. Moffatt had agreed to be Godfather, and had obviously marked the occasion by a generous present, for writing to him after the event on 19 August, when he and Kate were about to set off on their holiday, Cobden says to his friend: 'I have seen from my wife's letter from you what elegant and substantial forms your and Mrs Moffatt's kindness to your little God-daughter is assuming.'

Lucy Moffatt gave birth to a daughter while the Cobdens were in Scotland, and on 9 September Cobden wrote to congratulate his friend: 'My dear Moffatt My wife and I are delighted that your anxiety on Mrs Moffatt's account is at an end. I don't sympathise with you at not having another son born to you – In cases where an ample fortune is insured to them, and where they are sure to be brought up under good training and example, girls have a better prospect of being more happy – because they are more virtuous – than our own sex. It is a relic of barbarism, or at least of feudalism, in our nature, that we are disposed to undervalue, and even apologise for, the birth of girls...My wife begs to be most kindly remembered with many affectionate expressions to Mrs Moffatt. She abstains for the present from troubling her with written communications...I forget politics and Palmerstone [*sic*] in this grand scenery.'

After six weeks in Scotland Cobden wrote to Nelly at her new school – Miss Jeafferson's in Sussex Square, Brighton: '...I hope God will spare me life and health to accompany you to see the beautiful scenes in Scotland after you have finished your education. Your dear Mamma and I have often talked of you when we were looking at the old castles and celebrated places for which this country is so famous, because we knew how much you would have been interested to see them. But my dear Nelly you must not resign yourself to a too implicit belief in all the guides and guide books tell us about the old ruins and castles of this romantic land. For instance, when we were at *Glamis* Castle the housekeeper showed us the bed in which Duncan was murdered by Lady Macbeth. Now I hope for the honor of the female nature that there never was such a human monster as Madam Macbeth. But certainly there is no historical proof that she ever received the King of Scotland as her guest at Glamis, and as for the bed in question, I am sure it was made at least five hundred years after the death of Duncan. But notwithstanding there is much that is told by housekeepers and guides about these famous places which we must not swallow too greedily, yet is a very pleasant excitement of the imagination to visit the spots renowned in history and romance, or associated with the works of men of genius – it lifts us out of the daily routine and drudgery of real life into something which we can at least dream about as being of a more romantic and heroic character. This is I know only a dream, for the world was certainly not more truthful, or courageous, or virtuous in former times than it is now. On the contrary, the world grows better as it grows older. If it were not so it would not be permitted by God to continue to exist at all.

'Talking of the pleasure of seeing the places renowned in history reminds me how very odd it seems when we are passing along a railway to read the names of the Stations when they are places that we had only heard of before in the writings of Shakespeare or

Scott, such as Glamis, Cawdor, Melrose, and Bannockburn. There is something droll in the contrast between the railroad and these scenes of ancient and romantic incidents.' At the start the letter is carefully and clearly written, but there are signs that it was finished in a hurry after a visit to Scott's grave at Abbotsford.'Your Mamma will send you a book containing a description of Melrose and Dryburgh abbey. Tomorrow we go to Manchester.'

In spite of the 'open air and sunshine' which he told Bright in one of his letters during the holiday 'are I believe allowed by all medical men to be the one medicine of which we cannot take too strong a dose', both Cobden and Kate were soon complaining of colds. Kate, writing to daughter Jane from Rochdale on 29 October tells her: 'I am writing this in my bedroom where I have spent most of the day with a bad cold which has rendered me unable to go with Katie to the meeting tonight to hear your dear Papa speak. – tomorrow we shall spend in visiting some of the industrial schools for the Factory girls out of work and in calling upon friends. And on Friday we shall return to Broughton for a day...'

From Manchester on 21 November Cobden complains to Hargreaves: '...I have caught a cold, with my old affection of the throat, and feel the absolute necessity of getting home again to be quiet.' So much for the hoped-for effect of Highland air on the Cobdens.

The Scottish holiday was to be the last they took together.

CHAPTER FOURTEEN

The days shorten

'I am alone here, all my family being in Town,' Cobden told Hargreaves from Dunford on 19 January 1863.'...Kate and four of the children are in Town, where they have been for a week consulting dentists, visiting friends, and seeing pantomimes. I expect them home on Saturday...Katie and I are going on Thursday to pay a long deferred visit of a few days to Sir Joshua Walmsley at Wolverton Park nr Basingstoke.' 'Domestic tethers,' he wrote, prevented Kate from going.

In April Kate was with Cobden at their Victoria Street flat when the current Dunford governess, Miss Amos, reported to her on 22 April that Mr Ingram had been to vaccinate the inmates: 'All have been vaccinated, and the children were agreeably surprised as to the pain vaccination causes. Poor Lizzie [Elizabeth Clare] would have fainted if Mr. Ingram had not taken her into her garden, and applied water to her face. The children had serious intentions of having their dogs vaccinated yesterday, as Mr Ingram told them it prevented them having the distemper.' But it seems Mr Ingram had not enough vaccine. Miss Amos was about to leave, creating another recurring problem for Kate. Her confidant, Alice Hargreaves wrote her from Ripley on 25 August: 'I am truly sorry to hear of all your cares and troubles – You looked ill when I saw you in London – I fear you will be quite knocked up – How I wish you could hear of a really trustworthy Governess. – I do not see how you can leave your children for the winter unless you can place them in Safe keeping. – there is a Mr. Hatchard, a bookseller in Piccadilly, whose partner, I forget his name, interests himself very much in procuring good situations for Governesses – '

Another subject very much on her mother's mind at this time was Katie's wish to marry Richard Fisher, son of their neighbour at Hill Top, Midhurst. The Hargreaves had heard the rumour of an engagement, although certain members of the family in Manchester had not. Mrs Hargreaves, in the same letter, is frank about Katie's choice: '...I can fancy that Mr. Cobden had hoped that Katie would marry some distinguished man, and in his position it is no wonder...Still I am sure he will be reconciled to see the child happy in her own way...we cannot choose for our children and in this case there seems so much to be pleased and contented with. I fully sympathise with your anxiety in this matter dearest friend. Is the gentleman of liberal views in political matters? No doubt it would be much more agreeable to Mr. Cobden if he were, I am afraid my Husband would rebel against a Tory son in law. I will hold your confidence sacred until you give me leave to break it...'

It was not until 6 October that Cobden wrote to his sister, Priscilla Sale, and to Thomas Potter the following day, about the full facts of Katie's engagement.'If there had been the prospect of an early marriage of our dear Katie, we should not have left you and Mrs Potter to learn the news indirectly...*Personally,* I may say that the suitor for dear Katie's hand is all that I could wish.' He tells Hargreaves on 3 November: 'There is a long time to wait.' Cobden admits to a friend that he would have liked Katie to live in Lancashire.

Cobden was in autumnal mood as 1863 drew to its end, and writing to Henry Ashworth about his monotonous life at Dunford he tells him 'It suits me as a variety and a relief from the wear and tear of London politics. It suits my vocal organs especially to be free from the temptation of much talking. But there is one terrible feature in this life. Time gallops away and seems to leave no landmarks behind. When Sunday returns it seems only like a day instead of a week. It is only when crowded with incidents that the retrospect of existence is satisfactory. Otherwise I am not afflicted with ennui, or troubled for want of mental occupation.'

Things on the educational front were seemingly too unsettled for Kate to consider going abroad that winter, but Nelly's diary, which she called her 'Memoranda', shows they had a merry time at New Year, with the annual party for the village children. On New Year's Day 1864 they were: 'All very busy cutting up cake and sandwiches and decorating the laundry – the crown was put up in the farther laundry' (made by Dick Fisher, by now an accepted member of the group).'A most gorgeous production,' Nelly proclaimed it, 'and the Welcome opposite the door – two flags were put in each corner of the room – a huge clump of evergreens were on the walls, and the whole effect was very pretty – the children came at about 3 o'clock, they had soup and played games – Dick showed them a magic lantern, which charmed them immensely, poor little things. They then had tea, and went away at about 8 o'clock, cheering and shouting nearly all the way home – there were upwards of 80. Three of the Collins were here to tea for which we all had good appetites as none of us had had time for dinner.'

There were the now customary visits to London for Kate and the older girls, and in March she and Cobden went together to the Paultons, from where she wrote to Mrs Leathley on 8 March: 'I and Mr. Cobden have just arrived here from Dunford. I could be ill spared from there, but I felt it impossible to allow Mr. Cobden to go away alone from home in the present state of his health. He requires watching of a night which no one can do so well as myself – Unfortunately I have a bad cold myself – and most provoking – I keep barking every moment at a friend's house...On the 18th Inst Nelly is starting for Paris and thence to the North of Italy with our friends the Potters...' She continues the next day: 'Wednesday morning. Mr. Cobden had a very bad night after being in the House of Commons last evening – a bad beginning for us...'

Nelly's continental tour lasted until July, and meanwhile her parents had returned to Victoria Street.'My throat has not given me much trouble lately,' her father told her, 'I avoid going to dinner parties, and do not stay late at the House in the Evening. Now that the weather is mild I find no inconvenience, and shall be able to take my part in the House as usual if there should be any thing worth attending to. You ask me if I saw Garibaldi. I called in the morning at Mr. Seely's and had a little conversation with him. He said to me "I am altogether for your principles; I am for peace and though a soldier, and therefore obliged to fight, yet I fight only for peace." I am afraid this is the excuse of all fighters...' and goes on to give her – and the Potters – a vivid account of the Italian patriot's visit to London.

Cobden was with the Moffatts at St Leonard's Hill, Windsor, when he wrote to Bright on 26 October. It is clear that he is having qualms about making his annual speech to his constituents at Rochdale the following month: '...I have symptoms of the old sort in my respiratory organs, caused by the lowering temperature of the weather, and it will be my safest course to get through my work in one day. Were I to attempt two meetings I might not be equal to the second. As I can only speak to a large meeting for about an hour, I will rely on your making a good speech.'

When on 30 October he writes again to Bright, one senses a feeling almost of panic: '...I see a letter in the *Rochdale Observer* suggesting a banquet as well as a meeting. If you have the opportunity I wish you would discourage this through your friends.' On 9 November he tells Bright that he does not wish an out of doors non-electors demonstration on his arrival, and tells him that he has written to the Rochdale Reform Association 'to deprecate this on the score of my health'.

By a cruel coincidence, Bright's six year old son died at this moment of scarlet fever. On 10 November Cobden writes his condolences: 'What an awful mystery is the death of the young! My wife and I know all that you and Mrs Bright are suffering-...How insignificant do the affairs about which we trouble ourselves become in the presence of such a calamity as this. My wife begs her kindest love to Mrs Bright.' On 19 November he tells his old friend: 'I am glad you have gone to Leamington for a change. Change of scene is wise under the circumstances. But *retirement and seclusion are not good*. With my sad experience, I often think that if I had carried my wife to London and Paris, *to have lived in the streets as much as possible*, for some months after our great blow it would have been better than the course I took in going with her to Wales.'

Undeterred by this setback Cobden travelled to Rochdale on 23 November. When he wrote to Kate after the meeting he told her that never again would he address a meeting later than September: 'I have been much affected in my breathing,' he told her, 'and have a cold. This climate of Lancashire is enough to kill anybody, except those who have native constitutions.'

Cobden's last speech to his constituents took him more than two hours to deliver and was reported in close on seven newspaper columns the following day. Instead of being able to rest and recover from his efforts, there was 'a reception of two hundred of the leading Liberals' the next day, when, as he later told William Paulton, 'I spent the whole evening in shaking hands and incessant talking to relays of friends.'

When this ordeal was over Cobden headed straight for Dunford, without spending a night with friends in London as he might well have done: he was afraid that if he did he would be too ill to complete the last lap of the journey. He took at once to his bed on reaching home and it was not until 14 December that he was able to write to thank Bright for kind enquiries: 'I am to-day for the first time out of my bed-room since I got back from Lancashire and though weakened by blistering and doctoring I am very much better. It was imprudent in me to go at so late a period. My constituents are not to blame. I had not realised as I now do that I am not equal at 60 to do the work which I could master at 40. I was completely upset in every way from top to toe. In addition to a recurrence of my besetting and capricious affection of "nervous asthma", I had a most violent cold and a disordered stomach. Thanks to kind nursing and a very experienced and attentive doctor the bronchial attack was arrested before it invaded the lungs, and now I want nothing but care and time to put me to rights. A fortnight's July weather would be the true remedy, but that is beyond the power of parliament.'

Elizabeth Clare remembers that last winter of Cobden's life: 'he used to be in his bedroom a good deal. He had Broncitis [*sic*]. Mrs Cobden used to keep his bedroom fire up all night. she used to have in her room, small pieces of wood and coal to light it, in case it whent out. I waited on Mr. and Mrs Cobden for their breakfast at that time To go downstairs for any thing they wanted. and take the letter bag up to them. The little bullfinch used to fly abut their bedroom. Mr. Cobden used to put his finger up, and the little bird used to settle on it, and then fly across the room, and back again.'

Life for Kate must have been claustrophobic that winter, with Cobden housebound after what he described to Paulton as his 'shake'. Katie was happy enough in the companionship of 'young Fisher', and Kate arranged for seventeen year old Nelly to go and stay with their friends the Scrivens in Hastings, where she could be with girls of her own age and have 'a little gaiety'. On 7 February Kate told Mrs Leathley: 'You, like many more of our friends have had no idea how ill he has been I am sure – The first fortnight in December or rather the end of November and the beginning of December he was confined to his bed without being able to speak or move scarcely – and it is only within the last three weeks that he has been able to spend his days in an adjoining room to his bedroom. [This was the old schoolroom.] Now, on fine days, he joins our family meals downstairs. I have been his nurse night and day and have only been out of doors as far as Midhurst about three times since he has been taken ill.'

As Priscilla McLaren wrote to Kate: '...That Rochdale meeting was a great success, tho' I fear too dearly purchased.'

CHAPTER FIFTEEN

'Sunless winter'

Not surprisingly, Cobden was in sombre mood during what he called that 'sunless winter' of 1865. He told Bright on 22 January he would not be in London at the opening of the Session: 'Although much better I have not yet been out of doors. I lie in bed till 10 or 11, and am useless when I get up.' His letters to Bright and Chevalier are full of his feeling the effects of age, and on 1 February he told Parkes that 'old people require no winter – it is in their bones.' But he had not altogether despaired of recovery, and by 6 February he was telling Bright he hoped to be in town soon, when he would 'take an opportunity of consulting a London doctor eminent in throat cases. Our country apothecaries are very good nurses and little more. The drawback in the case of the London physicians in great practice is what you never feel that you have their whole minds owing to the multitude of cases dividing their attention...' On 11 February the devoted Nelly writes in her diary that a visitor to Dunford 'thought Papa altered'.

By St Valentine's Day Kate had escaped to London with Nelly. Cobden wrote to her there that day, assuring her of his well-being: 'Do not hurry home on my account. I had a good night so far as absence from coughing goes, and in regards to a good sleep. But the weather is far more severe than we ever had it. The snow though not thick, lies all day without the slightest thaw.' Convalescent now he was showing his old interest in international affairs, particularly the American Civil War: 'Have you any Americans at Edwards Hotel?' he asks Kate.'The last telegram really looks as if the Richmond government were inclined to try the way for peace negotiations. The children have been very merry with their Valentines to-day – Maggie burst into my room the first thing with hers quite wild with delight.'

Neither of them knew it, but this was to be the last letter Cobden wrote to Kate.

Gladstone now offered Cobden the post of Chairman of the Board of Audit, at a salary of £2,000 per annum. On 13 February he wrote declining the offer, giving as his reason attacks of nervous asthma, but adding that even were his health good it would be 'a nauseous ordeal' to audit the finance account: he considered government expenditure 'to the last degree wasteful and indefensible'. He had no intention, however, of giving up his seat in Parliament, 'as long as I am able in any tolerable degree to perform its duties, where I have at least the opportunity of protesting, however unavailingly, against the Government expenditure.'

On 16 February Cobden tells Ashworth: '...I have been for a long time quite out of health. Indeed for more than two months I have not been out of doors. It is all attributable to my own indiscretion in paying so late a visit to my constituents, and to my misfortune in having had to address 6,000 persons not only for myself, but for Mr Bright who had the greater misfortune to be prevented from attending by the sad death of his son...' He goes on: 'I rather like the following verse from the old Greek poet, Hesiod: "Let youth in deeds, in council man engage, Prayer is the proper duty of old age". And surely this must apply with additional force to an old politician and diplomatist whose life must require at least a closing year or two of atonement in the form of prayer and repentance.' Cobden was not to be granted so long a stay of execution.

On 21 February Kate was off again, with her older daughters and Elizabeth Clare to attend the wedding of Sally Ashburner at Tilgate, near Crawley. Cobden was not well enough to join the party. In the fly from Petworth Kate told the girls their father had been offered the Chairmanship of the Board of Audit but had refused it. At this time Nelly was obviously still hopeful of her father being able to work again, for she writes in her diary that she is glad of his decision, as the appointment 'would have completely shelved him in Parliamentary life'.

While the wedding guests were pulling crackers the post brought Cobden a letter from Bright, written on 23 February which, given the circumstances, it is not over melodramatic to describe as his death warrant, for in it Bright told him there was to be a debate in the House on the question of the proposed Canadian fortifications, and Bright wished that his old friend could be there to vote against the proposal to spend vast sums of money in this way. Cobden replied on 1 March, inviting Bright to Dunford. 'We have a railroad now into Midhurst,' he told him, 'You can start from Waterloo Station at 11.30 and arrive here before 2, changing carriage at Petworth...I should have something to say about Canada and America.'

When Kate returned on 24 February she had found Cobden better, and she now started the girls on preparations for the belated Christmas party for the village children. Next day Cobden went out for the first time since his illness. The weather improved further during Bright's visit, and they were able to go out walking together in the middle of the day. The two old war-horses strolled on the terrace and in the lanes, but Cobden's mood, it seems, was still sombre, for on one of these outings he looked in the direction of West Lavington churchyard and told Bright he would shortly be joining his dear boy there.

By Friday 17 March the weather had turned very cold again when Kate paid her next visit to London, taking the early train. The object of this journey was to find lodgings for Cobden, who, after his talks with Bright, was determined to attend the debate on the Canadian fortifications. Had she tried to dissuade him? It seems unlikely, for she knew, after a quarter century as his wife, that once his mind was made up not even his 'dearest Kate' could hope to change it, especially if what he considered to be his duty was involved. She returned the same evening, having found rooms in the house of a Mrs Strickland at 23 Suffolk Street, Pall Mall, conveniently near the Athenaeum and the House of Commons. Mrs Strickland's visiting card survives, with notes of her charges.

On 21 March, the first day of spring, Cobden, Kate and Nelly travelled to London, first in a fly to Midhurst, with other members of the family accompanying them in the Fishers' pony chaise. At Midhurst they took their leave and boarded the 3 o'clock train. Trains were still unheated at that time but for foot warmers filled with boiling water and known as 'tins'. Arrived at Suffolk Street, no sooner had Cobden climbed the stairs than, according to Nelly's diary, 'he complained of an Asthamatical [*sic*] feeling'.

Next day there were many callers, and by evening Cobden was so much worse that at 8 o'clock Kate and Nelly went to Hooper the chemist to ask if they knew of an Asthma hospital. Hoopers could not help them, so Kate drove on to the chemists, Savory and Moore in Bond Street, where she was told that no such hospital existed. They recommended a Dr Roberts at 75 Grosvenor Street, so after buying some cigars for asthma they went there. Roberts was out, but Kate left word for him to call at Suffolk Street that evening.

Next day Cobden was well enough to write to Thomas Potter – the last letter he ever wrote. On 23 March he got up, Roberts called again, and again there were many visitors; and in the evening Kate went again to Savory and Moore, presumably to have Dr Robert's prescription made up. She seemingly made a note, or perhaps Nelly made it, for two small slips of paper survive to show what treatment Cobden had: '30th. Take a pill immediately and in three hours after a dose of the Mixture and so on alternatively – drink Barley Water – Take nourishment every two hours – consisting of Beef tea, Mutton broth, Sago – or Arrowroot, &c. Take one of the night pills at half past 10.'

On 24 March, Cobden stayed in bed all day and was so much worse that Kate telegraphed for Mr Ingram to come up from Midhurst. Ingram caught the last train and had a consultation with Roberts, and seemingly spent the night at Suffolk Street before going home the following day, with his fee.

'My dear friend,' Alice Hargreaves wrote to Kate, 'We are most grieved to hear of Mr Cobden's severe illness – when we heard he had ventured to travel we were very much afraid of the consequences – What a grievous thing that he should have left his warm home in March after such long and patient confinement...'

On 25 March Kate's task was made lighter by the arrival of Ann Munday to help with the nursing, and on the same day Nelly had a letter from Jane: 'I was so sorry to hear from your letter to Katie this morning that dear Papa is worse...In the hamper which Ann Munday is going to take up this afternoon I send a box of ferns and moss, be sure you arrange them nicely as the little ferns are getting scarce, and I don't think I shall be able to send many next week-...When the hampers are sent back don't forget to send a pair of riding gloves for me in one of them as I am so badly off for them, and I should also like a pair of warm ones like yours...I can't get any more conservatory flowers as there are hardly any there-...Adieu my cherubina Nelly – write soon – ' If Jane sounds heartless it should be remembered that she was only 14 at the time, and by now the children were accustomed to their father's periodic bouts of illness, from which he had always recovered.

When Bright, on his way to Clifton, called on 28 March he was obviously unhappy about Cobden's condition and asked Nelly to write to him with news the next day. At this stage only Kate and Nelly – and presumably Ann Munday – were allowed to see the patient. Dr Roberts was calling twice a day. Cobden was well enough for Nelly to read the newspapers to him. By 29 March he was said to be 'decidedly better'.

It would appear from receipted accounts preserved by Kate at the time that the Cobdens expected to stay for a while at Suffolk Street, and to entertain friends. The Beaujolais Wine Company had provided them with three dozen bottles (costing £3 a dozen) and there were purchases from Fortnum, Mason & Co including caviar (at 5/- a jar) which suggest that they had departed from their usual plain living.

The *Morning Star* had reported earlier that Cobden had had a severe relapse in consequence of his journey to town, with the result that letters from anxious friends and relations who had read the news began to arrive addressed to Kate, begging for reassurance. Sarah Fiers-Cobden, writing from Fallowfield on 26 March, was as frank as a member of the family had a right to be: 'It really did seem madness for a person with a delicate throat or chest to change his residence, in such a fearful Easterly wind – It seemed to search into the very marrow of ones bones...Do send us a line just to say how Richard is going on – I do hope that you continue to be satisfied with yr Medical attendant, and that dear Richard has confidence in him – '

When the Ashburners called on Thursday 30 March it was to find Nelly still in bed after a night when Cobden's condition had worsened and he had been delirious. Roberts now called in a colleague, a Dr Watson, for a second opinion. Moffatt was present and met the two doctors. Their verdict was reassuring. This raised what were to prove false hopes and caused Nelly to write on behalf of her mother on 31 March, to Thomas Potter: 'Mamma thinks you will like to hear how Papa is going on. Yesterday morning we were very much afraid that a change for the worse had taken place. Papa had been delirious in the night and the doctor thought it necessary to call in other advice. Dr Roberts brought a Dr Watson here in the afternoon and they had a consultation. We were very much relieved by the favourable opinion they came to. His heart and lungs they pronounced quite sound, but the latter are very much congested – and the bronchial tubes affected. But these with strict attention to rules and great care they think will soon recover themselves. He is extremely weak, and the great difficulty is to get him to take sufficient food. All our friends have been most kind and have brought him things such as soups and jellies, which we could not have so well made in lodgings...P.S. I send an American pamphlet which Papa thought you would like if you have not already got it, – He has had some sent him for distribution...'

Things being so much improved by Saturday afternoon that Kate left Cobden with Ann Munday in charge of the sickroom and went out shopping with Nelly to try and find a comfortable pillow for him. When they got back the girl reported that she did not like the look in Cobden's face – it was dark and blueish, and he had slept uneasily. When Bright learned of this he came to Suffolk Street after dinner and remained there with Moffatt until after midnight, but did not see his friend.

Cobden was nothing if not a realist and the remark he had made to Bright at Dunford that he would soon be joining Dick in the churchyard at West Lavington shows the approach of death was something he had already faced, in spite of medical reassurance. On that April Fool's Day he sent for his lawyer and dictated his Will, appointing as his executors 'Thomas and John Thomasson of Bolton, co. Lancs, cotton spinners, and Catherine Anne Cobden, his wife'. Called to the bedside to witness his signature were Richard Fisher, soon to marry Katie, and John Roberts, M.D.

On Saturday evening Fisher and Roberts both proposed that Bright should see Cobden, but Bright wrote in his diary that he feared to excite his friend and refused to go up unless he heard Cobden himself wished it. Fisher then told Cobden that Bright was in the house. According to Bright: 'Cobden turned to Dr Roberts and said: 'Doctor, I am in your hands perhaps those of death, ought I to run the risk of any excitement?' Roberts thought not, so Bright, greatly to his regret, never saw his friend *compos mentis* again. On his way home (and this must have been in the small hours of the Sunday morning if he had been talking with Moffatt until after midnight) Bright records that he called at the St James's Restaurant to get some 'Invalid Turtle soup', which Moffatt then took round to Suffolk Street. It seems that it was at this moment that Bright decided to send a telegram to Sale, which suggests there was an all-night Post Office in the neighbourhood.

On Sunday morning it was young Fisher who sent the note summoning Bright: Cobden was 'worse and sinking'. Bright set off at once for Suffolk Street and remembers how he heard the bell ringing for service at St Martin-in-the-Fields as he neared the house. He was at the bedside soon after 8 o'clock and found his friend 'insensible and sinking'.

Cobden died at 11.15 in the presence of Fisher, Roberts, Moffatt, with Kate and Nelly 'in and about the room'.'There was no apparent pain,' Bright was to write in his diary, 'not a limb stirred, he lay breathing out his precious life and for 3¾ hours I watched my greatest friend, of more than 20 years, as his life ebbed away...At a quarter past 11 o'clock the breathing ceased, there was a moment of suspense, a pallor spread over the face and the manly and gentle spirit of the noblest of men, passed away to the reward which surely waits upon a life passed in works of good to mankind, a life of unselfish benevolence and unspotted honour.' (The certified cause of Cobden's death was bronchitis and congestion of the lungs.)

After witnessing what he described as 'a scene never to be

forgotten', Bright passed a busy day about Cobden's affairs. First, he went to the Reform Club where he wrote to Ashworth and Thomasson with the news; then home to Gordon Street where he 'Found McLaren and dear Priscilla there – we all wept'. Then he talked to a writer from the *Morning Star* who had come to write a memoir. Returning to Suffolk Street he found 'the poor girls in grief and excitement, Nelly almost delirious'. So he carried her off, first to be comforted in his own home by his wife, then to the Hargreaves in Craven Hill Gardens. From there he took her for a walk in Hyde Park, then to a florist in Piccadilly to buy her 'a sweet nosegay – a red rose and a white rose and some lilies of the valley'; then back to Suffolk Street, where he saw her put the flowers 'over the heart which had loved her so tenderly.'

Alice Hargreaves called on Kate on the Sunday afternoon and wrote that day to her sister Martha Paulton, who was out of town: '...I found Mrs Cobden in his room with Nelly, both in sad grief. She will not leave him, did everything herself, knowing how reserved and sensitive he was. Happily, she can talk and express her sorrow but I fear when she gets down to Dunford she will suffer terribly – she says she doesn't know how she is to bear the sight of familiar places and things – but has resolved not to shrink from them as before – ' Alice Hargreaves said of the dead man: 'He is much thinner. That illness after the Rochdale visit must have changed him indeed...As far as I can gather he seems to have enlarged liver and congestion of the lungs...he has certainly thrown away his life, in his desire to do his duty. It is very sad to see him lying in the poor, hired room, with no home look or comfort about him. I cut off a lock of his hair – and kissed his brow...There are many friends, all ready to do something. Mr Williams is there – I will go again tomorrow – Katie is coming up.'

At a quarter past six Bright 'saw the sad family off from the Waterloo Station...'

The certified cause of Cobden's death was bronchitis and congestion of the lungs.

CHAPTER SIXTEEN

'The Widow of a public man'

Cobden chose to be buried at West Lavington, alongside his son. Mahomet, then came in large numbers to the mountain, including Gladstone, Chancellor of the Exchequer. On 11 April a special train was run from Waterloo to the new station at Midhurst, a journey of some sixty miles. Upwards of 400 people availed themselves of this gesture on the part of the railway company.

Arriving at Midhurst about midday on that beautiful spring day the mourners formed up and walked to Cocking Causeway. The local press estimated that between three and four thousand persons walked in the funeral procession. As the cortège approached from the hanger road from Dunford and joined the causeway, Moffatt invited his fellow members of parliament to lead the way to West Lavington. This they did led by Gladstone. The press reported that the 'whole mass of gentlemen' doffed their hats. The national press gave the funeral extensive coverage – black borders and column upon column of eulogy – and the *Illustrated London News* sent an artist who vividly recorded the scene on the causeway – surely one of the most spectacular and theatrical in that era of elaborate obsequies, and all the more striking against rural surroundings.

The Rev. Caleb Collins took the service, the Rev. J. Currie, incumbent of the parish, reading the concluding sentences. According to the local press Bright sobbed audibly when the coffin was lowered into the grave. Gladstone 'remained with closed eyes and joined in the responses audibly'. After the interment he and Milner Gibson visited Kate, 'who', reported *The Morning Star*, 'in the midst of her great grief desired that all the old friends of her husband should call upon her, and, when they did so, in a firm and dignified manner expressed her gratitude. Around the house were still assembled groups of sorrowing friends who were unwilling to disturb the privacy of the family.' The emotional Bright was one of those who held back.

Kate outlived Cobden by twelve years. They were troubled years but she used them as well as any woman of her time and circumstances could have done and, true to her word to Alice Hargreaves, did not shrink from what she saw would be her unenviable role as 'the widow of a public man'.

In the early days she was supported by the family and her future son-in-law, Richard Fisher, and by many of Cobden's wealthy and influential friends, among them her co-Executor Thomas Thomasson, Moffatt, Paulton and Bright. Without their guidance Kate might have made awkward mistakes. The matter of her refusal of the National Bounty was an example. On behalf of the Government Palmerston had written offering her an annuity of £1,500 a year. This she turned down in terms which struck Thomasson to whom she had sent – *after* replying to Palmerston – a copy of her letter as 'rather curt and quite formal and scarcely polished over with the usual diplomatic gloss'. On his advice she consulted Moffatt, whose reaction was that her letter 'would not do'. She agreed to his redraft and this was substituted by agreement with the Prime Minister. The switch was made and the situation retrieved.

The press on 6 June had reported that '...the public will be glad to know that the family of the lamented statesman are left in circumstances that make any provision on the part of the Government unnecessary'. What the public did not know was that it was Cobden's friends who provided the means to enable Kate and her five daughters to live in comfort if not in affluence. The Cobden Tribute Fund they raised had resulted in upwards of £25,000 being invested under Trust for the benefit of Kate and the children.

Within a few months of Cobden's death she was corresponding with Gladstone over the reprinting of his *Political Writings*, a project in which she had the help of Chesson of *The Morning Star* and of Thomas Potter, and which she paid for out of her own funds. Queen Victoria and Disraeli were among those who received presentation copies when the work appeared.

Kate lived to see only one of her daughters married. In June 1866 Katie and Fisher were married from the Hargreaves' house in Craven Hill Gardens – 'the quietest thing possible' Kate had insisted, as the family were still in mourning. Even the young bridesmaids' dresses were violet and white, but at least there was a huge cake, according to the bride.

Kate found herself involved in correspondence with Thomas Woolner, the sculptor, about his bust of Cobden which the Dean of Westminster had assented should be placed in the Abbey. Correspondence with Michel Chevalier was another task, for he was arranging for a copy of the bust to be presented to the French Emperor, where it eventually found a place in his personal apartments at Versailles. There was correspondence with The British and Foreign Marble Galleries about the stone over Cobden's grave, correspondence with Thomasson over trouble at Warrington Lodge, Maida Hill, where Jane and Anne were at school, and where there had been what Kate called 'disagreeables' between the head mistress and her staff which had led to the girls being removed, and in Kate's words 'thrown upon my hands'. There were complications over governesses for Maggie, there were – surprisingly – money worries, borrowings from relations, a falling out with her brother John over interest on a debt he had paid, and other problems which caused her endless headaches.

Then there were the projects for the raising of memorials, including the Camden Town memorial statue, which caused her concern. Kate had told Chesson, who acted as her intermediary with the Memorial Committee, that she was against the erection of any such memorials 'unless they be works of genius'. But good manners required her to withdraw her objections for fear of offending the good men of St. Pancras. She consulted the devoted Moffatt on this subject, and as ever the advice he gave her was sound: that no such scheme should be attempted 'unless the promoters were quite secure as to the means for an efficient performance', and he counselled her to make her consent subject to the condition that funds should be in hand before work began. In the event the Committee went ahead regardless, and even on the day the statue was unveiled in her presence – 28 June 1868 – were still collecting money to pay for the work. A few weeks later the French Emperor donated 1,000 francs and now has his name on what has been described by one critic as 'the worst statue in London'.

Kate decided to let Dunford furnished, and after much effort succeeded in finding a suitable tenant. It was in February 1867 when she wrote to Mrs Caleb Collins, putting her in the picture about the new inmates of the house, that she uttered her often quoted *cri de coeur* 'God help the widow of a public man!' With the maid Lizzie Clare (now senior enough to be called Elizabeth) and the three youngest girls, Kate moved to the Angel inn in Midhurst, before starting on a round of visits to relations and friends.

With Mrs Tiller to act as cook Kate then settled for a while at Walkers, then to be known as The Hurst, and later Oatscroft.

In June 1869 the contents of Dunford were disposed of in a three day sale at the house, a sale reported as being 'but scantily attended'. No pictures or ornaments were included but on the second day six hundred books went under the hammer. The

Sevrès porcelain vase which the French Emperor had given to Cobden after the successful conclusion of the Commercial Treaty was sent to the 'Kensington Museum' (Victoria and Albert Museum). Resembling rather a baptismal font than a flower vase, it was obviously considered too handsome to find a place at The Hurst. Among the pictures retained was a large oil painting of Kate, showing her at the height of her beauty. This portrait, which is unsigned, is listed in the Dunford inventory as being of the French School, but is the work of an Italian artist named Cittadini, for whom Kate sat when she was living at Victoria Park. In the painting Kate is wearing the brooch with the 'likeness' of Dick, which a Manchester silversmith made for her at a cost of £6 .16.6d in 1848, but it was not until 1867 that the painting came into her hands in a very strange manner.

On 4 December that year a clergyman named Thomas Orr wrote to Kate from an address in Chiswick at the request of a lady who had the picture in her possession, and who wished to sell it to raise money for the artist's wife who was 'in great distress'.'On account of some misconduct', Cittadini had had to leave Manchester before completing the portrait, which had therefore been refused by Kate. Orr asked whether under the circumstances she now saw any reason for altering the decision she had then made. It would seem that Kate, known for her kindness of heart, must have responded to this appeal, for the picture hangs to-day in the former drawing-rooom at Dunford House.

After the 1869 sale the house was let unfurnished, and Kate and her youngest daughter Maggie and 'the little careful staid Elizabeth' Clare began their wanderings.

At this time Kate had acquired a house in Petersham Terrace, South Kensington, which she shared on a part-time basis for a while with Nelly, Jane and Anne. But the experiment proved a disaster. The girls were rapidly growing away from their mother, and in spite of their sporadic education were all three destined for life in a wider, more emancipated world. There were differences over money and the arrangement came to an end.

Kate then embarked on a radical change in life style. With Elizabeth Clare and Maggie she went to live in North Wales, at Llanddulas, a house at Abergele near Colwyn Bay. According to Clare's Autobiography they were at various addresses in Wales for several years, during which Hugh Williams died. When she returned to The Hurst in 1874 Kate had evidently now made up her mind not to go back to Wales, for Clare recalls: 'Then we whent back to Walkers [The Hurst] and Mrs Cobden thought she would not go back to Llanddulas again, so I had to go and pack all the things belonging to Mrs Cobden, and bring them back to Walkers. Their were the 3 dogs to bring back Topsy and her two Sons. Harry Bertram and Hyawatha and two birds a canary and goldfinch in two cages. I got three hampers to put the dogs in. They were in the hampers early in the morning till late at night.'

After that there were no more wanderings and for the remaining years of her life Kate settled in self-sought seclusion at The Hurst. The winter of 1876–77 had been long and wet, but in April the primroses and wood anemones appeared in their usual profusion in the hanger. But spring brought no return of strength to Kate, who had been complaining of weakness for some time. For the fourth time, the month of April, which had seen the deaths of Dick, Frederick and Cobden himself, was to prove fatal to Kate.

'Poor Mrs Cobden...did not keep her bed many weeks...All her daughters were at Walkers when Mrs Cobden died, except Mrs Fisher, and she was in Florence.'

By the end of March Kate was confined to bed, suffering from 'extreme weakness', and on 18 April she died, as her mother had done, at 6 o''clock in the morning. Like Cobden she was 61. Among other causes of death certified by Dr William Attwood were liver and heart disease.

A paragraph which appeared in an unidentified newspaper after Kate's death states that 'Cobden used to say that he owed any success he had achieved in life to his wife, the "ignorant Welsh girl", whom his friends looked on with so much suspicion as an unsuitable helpmate for him. The union, "begun in romance and indiscretion" was cemented by a long life of mutual sorrow and struggle, through which Mrs Cobden's bright spirit buoyed her husband to success.' Kate had a peaceful end to her life, the press reporting that she had died 'apparently without any suffering.'

Elizabeth Clare was to write later: 'Mrs Cobden left me £500, and dear Miss Nelly had great trouble to get it for me...' It was a handsome legacy considering that Kate left less than £4,000. Elizabeth Clare was to continue with the family, and completed sixty years' service before she finally retired.

At her own request, Kate's funeral had nothing of the pomp and ceremony of Cobden's: 'A two-horse hearse and three private carriages' the local paper told its readers. The Rev. Caleb Collins officiated but the Rector of West Lavington was unavoidably absent.

On 24 April it was reported that 'Mrs Cobden was buried yesterday at three o'clock...A considerable gathering was anticipated by our correspondent' (who apparently left prematurely to attend to a more newsworthy event). Bright, in his diary for 23 April, gives the true picture of the laying to rest of Cobden's Kate: 'To Midhurst to the funeral of Mrs Cobden. A small party...'

The Main Characters

ASHWORTH, Edmund and Henry. Brothers of Quaker parentage. Wealthy and influential, they managed the Friends Mills at Turton. Staunch non-conformists and founding members of the League, they were close friends of Cobden.
BENDER, Dr. H.B.C. Physician at the school at Weinheim.
BENDER, Dr. L. Director of Dick Cobden's school at Weinheim.
BRIGHT, John, MP. Leader, with Cobden, of the Anti-Corn Law League; a Quaker.
CLARE, Elizabeth ('Lizzie'). Faithful servant of the Cobden family for over sixty years.
CLARK, Sir James. Physician to Queen Victoria. Cobden sought his advice on numerous occasions, including Frederick's last illness.
COBDEN. Charles. Cobden's youngest brother. Involved in the calico-printing business.
COBDEN, Ellen Millicent Ashburner ('Nelly') (1848–1914). Daughter of Cobden and Kate.
COBDEN, Emma Jane Catherine (Jane) (1859–1935). Daughter of Cobden and Kate.
COBDEN, Frederick. Cobden's eldest brother. After some years in America, was with Richard in the calico-printing business. Acted for Cobden in overseeing the work of rebuilding Dunford, then made his home there with Cobden and Kate. Died at Dunford after a painful illness in 1858.
COBDEN, Julia Sarah Anne (Annie). Daughter of Cobden and Kate.
COBDEN, Kate. Daughter of Cobden and Kate; died in infancy.
COBDEN, Kate (Katie) (1844–1916). Daughter of Cobden and Kate. Married Richard Chester Fisher ('Dick'), son of neighbours in Midhurst, a barrister.
COBDEN, Lucy Elizabeth Margaret (Maggie) (1861–1891). Eighth and last child of Cobden and Kate.
COBDEN, Richard (1804–65). Joint founder of the Anti-Corn Law League, Member of Parliament. Husband of Kate.
COBDEN, Mary. Richard Cobden's youngest sister.
COBDEN, Sarah. Sister of Richard Cobden, married to Charles Fiers, a Swiss.

COBDEN, Richard (Dick) (1841–56). Firstborn son of Cobden and Kate.

COBDEN, William. Father of Richard; unsuccessful timber merchant.

COBDEN, William. Son of Cobden and Kate; died in infancy, 1849.

COMBE, George. Moral philosopher and writer on Phrenology; much admired by Cobden.

ELLENBERGER, J.L. Headmaster at Dick Cobden's school at Worksop.

EVELEIGH, Miss Elizabeth. Later Mrs Fell. Quaker lady who ran a nursery school and had the care of Dick Cobden while his parents were on their Continental tour in 1846.

FITZMAYER, Colonel (later General) James William, CB, RA. Friend and correspondent of Cobden at the time of the Crimean War and after.

GLADSTONE, William Ewart. Chancellor of the Exchequer (and later Prime Minister). Entrusted Cobden with the negotiation of the Commercial Treaty with the French.

HAGEMANN, Miss. German governess, popular with the Cobden children and with Kate.

HARGREAVES, Alice. Wife of William, sister of Martha Paulton, née Mellor.

HARGREAVES, William. Close friend of Cobden, who sometimes stayed at his house in Bayswater.

HELDENMAIER. Proprietor of Worksop school where Dick Cobden went before being sent to Germany.

LAMBELET, Monsieur. Housemaster at Weinheim school, present at Dick Cobden's death.

LEATHLEY, Mrs Mary. Widow. Roman Catholic mother of son Dudley, lived at Easebourne. Friend of Kate Cobden. Known to the family as 'Aunt Mary'.

LINDSAY, W.S., MP. Wealthy shipowner, lived at Shepperton Manor, wrote an account of a visit to the Cobdens at Dunford.

MOFFATT, George. Wealthy friend of the Cobdens, with whom they stayed in Belgravia and Surrey.

MOFFATT, Lucy. Wife of George. Maggie Cobden's godmother.

NAPOLEON III. Emperor of the French, associated with Cobden over the Commercial Treaty negotiations.

PARKES, Joseph. Parliamentary solicitor, friend and correspondent of Cobden.

PAULTON, A.W. Journalist; married to Martha. Cobden stayed at their mansion in Cleveland Square, Bayswater, when parliamentary duties kept him in London.

PAULTON, Martha, née Mellor. Wife of A.W. Paulton.

POTTER, Sir Thomas. Politician who founded the *Manchester Gazette*, later incorporated with the *Manchester Times*. A founder of the Anti-Corn Law League.

PRENTICE, Archibald. Journalist. Helped to found the *Manchester Gazette*. A founder of the Anti-Corn Law League.

SCHWABE, Julie Salis. Wealthy friend of the Cobdens, who, with her husband, shared part of their Continental tour. It was to her house, Glyn Garth on the Menai Straits, that Kate withdrew to mourn her son Dick.

SMITH, J.B., MP. Chairman of the League Council until succeeded by George Wilson.

STURGE, Joseph. Philanthropist, one of the first to join the Anti-Corn Law League.

VILLIERS, Charles Pelham. Statesman, barrister, Corn Law reformer, MP for Wolverhampton for over 60 years. Judge-advocate general and a Privy Councillor.

WALMSLEY, Sir Joshua. Friend and neighbour of Cobden.

WEYNERT AND ASHDOWN. London architects who rebuilt Dunford, the ancient farmhouse where Cobden was born, near Heyshott, Sussex.

WILLIAMS, Catherine Anne (1815–77). Married Cobden in 1840. Bore him eight children. Always called his 'Dearest Kate'.

WILLIAMS, Hugh. Father of Kate; timber merchant in Machynlleth, North Wales. In 1815, in partnership with John Pugh, he struck lead at Dylife, near Machynlleth. At his death in 1852, the interest in the mine was acquired by a partnership including Cobden and John Bright, and became the cause of much trouble.

WILLIAMS, Hugh. Kate's elder brother, practised law in Verulam Buildings, Gray's Inn, with his younger brother John. Political agitator.

WILLIAMS, John. Kate's younger brother. Solicitor. Helped in the agitation against the Corn Laws.

WILSON, George. Succeeded J.B. Smith as chairman of the League Council.

WOOLLEY, Mrs Elizabeth. Widowed friend of the Cobdens' Manchester days. In straitened circumstances she took in boarders at her house in Paris where the Cobdens lodged during the Commercial Treaty negotiations.

Select Bibliography

ASHWORTH, Henry, *Recollections of Richard Cobden M.P. and the anti-Corn Law League.* 2 vols (London 1876).
BRIGGS, A. (ed), *Chartist Studies* (London 1962).
COLE, G.D.H., *Chartist Portraits* (Cassell 1941, paperback 1939).
EDSALL, N.C., *Richard Cobden, Independent Radical* (Harvard 1987).
HINDE, Wendy, *Richard Cobden: a Victorian Outsider* (Yale 1987).
HOBSON, J.A., *Richard Cobden: the international man* (London 1919, rept 1968).
MORLEY, John, *Richard Cobden,* 2 vols (London 1879).
READ, D., *Cobden & Bright: a Victorian political partnership (London 1967).*
SCHWABE, Mrs Julie Salis, *Reminiscences of Richard Cobden* (London 1895).
STOWE, Harriet Beecher, *Sunny Memories of Foreign Lands.*
WATKIN, Sir E.W., *Alderman Cobden* (London 1891).

Chester, 52

Index